JEWISH AND CHRISTIAN TEXTS IN CONTEXTS AND RELATED STUDIES
VOLUME 35

Executive Editor
James H. Charlesworth

Editorial Board of Advisors
Motti Aviam, Michael Davis, Casey Elledge, Loren Johns, Amy-Jill Levine,
Lee McDonald, Lidia Novakovic, Gerbern Oegema, Henry Rietz, Brent Strawn

Hellenistic Inter-state Political Ethics and the Emergence of the Jewish State

Doron Mendels

LONDON • NEW YORK • OXFORD • NEW DELHI • SYDNEY

T&T CLARK

Bloomsbury Publishing Plc

50 Bedford Square, London, WC1B 3DP, UK
1385 Broadway, New York, NY 10018, USA
29 Earlsfort Terrace, Dublin 2, Ireland

BLOOMSBURY, T&T CLARK and the T&T Clark logo are trademarks of Bloomsbury Publishing Plc

First published in Great Britain 2022
Paperback edition published 2023

Copyright © Doron Mendels, 2022

Doron Mendels has asserted his right under the Copyright, Designs and Patents Act, 1988, to be identified as Author of this work.

For legal purposes the Acknowledgments on p. ix constitute an extension of this copyright page.

All rights reserved. No part of this publication may be reproduced or transmitted in any form or by any means, electronic or mechanical, including photocopying, recording, or any information storage or retrieval system, without prior permission in writing from the publishers.

Bloomsbury Publishing Plc does not have any control over, or responsibility for, any third-party websites referred to or in this book. All internet addresses given in this book were correct at the time of going to press. The author and publisher regret any inconvenience caused if addresses have changed or sites have ceased to exist, but can accept no responsibility for any such changes.

A catalogue record for this book is available from the British Library.

Library of Congress Cataloging-in-Publication Data
Names: Mendels, Doron, author.
Title: Hellenistic inter-state political ethics and the emergence of the Jewish state / Doron Mendels.
Description: London : T&T Clark, [2022] | Series: Jewish and Christian texts; 35 | Includes bibliographical references and index. |
Summary: "Doron Mendels demonstrates how inter-state political ethics gave rise to the emergence of the Jewish state during the years 200–168 BCE and provides an overview of how these values functioned"–Provided by publisher.
Identifiers: LCCN 2021026018 (print) | LCCN 2021026019 (ebook) | ISBN 9780567701398 (hardback) | ISBN 9780567701404 (pdf) | ISBN 9780567701428 (epub)
Subjects: LCSH: Jews–History–586 B.C.–70 A.D. | Jewish nationalism. | Judaism and state. | Ethnicity–Religious aspects–Judaism. | Livy. Ab urbe condita. | Bible. Maccabees, 1st–Criticism, interpretation, etc. | Bible. Maccabees, 2nd–Criticism, interpretation, etc. | Rome–History–Early works to 1800.
Classification: LCC DS121.65 .M447 2022 (print) | LCC DS121.65 (ebook) | DDC 909/.04924–dc23
LC record available at https://lccn.loc.gov/2021026018
LC ebook record available at https://lccn.loc.gov/2021026019

ISBN: HB: 978-0-5677-0139-8
PB: 978-0-5677-0143-5
ePDF: 978-0-5677-0140-4
ePUB: 978-0-5677-0142-8

Series: Jewish and Christian Texts in Contexts and Related Studies, volume 35

Typeset by Newgen KnowledgeWorks Pvt. Ltd., Chennai, India

To find out more about our authors and books visit www.bloomsbury.com and sign up for our newsletters.

Contents

Preface	vi
Acknowledgments	ix

Part I Mapping the Hellenistic Political Inter-state Ethical Code

Introduction   1

1	Dialogue, War, and the Public Declaration of Liberty (200–196 BCE)	9
2	Two Zones of Influence—One Ethical System	41
3	Hearings Granted to Enemies through Dialogue	51
4	The Use and Abuse of an Inter-state Ethical System—Rome's Slide into Dominance	85

Part II Ethical Climate, Patterns of Behavior, and the Emergence of the Jewish State

Introduction   125

5	The Hasmonean State as a Test Case for Patterns of Relationship between Empire and Subject State—the Book of 1 Maccabees	127
6	The Subject State Corresponds and Reacts to the Hellenistic Inter-state Ethical System—the Book of 2 Maccabees	143

Bibliography	165
Index of Ancient Sources	169
Index of Authors	174

Preface

This study is based on primary sources, while the secondary literature is reduced to a minimum. The use of Latin and Greek terminology is also minimized since my intended readers are not merely scholars in the field and beyond (scholars who are, for instance, in the field of ethics) but interested people to whom ancient ideas are made accessible first hand. Whereas in Part I we view the events through the narrative of Livy's *Ab Urbe Condita*, for Part II we draw mainly on 1–2 Maccabees. Livy, who presents us with the fullest and most comprehensive description of the years 200–168 BCE, used important sources, most of which disappeared or remained in fragmentary form such as the Roman Annalists and Polybius.[1] Livy as well as 1–2 Maccabees narrated the events through the lens of the politics and cultural systems of their own times.[2] Nevertheless, reading the abovementioned sources with a critical eye, taking into account the modes of interpretation and the ideas of the narrators themselves, we have identified a comprehensive inter-state ethical system. This virtual code,[3] not yet discovered by scholars, alongside patterns of behavior of

---

[1] For cannibalism of sources, see Mendels (2004: 1–29).

[2] My purpose in this essay is limited to the presentation of a general survey of patterns of relationships between states and between ruling powers and their subject states; as well as an attempt to reconstruct the virtual inter-state ethical code that emerged (or was invented) during the years 200–168 BCE. Hence, I follow Livy's extensive narrative that reveals those two aspects in a comprehensive manner without interrupting the flow of my survey with scholarly discussions and long footnotes on side issues that are not relevant to my study. For the benefit of my readers, I will also avoid discussions about textual matters and comparisons with other fragmentary and later sources such as fragments in Appian, Cassius Dio, Plutarch, and Josephus (which I leave for the younger generation to pursue). Also, I extensively adduce important quotations from Livy, my wonderful main source, so that my readers will have direct access to the ideas of the active heroes in their own words (obviously through Livy's and Polybius's presentations). This is also the reason for which I preserve the order of events in Livy's narrative and accentuate the ethical inter-state aspect where it has a bearing on the emergence of the Hasmonean state told in Part II. I have used the text and translation (with slight changes) of the Loeb edition. For the interpretative issues that I do not tackle here (also because of brevity constraints), the readers can consult the following commentaries: Briscoe (1989–2012) for Livy; Walbank (1957–79) for Polybius; Doran (2012) and Schwartz (2008) for 2 Maccabees; and Mendels and Darshan (forthcoming) for 1 Maccabees. The well-defined scope of my essay accommodated also with the requirement of the publisher for brevity. Josephus on the Hasmonean state will not be tackled here since it contaminates the authentic picture about ethics and patterns in 1–2 Maccabees (for contamination of historical texts, see Mendels 2004).

[3] Virtual, because as the reader will discover such a code was, as it were, only written down in the historiography of the period and did not exist as a written code in reality. Thus, some experts may argue that the ancient historians' own perceptions and interpretations overshadowed the reality that they relate. To appease those imagined critics, I will argue in the following that whether the inter-state ethical code was an ideal concept of the above-mentioned historiography (Livy in particular) or an emergence of it in the real world, in either case the code signifies a milestone in the cultural history of the West. I can add here the observation that if Livy's picture was an invention or rather a formulation of a reality, Livy can be considered as the inventing father of the inter-state ethical system, whereas Hugo Grotius in the seventeenth century the founding father of international law.

empires and individual states will constitute the cultural political and ethical world against which we have to reassess the Hasmonean state. We wish to emphasize that the abovementioned ancient historians, who were still close to the world of inter-state patterns of relationships and ethics in time and in spirit, reflect the climate of the period they have portrayed.

The book consists of two parts. Part I is a history of the gradual emergence of an inter-state ethical system (virtual code) that during the years 200–168 BCE became the framework of an inter-state network. We discover that in this process Rome played a major role, yet her motivations for launching the three Macedonian wars as well as the Roman-Syrian war, which signified the beginnings of her imperialism in the Hellenistic east, will not be the main theme of this book.[4] My story will also not deal with legal aspects concerning her impressive republican legal system, some of which Rome may have applied on others during her imperialism.[5] I will rather focus on mechanisms of her ethical interaction with the Hellenistic states and the relationships among the latter during the first three decades of the second century BCE and reflected in the Hellenistic kingdom's conduct henceforward. In short, only the events that have a clear bearing on the gradual formation of a political ethical inter-state code are discussed. Hence my reader will get some close acquaintance with dialogue and talk adduced by our sources. By introducing some of the speakers in their words, rather than paraphrasing them, I hope that the reader will experience the authentic spirit of some of the most wonderful dialogues and speeches of politicians dealing with inter-state ethics.[6] By and large, we shall see how at the beginning of this period Rome posed as a more or less equal partner in an inter-state ethical network that she helped to create. Yet, within three decades Rome had abused the system by interpreting its values in such a manner as to justify her slide into dominance. When she finally subjugated the Greek world in 146 BCE, the inter-state ethical code became irrelevant but left a significant trail of fragments in the Hellenistic world.

Thus, Part I presents a detailed picture of mainly two aspects one is a history of the emergence of an inter-state ethical code, and the other, an overview of patterns of inter-state relations between equals as well as between empire and subject states. Part II consists of two chapters, the first of which will answer the question whether the emerging Jewish state can at all be considered as a typical subject state of a Hellenistic empire. Viewing the relationship of the Seleucids with Judea from the standpoint of the

---

[4] Time span: 213–168 BCE, but I start my survey only in 200 BCE. Rome's imperialism in the Hellenistic East was the theme of many excellent studies, such as Frank (1921), Scullard (1951), Badian (1958), Harris (1979), and Gruen (1984). The latter is the last comprehensive one of which I am aware.

[5] A law code differs from an ethical code mainly because the latter has no index of sanctions. A law code expresses inter alia rules of ethical nature but with sanctions attached; an ethical code can just be a list of rules of the correct behavior without mentioning sanctions. To what extent was the legal system of the Republic influential on Rome's dealings with her Greek neighbors requires a separate study, the closest of which is still Badian (1958). Also, the legal classification of cities and states is not the topic here and was tackled in Badian and the Oxford Classical Dictionary. For law and ethics in the individual city in the classical period, see Herman (2006).

[6] Their compositions are anyhow not very accessible to wider audiences in the humanities to whom this book is targeted. Moreover, the orientation that is needed in narratives that are quite detailed and complicated would be for the general reader a difficult task to acquire.

Seleucid empire, mainly through an examination of the book of 1 Maccabees, we come to the conclusion that Judea was treated similarly to other states that were subjected to Rome and the Hellenistic empires. Chapter 6 focuses on the book of 2 Maccabees and reveals a correspondence with inter-state and communal ethics against the background of the inter-state ethical code that we reconstruct in Part I.

Acknowledgments

I would like to thank my friends and colleagues for their readiness to read the final draft of the manuscript and for their excellent advice in matters of content and English style: Jeffrey A. Barash (Political Philosophy, University of Picardie), James H. Charlesworth (PTS and executive editor of the series), Guy Darshan (Bible, Tel Aviv University), Etan Kohlberg (Islamic studies, Hebrew University of Jerusalem), Loren T. Stuckenbruck (New Testament and Jewish studies, Maximilian University of Munich), Alexander Yakobson (Roman history, Hebrew University of Jerusalem), and Moshe Zimmerman (Modern History, Hebrew University of Jerusalem).

I also wish to express my gratitude to the editors of Bloomsbury T&T Clark, Dominic Mattos and Sarah Blake and to their staff.

This book is dedicated to my wife Michal and to our family for their unfailing encouragement and support.

Doron Mendels
The Hebrew University of Jerusalem
Tel Aviv, April 2021

Part I

Mapping the Hellenistic Political Inter-state Ethical Code

Introduction

The emergence of a nonwritten inter-state ethical code in the first thirty years of the second century BCE can be defined as one of those hidden revolutions in Western cultural history. Why revolution? Because the thirty years discussed in the following signified a relatively fast process in which an evolved set of ethical principles, many of which had sporadically been on the historical scene beforehand, turned into an inter-state arsenal of values that became gradually embedded in the collective system.[1] But what do I mean by system? Rome and the Greek states to her east became an international system, if we follow Buzan and Little's "sources of explanation." They claim that "sources of explanation refer to variables that explain behavior. In the study of international relations, three sources of explanation encompass most of the debate: interaction capacity, process, and structure. They are the key to theory on any given level of analysis and in any sector."[2] Since this analysis is crucial for the understanding of what follows, we will elaborate a bit.

Examples of the processes that can be observed in the international system extend across fighting, political recognition, trade, and identity formation. Process is distinct from structure, which is about how units are arranged in a system, and which is therefore more static and positional. In the following the authors conclude that:

---

[1] This process is reminiscent of the years leading to the French Revolution during which many of the components and ideas of the new ethical code were created. When the revolution broke out in 1789, those and the additional ones molded by the revolutionary events became one comprehensive ethical code that within ten years changed France altogether. See in general for a survey Schama (1989). This is also the case with the Russian 1917 revolution. Several ingredients and sociopolitical aspects of the ethical code of communism and other revolutionary ideas were circulating in Russia long before the revolution (Tolstoy in *Anna Karenina* on communism inter alia mentions them) yet soon became an ethical code during the revolution of 1917 and beyond. In the later years this code was abused altogether. See in general Brown (2009). Some ethical terms and concepts relating to international relations can be found in the remaining epigraphical evidence of 212–168 BCE, translated and interpreted by Sherk (1984: 1–25).
[2] Buzan and Little (2000: 77, 73–4). Sector being the lens through which the scholar views the international relations (specifying the various sectors; my sector/lens here is the ethical one, not specifically mentioned by the two).

perhaps the most interesting aspect of process for IR [International Relations, the discipline] is the durable of recurrent patterns that occur in relations among units ... Other processes, which we label process formation ... These are durable or recurrent patterns in interactions among units. Process formations include war, arms racing, balance of power, the security dilemma, security complexes, alliance, diplomacy, regimes, international organizations ... Process formations often embody action-reaction theories of unit behavior, and so are conditioned by structure, both at the system level (whether anarchic or hierarchic), and at the unit level (for example whether units are ideologically compatible or incompatible).[3]

Interaction capacity:

refers to the amount of transportation, communication, and organizational capability within the unit or system: how much in the way of goods and information can be moved over what distances at what speeds and at what cost? It is about the technological capabilities (e.g. caravans, ships, etc.), and the shared norms, rules, and institutions, on which the type and intensity of interaction between units in a system, or within units, depends. Interaction capacity is about capabilities that are spread throughout any given system or unit (for simplicity sake we will just talk about systems). It refers to the carrying capacity of a social system, its physical potential for enabling the units within it to exchange information, good, or blows. If process defines what units *actually* do when they interact, interaction capacity defines what they *can* do ... interaction capacity is implicit in definitions of systems, all of which stress that units must be interacting in order for a system to exist. Interaction is fundamental to any conceptualization of a system. But other than pointing out that this interaction must be sustained, and in some way influential, the literature is generally silent about the nature of interaction. It can be inferred from some realist writings that the ability to wage war is the key to interaction that defines international systems ... From this perspective, a set of states that cannot pose each other a military threat fail to constitute an international system. It is the ability of states to create and communicate mutually credible military threats which generates a systematic relationship.[4]

Structure:

suggests that the behavior of units is shoved and shaped not only by their internal processes and their interactions with other units, but also by the way in which their environment is constructed. Structure focuses on the principles by which units are arranged into a system, how units are differentiated from each other, and how they stand in relation to each other in terms of relative capabilities ... Although the structures of military-political systems, economic systems, and socio-cultural

---

[3] Buzan and Little (2000: 79).
[4] Buzan and Little (2000: 80).

systems are different (e.g. anarchy, market, international, and world society), they all share these general characteristic.[5]

All of these give us a good theoretical framework. Henceforward we can say that what we are going to relate in the following is a history of an inter-state system that shared an embedded ethical code. Let me clarify my last statement.

During 200–168 BCE, as a result of the encounter of the Greek world with the interventionist activities of Rome in the Hellenistic east, a network that included all states, enemies, as well as allies was created, which shared an ethical inter-state code. This is at least the impression we get from the historiography of the period. In contradistinction to ethical codes that were and still are created and written down by committees at companies and institutions, this ethical code came into existence as a result of historical processes and underwent a gradual development during the evolving events. Early on during this period, it was realized by almost all states in the region that the Roman senate actually took upon itself the role of arbitrator and what we call today the regulator of the right conduct in world affairs. This view was conducive for the creation of an ethical inter-state code recognized by many states that cherished its operational mechanisms. There is no precedent to it in the world before the rise of Rome.[6] Even in Rome's interventionist actions in the West such a code was not apparent. Since this inter-state ethical code remained oral during its emergence, we are lucky that ancient historians on whom we rely for our survey have written down and enhanced its emergence.[7] By doing so they actually converted the code from an oral into a written one. This enabled us to reconstruct much of this ethical code and map its ingredients.

But how did I manage to locate the evidence for such an inter-state ethical code and even map it? The answer is quite simple: In the many speeches, assemblies, and deliberations throughout the three wars that occurred during 200–168 BCE and between them, the representatives of the participating states frequently refer to inter-state values, manners of conduct, and stately etiquette. For instance, when in dialogues it is contested that the state of which a discussant was representative has breached or fulfilled something, such as loyalty or promises for liberty, an inter-state value system as distinct from a code of local laws is referred to. In other words, as the following survey will demonstrate, we are dealing here with what Habermas called "discourse ethics," which is achieved by procedural processes in which "moral rules are liable to justification through agreement by all those affected by them in a discourse situation characterized by symmetry, reciprocity and mutual perspective-taking."[8] His proceduralist discourse theory can easily be applied to inter-state relations where the states are viewed as individuals within a community who talk constantly to each other. In our present research we have mapped a code of values

---

[5] Buzan and Little (2000: 84).
[6] The king's Peace of 387/6 BCE is not a precedent; it is more of a dictate as the wording implies, see Eckstein (2006: 41). The relations between states in classical Greece can also not be an example for the creation of a comprehensive ethical code.
[7] Written pacts and *Senatus Consulta* can still be viewed in museums.
[8] See summary in Pensky (2010: 46).

serving as a framework for an inter-state network that developed its own discourse and political ideas. Thus, we can speak here of a significant ethical revolution created by dialogue during circa thirty years.[9]

* * *

The (Greek) Hellenistic world at the end of the third and during the second centuries BCE was a world that enjoyed intense inter-state relations led by a few dominant powers: Macedonia, the Seleucid and Ptolemaic kingdoms, and Rome. Other states such as Pergamum and a few leading states such as Athens, Sparta, Rhodes, the Achaean, and Aetolian leagues were dominant as well within the inter-state scene. Relationships between states at that time were mainly orderly and sequential, but in general not anarchical as Arthur Eckstein once argued.[10] This political backdrop will serve us to demonstrate how the Hasmonean brothers, and/or the authors of 1–2 Maccabees, corresponded with the narratives of behavior prevalent in the Hellenistic environment. Not again the familiar topics of the Hellenization of their court and etiquette, but a much broader picture will be discussed. That is, against the background of the creation of a virtual inter-state ethical political code and patterns of conduct on the one hand, and the lack of a systematic international law code on the other, the question will be raised whether the emerging Hasmonean state was exceptional or in line with general Hellenistic political ethics and conduct. Before starting our survey, a concise survey of the historical background is needed.

The era of the Hasmonean brothers, the years 168–134 BCE, followed a great shake-up of all the inter-state relationships in the territories east to the Italian peninsula (henceforward the "Hellenistic world/era"). Rome defeated Carthage led by Hannibal in 201 BCE, and shortly thereafter entered a war with the Macedonian king Philip V who had concluded a pact with the Seleucid king Antiochus III with the aim of dividing the treasures and subject territories of Ptolemaic Egypt.[11] The latter empire showed signs of weakness toward the end of the third century BCE, hence the roving eyes of both powers is understandable.[12] In line with this policy Philip V pursued a series of conquests to his east whereas Antiochus III started a conquest of Palestine, the latter being under Ptolemaic rule for a century as of c. 300 BCE. After the decisive victory, the Seleucids annexed Palestine, while its king Antiochus III behaved benevolently toward the Jews and their Temple as we know from the account of Josephus (he was *euergetes*).[13] At that time, with the invitation of Greek cities and the king of Pergamum, Rome intervened and fought for three years on Greek soil against Macedonia. The so-called Second Macedonian War

---

[9] The making of a virtual corpus of inter-state ethics is what I see as a real novelty in international relations and hence enhanced here. Jewish law and ethical traditions were as well oral for centuries until they were transformed into written corpora (cf. Sussman 2020: 29–53).
[10] Eckstein (2006).
[11] From modern history we know of many agreements between states which divide neighbor states such as the three partitions of Poland between its neighbors.
[12] See Eckstein (2006: 269–76) for an excellent survey on this pact.
[13] Josephus, *Ant.* 12.138–146; Stern (1983: 32–42).

ended in 197 BCE at the battle of Cynoscephalae with a decisive Roman victory. Then, the Roman victor, Titus Quinctius Flamininus, announced at an impressive gathering at Corinth that the Greek leagues and cities (henceforward "states") will be free. Yet Rome did not hurry to evacuate Greece since she wanted to settle affairs with Nabis the tyrant of Sparta who still posed a threat to the peace achieved in Greece. When this was done, Rome evacuated Greece, but not for long. Some years later Rome returned and had defeated Antiochus III who invaded Greece in the so-called Roman-Syrian War (192–189 BCE). The settlement reached at Apamea between Rome and the Seleucid kingdom in 188 BCE resulted in a peace treaty that had severe repercussions for the Jews almost twenty years later when the Seleucids were short of money which they were obliged to pay to Rome as reparations; the attempts made by Antiochus IV to extract money from the Temple in Jerusalem ignited the Hasmonean upheaval against the Seleucids. In 171 BCE the Third Macedonian War broke out, this time of Rome in cooperation with several states in the Greek sphere against Perseus king of Macedonia, Philip V's son. This war ended yet again with a Macedonian defeat at Pydna in 168 BCE. We shall see in Part II that the Hasmonean war against the Seleucids should be told against the background of the peace at Apamea and the Third Macedonian War, its end being a point at which change of balance between the powers was created. In addition, we should mention that twenty years after the outbreak of the Hasmonean uprising (168 BCE), a revolt of the Achaean league against Rome broke out in 146 BCE (probably mentioned in 2 Maccabees 8). Subsequent to its suppression, Greece finally became a Roman province. Not long thereafter the last king of Pergamum (Asia Minor) bequeathed his kingdom to the Romans (133 BCE). This is a short historical outline of the international scene in the Hellenistic east during 200–146 BCE. Now we have reached our main topic in this part of the book.

In our modern world, political inter-state ethics has become a major topic since universal morals are breached daily and very little is done to repair it even though an international law code exists and a central institution, the United Nations, is responsible for its enforcement. Yet at the time under discussion when a political inter-state ethical code was not written down in codices or inscriptions, it comes to the fore in speeches, agreements, and dialogues that are adduced by the historiography of the period. It is quite clear that talk about ethical inter-state relations cannot be dissociated from current events, as we learn once and again in the course of human history. Hence in order to unveil and to map the components of such a code, we will write here for the first time a linear survey of the development of an inter-state ethical code as linked to the events, something like "the history of inter-state political ethics of the Hellenistic world during the years 200-168 BCE as adduced by historians of the period." It should be emphasized that for centuries the concept of law (oral and written) was deeply rooted in the city-states of the Greek world as well as in the Roman Republic whose codes of law had a prominent visibility in the poleis.[14] That makes the absence of a systematic written international law code

---

[14] Cf. the laws inscribed on stone positioned in the marketplace and temples of Greek city-states.

quite surprising.¹⁵ However, two factors helped build up an inter-state ethical code while the encounter with Rome and the ensuing wars became the catalyst for its formation. First, representatives of states during the years 200–168 BCE entertained a vast and intensive dialogue about political ethics in conferences and presentations in the Roman senate as well as in assemblies of Greek states. They frequently used ethical terminology drawn from the ethical systems of the individual states, thus creating an arsenal that became a rich source for inter-state ethical discourse. In other words, before 200 BCE, sophisticated local law codes of states never took off to become a systematic international and accessible law code,¹⁶ yet provided some of the components for the creation of an international ethical code. My reader should note that an ethical code was not just a list of values such as loyalty, honesty, and reciprocity but an arsenal of terms, each symbolizing a complex set of sociopolitical and cultural relationships. Reciprocity, for instance, as we shall see later, has different connotations in different circumstances in international bargaining. Second, the term *Ius gentium* was used by the Romans as a self-assuring term (or rather concept) for receiving the legitimacy within Rome to launch wars outside it. Cicero (*De Legibus*) in the first century BCE defined it as "natural law." The belief that some sort of "natural law" shared by all states had existed was yet another fundamental concept that enabled the formation of an inter-state ethical code that was a more realistic expression of the abstract construct of "natural law." Whereas law codes of the individual states usually settled affairs of citizens among themselves and their relationships with the state, ethical codes were universal in nature and could have easily been shared by many nations. Laws of states or agreements on inter-state pacts usually had a sanction attached, whereas ethical rules did not. I will return to this issue when I discuss ethical discourse and its operational modes. It goes without saying that in spite of the fact that treaties between states in Antiquity did sometimes contribute to our understanding of the inter-state value system, they certainly did not serve as evidence for the existence of a comprehensive international law code.¹⁷ Also, as already mentioned, during the encounters of Greek states and monarchies with Rome, the latter's senate (and magistrates) turned during the period under discussion into a formal international institution with authority for arbitration, regulation, and implementation, a phenomenon we have not yet encountered in such a magnitude in Antiquity. Moreover, dialogue between states during wars and cease-fires was already practiced long before the Hellenistic period, yet neither did it develop into a functioning international law code with a regulatory mechanism to

---

¹⁵ That the somewhat monotonous written agreements between Rome and her allies in the period under discussion constitute the beginnings of an international legal system is common knowledge; but very far from the views of Hugo Grotius in the seventeenth century and certainly from the systematic and holistic inter-state legal system, which it became in the next centuries. In contradistinction, the concept of a comprehensive ethical system, theoretical or real (or both), is discussed in the following, which obviously takes the latter agreements of Rome and her allies into account. For the pacts and settlements of Rome during the third and second centuries, see the important surveys of Badian (1958), Dahlheim (1968), and Gruen (1984), all with the older bibliography.

¹⁶ Cf. for getting some idea about such an issue in modern times, see Burset (2019: 483–542).

¹⁷ See for Rome's pacts before 200 BCE Schmitt (1969), and during the period under discussion and beyond Sherk (1984).

enforce such a law nor did it become a comprehensive ethical system.[18] This is not a history that is focused on events, wars, or diplomacy but an attempt to demonstrate the birth of an ethical international virtual code associated with the historical course of events.

---

[18] This observation gets some support from the conclusions of J. Price (2001) concerning Thucydides' stance about the Peloponnesian War. He claims that Thucydides portrayed the war as being a regular internal *stasis* in a Greek city. I would argue that Thucydides just used terms of a typical *stasis* because terms for inter-state ethics were lacking, yet described the war as a regional war between city-states that were organized in two separate leagues, the Delian and the Peloponnesian ones. It should be clarified yet again that values that I mention throughout my survey are not necessarily an invention of the period I discuss here, but their assemblage into one virtual ethical code is what makes it an inter-state ethical revolution.

1

Dialogue, War, and the Public Declaration of Liberty (200–196 BCE)

The beginning of the Second Macedonian War (200–197 BCE) reveals that a strong awareness of inter-state political ethics was already embedded in the discourse of the warring parties and was on the agenda of inter-state relations. The abrupt transition from peace to war in Greece in 200 BCE demonstrates that orderly public procedures for starting a war and deliberations during a truce were shared by Rome and the Greek Hellenistic states. Procedure was not just a technicality; it was a significant mental concept and a state of mind of the participants. The procedures entertained by the Romans during their first encounters with Greeks were basically not foreign to the latter whose conduct shows smooth and natural participation for both Romans and Greeks in public democratic inter-state deliberations. The orderly and frequent procedures, which included a vast diplomatic operation,[1] became vehicles for the acknowledgment, debate, and implementation of political ethical conduct on the level of not only the city-state but also inter-state relations. It would not be an exaggeration to say that there existed a symbiosis between procedure and value. In other words, when political ethics was on the agenda, the Greek cities, states, and kings quite easily understood Roman ideas, and vice versa.[2] On the one hand, the Romans accepted Greek systems of state with which they had frequent encounters, before, during, and at the conclusion of wars; they usually listened patiently to speakers even if they had opposing views (assemblies, voting, speaking, etc.). On the other hand, the Greeks quite naturally accommodated with Roman ideas about inter-state ethics and its procedures (such as the appearances and deliberations in the Roman senate). This mutual understanding and amalgamation in praxis brought about the great inter-state ethical revolution of 200–168 BCE. I will now start with my survey following Livy's account, which is the most complete one and quite dependent, alongside other sources, on Polybius's history, great parts of which were lost.[3]

---

[1] Cf., in general, Grainger (2019).
[2] In the following I will emphasize the understanding of Romans and Greeks of one another's ethics through similar terminology in the two languages.
[3] Cf. Briscoe (1989: 1–48). Livy wrote during the formation of the "Principate," the atmosphere of which surely influenced his writing. See also the discussion of the first five books of Livy's *Ab Urbe Condita* in Vasaly (2015). Nevertheless, Livy was an expert on the Roman Republic and hence a quite reliable source of information. See remarks in the following, *passim*.

A few months after peace had been concluded in the war with Carthage (Second Punic War), war was declared on King Philip V of Macedonia.[4] Around this a vast amount of diplomatic and procedural activity was evident, starting with deliberations in the Roman senate and the *Comitia Centuriata* (allowed only to vote, no discussion). The latter assembly voted first against launching a new war shortly after the one with Cartage was finished, yet after a speech in favor of the war against Philip V presenting the war as defensive on behalf of Rome, the assembly voted in its favor. Receiving approval of the gods was a common ritual toward declaration of wars. The fact that states in antiquity cherished some of their gods who symbolized values such as clemency, justice, mercy, and victory should be kept in mind throughout the following survey. A crucial factor for reaching a positive decision in favor of war was the fact that various Greek states (such as Athens, Rhodes, Pergamum) sent embassies to Rome to complain about Philip's aggressive behavior toward the Greek states to Macedonia's east, followed by a hearing in the senate. Livy's narrative about this period reveals that inter-state principles and values were already imbued in the political discourse that had considerable influence on the events. First and foremost, he emphasizes prayer and ritual for receiving approval of the gods so that the decision to launch a war would turn out "well and happily" not just for Rome but also for participating allied states outside Italy and the Latin colonies;[5] as said, some gods were associated with values such as clemency and victory. Then the question of loyalty in inter-state relations is brought forward through the example of the relationship with the Ptolemaic empire. Livy mentions that three ambassadors were sent to King Ptolemy of Egypt to announce the defeat of Hannibal and the Carthaginians and to thank the king because in critical times when even allies near home had revolted, he had remained loyal, and to ask that if the Romans, compelled by their wrongs, should declare war on Philip, "he should preserve his ancient attitude toward the Roman people" (31.2.3-4). Later Ptolemy sends an embassy and assures the Romans of his loyalty. From the conduct of Ptolemy's ambassadors (31.9.1-5) we get the impression that inter-state relations were at that juncture orderly and even fairly managed between allies. The Ptolemaic empire was requested by Athens to come to her assistance against Philip V but went first to the senate to ask for Rome's permission since both Athens and the Ptolemies were allies of Rome. Rome wanted to settle the affair with Philip V on her own yet showed thankfulness to Ptolemy and gave the ambassadors gifts for the king whose resources were "firm and trustworthy supports of the Republic" (*subsidia firma ac fidelia suae*). This accords with a decree that was reached formerly by the Roman senate that the allies should be thanked because, though long harassed, they had not been led to break their faith even by fear of siege. The crucial terms here are *gratia* and *fide* as opposed to injury (*iniuria*),

---

[4] Livy 31.5.1; Gruen (1984).
[5] Livy 31.5.4. For reasons of brevity, textual problems and comparisons with other fragmentary sources will not be tackled here. The two main commentaries that will accompany our narrative are those of Frank Walbank on Polybius and John Briscoe on Livy, which will henceforward be occasionally mentioned. For Livy Book 31 and its comparison to Polybius and other fragments, see the detailed commentary of Briscoe (1989: 49–165), and for Polybius's fragments of this period, see Walbank (1967: 530–47).

disgrace, fortune, and power (in its different manifestations), all terms that became common in the international discourse henceforward (31.5-6.6). An example of disloyalty is adduced in the speech before an informal meeting of the assembly (*contio*) where a case is presented of allies who revolt when an opportunity arises.[6] Livy, as well as other ancient historians, is well aware of another level of political interaction, namely, the one of feelings and state of mind of decision makers. Hence already in this episode of the preparations for the Second Macedonian War, we hear of weariness of the hardships of war, enjoyment of peace, annoyance (of the senate), apathy, happiness, favorable opinion, and so on.

Declaration of war, as Livy presents it, was not just a technical matter. It was a formal statement that was usually considered as part and parcel of inter-state political ethics; in other words, fair play. Warning before wars was a basic rule of the right conduct in inter-state relationships. Even during fighting, a certain degree of honesty was expected, sometimes viewed as a last opportunity to grant one's opponent a chance to avoid war. Livy emphasizes that the fetials were consulted by the consul about the question whether the declaration of war against King Philip be delivered to him in person or whether it was sufficient to announce it at the first fortified post in his territory. The fetials' reply was that in whichever way he acted he would act correctly (*recte facturum*, 31.8). This correct action is portrayed as one of the cornerstones of inter-state ethics. Correctness, as it were, also plays a role in the decision of the college of priests who decided that a vow to the gods could also be on an indefinite sum.[7] I will come back to vows as an international value.

Another important inter-state ethical rule was the acknowledgment of the ancestral possessions of others. Being ancestral was at that time equivalent to being legitimate in the international discourse. Not that this ethical rule—like all other rules—was necessarily honored during wars and annexation, but it was high up on the value scale; we will encounter it quite frequently in our survey henceforward. A typical example adduced by Livy is the one of King Masinissa from North Africa who was congratulated by Rome (*Masinissae gratulari iussi*) because he had not only recovered his ancestral possessions (*patrium recuperasset regnum*) but had also enlarged them by the addition of the most prosperous part of the territory of a neighboring kingdom (31.11). This theme of ancestral territories as part of the value of ancestrality in the negotiation between states will be emphasized later.

Another value that we will meet in our text quite frequently later on is the one of reciprocity. The latter value was high up in the value system since it was a stabilizing factor in inter-state relationships. Failure to reciprocate brought states frequently into conflict. In many instances the term assumed that physical exchange of commodities in return for support and/or other favors had to take place. Emphasis is laid by our sources on equal relationships (usually between nonequals, such as Rome and her allies[8]) in which, for instance, gifts were measured according to the status of both giver

---

[6] 31.7. The term *auxilium* (assistance) as a value in inter-state relations will be mentioned later.
[7] 31.9.8: *Posse rectiusque etiam esse pontifices decreverunt*.
[8] See later Rome and the Hasmoneans in Part II.

and receiver, depending on the circumstances in which things were exchanged.[9] In order for gifts and/or other commodities to be valid they had to transfer hands and become the ownership of the receiver.[10] Later in the text we even hear of reciprocity in the grant of citizenship between two states of equal status, like Athens and Rhoads (31.15.6-7). The terms "praise," "excuse," and "blame" are sometimes associated with the notion of reciprocity (supplementation)[11] and will be discussed later in connection with the ancient (positive) connotations of revenge, which should also fall into the category of reciprocity.

An incident that took place at Athens at the beginning of the Second Macedonian War reveals other components of a value system that played a significant role in inter-state relations.[12] According to Livy, the provocation that started the Second Macedonian War occurred in Athens when two Acarnanians "during the celebration of the mysteries at Eleusis, though not initiated, had entered the temple of Ceres, unaware that they were committing a sacrilege" (31.14.7-9). They were sentenced to death as if they "committed some heinous crime."[13] This had been reported to Philip V, who viewed the matter as a "revolting and unfriendly act" on behalf of Athens toward another state. The Acarnanians revenged by an attack on Athens. "This was the original provocation; later regular war was declared and waged by decree of the state after formal notification" (*iustum bellum decretis civitatis ultro indicendo factum*) (31.14.10). Desecration of temples was regarded as a significant breach of inter-state ethics that aroused a great deal of bad feelings not just in the individual states but also within the international sphere. This means that it was expected from states and kingdoms to respect each other's holy places.

Respect in general, "secular and religious," as a central ethical rule in inter-state relations had several facets, some of which we find in the Athenian episode. For instance, the Romans and Greeks put much emphasis on the art of listening to each other's views whether in conferences, embassies, speeches, or unofficial parties.[14] Dialogue between states was a prominent expression of mutual respect, which also had ritual outlets. King Attalus of Pergamum who arrived in Athens in order to confirm the alliance with the Athenians, accompanied by Roman ambassadors, was received

---

[9] *Dona ampla*, 31.11.10-12: "Ample gifts—vases of gold and silver, a purple toga, a tunic adorned with palms, an ivory scepter, a robe of state and a curule chair—were given them to be presented to the king," and 31.9.5.

[10] Cf. Mendels (2013: 94-104) for an extensive discussion of gifts in the Hellenistic Near East and the Hasmoneans.

[11] Mendels (2013: 94-5).

[12] Livy 31.14-15. I follow in most of my survey the account of Livy that is complete and comprehensive since he drew on both Polybius and other fragmentary sources, mainly annalists (see for his sources Briscoe 1989: 1-48). Wherever possible I adduce the Greek terminology of terms that will appear in my reconstructed inter-state ethical code. Yet I am extremely economic in the use of Latin and Greek to simplify the narrative for the nonexperts who may read the book. I cannot delve here into a discussion of the different versions concerning the events adduced by Polybius and Livy. The comparison has been done ad nauseam and is not my topic here (see commentaries mentioned above).

[13] Reminiscent of Heliodorus's entrance into the Jerusalem Temple later in the century (2 Maccabees 3 and Part II, Chapter 6).

[14] See in the following where I adduce a reference of a beautiful dialogue in a private social gathering in Achaea. For their deliberations in private dinners and social gatherings, cf. Livy 32.29.

by the whole body of citizens (*civitas omnis, pantes hoi politai*) with their families who "poured out to meet him; the priests in their vestments and the very gods, so to speak, starting up from their thrones, welcomed him as he entered the city."[15] From Polybius's *Histories* we learn that the gathering became "such a demonstration on the part of the people of their affection for the Romans and still more for Attalus that nothing could have exceeded it in heartiness," using *philanthropia* and *hyperbole*, two most common ethical terms in the Hellenistic public sphere. The advent of a Hellenistic king— comparable to endless receptions of kings and their representatives in Hellenistic diplomacy (the most famous precedent is the visit of Alexander the Great in Jerusalem; Josephus Ant.11.329-339)—became a token of one state being honored by another. A written speech of Attalus, rather than an oral one that seemed "more consonant with his dignity," was read before the Athenian assembly of citizens (*ekklesia, populus*). The king's letter emphasized three matters: the king's generosity (*euergesia, beneficium*) toward Athens, an account of the campaigns he had already carried out against Philip V of Macedonia, and an exhortation to continue the fight against Philip while having the Rhodians and Rome as allies. The Athenians voted for war against Macedonia as a result of their *eunoia* for King Attalus of Pergamum.[16] The Rhodians were then given a hearing and their goodwill (*beneficium*) was enhanced. Then, after receiving extravagant honors, they and King Attalus of Pergamum received various gifts. This entire episode is filled with terms taken from the arsenal of political ethics such as liberty, glory, generosity, fame—terms that are recurrent in the narratives of that period and will be discussed later on as I proceed with my survey.

The war continues with ups and downs in the battlefield for both sides (we are still at the beginning of the war in the year 200 BCE). Yet at certain junctures talk and dialogue were resumed between the warring parties and the allies.[17] The episodes that exemplify values such as valor, treachery as opposed to loyalty, and voluntary submission of states to a super power rather than having a bloody encounter are enhanced.[18] That leads us to an episode where negotiations between the warring parties failed, and that the more powerful power determined the outcome of a conflict.

Abydus was under the authority of Pergamum, the ally of Rome, and a garrison was stationed there. Garrisons had a twofold purpose: to ensure the safety of one's subjects and to secure the interest of the empire. Philip V, who demanded its surrender, was rejected twice. Thus, Philip started a siege during which a Roman ambassador who was en route to another mission approached him and, in spite of the fact that the Romans were in the midst of a war with him, quite usual in antiquity, was received for a hearing. This meeting is interesting from our point of view. On Philip's claim that King Attalus of Pergamum and the Rhodians had made an unprovoked attack upon him, the Roman

---

[15] 31.14.12, and Polybius 16.25.5-6; Walbank (1967: 533–5).
[16] Polybius 16.26.7-8. Here we have yet another example of a value combined with an emotion that leads to a decision-making (defined as 'characteristic" in my *History as Repetition* where the model is exhibited for a more popular audience. Yet the model is universal and can be used as well in historical analysis addressed to experts in the field).
[17] Comparable to talk during wars in modern history, such as during the American civil war (enemies were talking during ceasefires).
[18] 31.16.4-5; Polybius 16.26.7 (using *eunoia*); and Walbank (1967: 535–6).

ambassador Aemilius asked: "Did the people of Abydus also take up arms against you, unprovoked?" Whether this dialogue really happened, presented a bit differently by Polybius who was apparently Livy's source here,[19] it reveals an interesting aspect in the politics of dialogue during war in the Hellenistic period. The Macedonian king,

> who was unused to hearing the truth [similar to authoritative rulers in our modern democracies], too arrogant for delivery in the royal presence, replied: "Your age, your good looks, and, above all, the Roman name, make you too arrogant. I should myself prefer first that you remember the treaties and keep the peace with me; but if you attack me in war, you will find that I too have the resolution to make both the kingdom and the name of Macedonia no less renowned than those of Rome." (31.18.3-4)

A dialogue to clarify conflicting positions of enemies at war that was still going on and intertwined in the events shows the awareness of both sides of the existence of an (undocumented) ethical code of the correct inter-state conduct that could be referred to. Clarification of a state's position, as in other instances that will be discussed later, does not mean consent but an urge to explain what the right conduct should be. Even if such dialogues are made up by the historians who were describing the events, they reveal a cultural atmosphere in which reference to inter-state values was part and parcel of the political game. This particular dialogue between the two representatives of states unfolds the notion that arrogance, as opposed to modesty, one might infer, was on the agenda in inter-state political discourse, as we will see later in my discussion of 1 Maccabees when Antiochus IV's arrogance is mentioned. We will also learn in the following that "renown" remained throughout the period a dominant value in the inter-state ethical scale of values.

Talk about ethics is not the only way to enhance certain values in inter-state discourse during war; ethical values were also put to the test through action. This can be learned from the episode of the conquest of Abydus by Philip V, which unfolds yet another set of ethical values such as valor combined with pride.[20] When Philip demanded unconditional surrender from the people of Abydus, Livy says that it "kindled such passion, arising from anger and despair together" that the people of Abydus launched a communal suicidal act alongside their brave fight with the enemy; to such a desperate decision they have arrived, since falling into the hands of a Hellenistic king subsequent to a stubborn struggle against him could, as the people of Abydus very well knew, turn into a bloody affair. On the other hand, a communal suicidal act as a result of an emotional arousal could be seen as a statement that was supposed to cross borders, and broadcast a message of steadfastness combined with pride to other states that might get into conflict with a super power. Communal suicide was a realistic option in order to avoid massacre by the enemy with or without fighting; both decision and act were

---

[19] For the episode of Abydus, see Polybius 16.29-35 and Walbank (1967: 538–44).
[20] Polybius 16.32.1 comments about the episode: "All this would induce one to say that the daring courage (*tolme*) of the Abydenes surpassed even the famous desperation (*aponoia*) of the Phocians and the courageous (*eupsuxian*) resolve of the Acarnanians."

a materialization of a strong group identity and independent thought. Suicide of a group became a visible (and last) expression of free thinking and its immediate result, a heroic death. This latter act was admired and followed by various states henceforward. Livy ends the story by stating that the people of Abydus

> hastily ran to kill their wives and children and then themselves sought death by every path. The king, astonished by this frenzy, checked the assaults of his soldiers and announced that he would give the Abydensians three days to die. At that time the conquered caused themselves more violence than they might have suffered from their enraged conquerors. No living man fell into Philip's hands save those whom chains or some other constraint forbade to die. (31.18.7-8)

This last comment enhances the association between being free and committing suicide and being enslaved and being incapable of making the choice between slavery and freedom. Philip, leaving a garrison at Abydus, returned to his kingdom.

Two conferences that followed these events will be discussed now. The first being the assembly of the Achaean league portrayed by Livy (31.25). It was King Philip V who retreated from his terrible attack on Athens and entered the council of the Achaean league convened at Argos.[21] Leagues were organizations of several cities as members with frequent and seasonal gatherings with a central elected council and magistrates. They were quite nationalistic, the passive sort.[22] Leagues were perhaps the closest political organizations to what we call today federal states. Be that as it may, Philip appeared at the meeting itself, to the surprise of the Achaeans while they were deliberating about a war against Nabis, the tyrant of Sparta (who was not a member of the league). Regardless of his real intentions, namely, to deceive the council and to involve his ally the Achaean league in the war against Rome,[23] he mentions two important terms, protection (of one country by another) and responsibility taken by an empire in order to relieve the smaller states of performing an independent act. His proposal was rejected by a procedural excuse: "it was not allowed under the laws of the Achaeans to vote upon other subjects than those for which the meeting was called, after passing a decree regarding raising an army against Nabis, [he] adjourned the conference that was held fearlessly and spiritedly" (31.25.9-10). Although this incident looks as a simple procedural matter, it offers more than meets the eye. First and foremost a law of the league is strictly obeyed and used to fend off even an approach of a king of a (ruling) empire. The king reluctantly accepts it and retreats (namely, respects the local law). Second, the emphasis on a meeting that is held "fearlessly and spiritedly" means that these values were appreciated and used in international discourse. This is at least what Livy thought of this gathering.

The second gathering is also intriguing from our point of view. A conference of the Aetolian league is adduced by Livy in which the warring parties led by Rome and

---

[21] Cf. for the Achaean league, Larsen (1968: 80–9, 215–40); cf. also Walbank (1979: 406–14).
[22] Polybius Book 2 (37.10-11) and Larsen (1968). For passive and active nationalism, see Mendels (2020: 564–70).
[23] See fragment Polybius 16.38. For Nabis, see Mendels (1998: 223–48).

Macedonia were invited to convince the Aetolians that they would be better off if they side with each of them in the war.[24] Through this meeting we get an opportunity to listen to a variety of views about political inter-state ethics and other related principles. The Macedonians spoke first, to deter the Aetolians, "this restless people" (*gens inquieta*), to change its allegiance with Macedonia upon arrival of the Romans (31.28.6). Hence their speech was built around the theme of loyalty in a relationship between states. The dialogue is concerned with positive values and brings to mind the negative ones: "Do you prefer," said one of the Macedonian ambassadors, "to imitate Roman presumption, or shall I call it fickleness?" He adds that the Romans complained about a breach of a contract between them and the Aetolians,[25] when the Aetolians concluded a pact with the Macedonians "without the authority" of Rome, who formerly pretended that they had taken arms against him on the Aetolians' account and for their sake; now the Romans forbid the Aetolians to be at peace with Philip V. The Macedonian ambassador here enhances the notion of loyalty as opposed to fickleness but even more so the question of who has the authority in inter-state relations to have the last word on international conduct. Here the Macedonian ambassador challenges Roman authority to enforce it on the Greek states, in this case on Aetolia. His arguments deserve an explanation. The speaker draws a distinction between Roman and Macedonian rule in reference to the concept of liberty, which with all its variant meanings was still high up in the ethical scale of inter-state relations and discourse. Through some examples from the past, the speaker makes clear that although the Romans came to "rescue and restore liberty" they subjugated the "liberated" (31.29.6-16). Moreover, the Romans left the council of the Sicilians intact, while "the Roman praetor presides at the council; the men whom he has summoned by his authority assemble. They see him seated on his lofty platform, rendering haughty justice, with a throng of lictors around him; their rods threaten their backs, the axes their throats; and year by year the lots grant them one master after another." The Macedonian ambassador goes on with atrocities that, according to him, Rome has inflicted on her subjects. He contrasts this with Macedonian imperialism that is quite mild: "The rule of Philip seems to interfere somewhat with your liberty; but he, though he would justly be angry with you [the Aetolians], has asked nothing from you except peace and to-day desires nothing but your loyalty to your pledge of peace."

He adds that if the Aetolians will be under Roman authority, it will be too late to call upon the Macedonians to assist them. In other words, his understanding of the term "liberty" is milder than that of the Romans. One additional argument of the Macedonian ambassador should be mentioned: The Greeks who are occasionally split by trivial causes are by nature united (creating a united identity) against common enemies with whom they have an eternal war since they are barbarians, referring to the Persians but having in mind the Romans. Namely, not a sporadic but a constant enmity is mentioned. From our point of view this means that the Greek world is united

---

[24] For the Aetolian league and this incident, see Larsen (1968: 78–80, 195–215); cf. in general Scholten (2000).
[25] Peace of Phoenice in 205 BCE that concluded the First Macedonian War, 213–205 BCE. See Gruen (1984: 389–90).

by language and culture, hence by a common set of codes of conduct that could not be shared with barbarians as the Roman Republic was at that time perceived by the Macedonians (around 200 BCE). This is of course a wild exaggeration since when the Romans crossed the Adriatic and started to intervene in mainland Greece, its islands, and the western shore of Asia Minor, the ethical code was easily shared with the Greeks. In spite of the difference of language and political antagonism, the mutual understanding of morals and ethics happened quite fast, as we discover in my survey here. A similar process had also occurred when the Hellenistic kingdoms conquered the Eastern countries where they immediately had a rapport, ethical and cultural, with the ruling Greek segment of the subjugated countries.[26]

The delegation of the Athenians came next (31.30). From their speech we can learn the extent of cruelty and savageness that Athens suffered from the Macedonian king whose devastation and miserable destruction of their land they lamented. Livy says that the Athenians

> did not complain because they suffered the treatment of an enemy from an enemy, for there are certain laws of war (*belli iura*) which are legitimately to be experienced as well as practiced: it is sad, rather than unjust to the sufferer, that crops be burned, homes be destroyed, men and animals driven off as booty; but they did, however, complain that he who calls the Romans aliens and barbarians had so polluted human and divine law alike (*omnia simul divina humanaque iura polluerit*) that on his first raid he had waged impious war on the gods of the world below, on his second, with the gods above. (31.30.2-4)

He goes on describing the desecration of holy sites and temples by Philip. Briscoe in his commentary on Livy, justifiably, referring to *belli iura*, comments that "the passage implies that these are the rights of the combatants to inflict injury, not a set of rules prohibiting certain actions," and that "there was, however, clearly no agreement on what actions were prohibited. To protest against acts considered excessive, appeal could be made to the more general 'Laws of mankind' as in Polybius 2.58.6, or to the *humana iura* here."[27]

The Roman delegate to the conference spoke at length; I will adduce only the ratio decidendi that concerns us here (31.31). He blames Philip for "grievous and cruel treatment wherever he had greater power to do harm." Rome is presented by him as a liberator that concerning her allies "each one's fortune is proportioned to his services". He even mentions what liberty means: restoration of possessions and lands alongside laws and liberty, and in some instances also a grant of Roman citizenship. By examples taken from the history of Rome he enhances the necessity to be loyal and to avoid ingratitude and ever. betrayal in inter-state relations (31.10-20). Other values in international ethics are also brought forward, such as to be free of guilt

---

[26] See Part II, Chapters 5–6 for the rapport of the Seleucid empire with the imitators of Greek culture in Judea.

[27] *Ton anthropon nomous*; Briscoe (1989: 133–4). Polybius mentions in 2.58.10 *tou polemou nomous* (and see 7.14.3; Walbank 1967: 61).

(he mentions suicidal acts as a result of guilt feelings) (31.31.14) and pity (granting liberty and peace to the subjugated who beforehand harmed the Romans). From Livy's interpretation of the reaction of the president of the Aetolian council, we learn that, at least according to him, repentance and wisdom were values to be reckoned with in inter-state relations: "nothing was so inconsistent with wisdom in a great crisis as haste; for repentance, swift yet non the less late and unavailing, followed, when hastily-formed plans could not be recalled and annulled" (31.32.2).

In the following chapters Livy mentions in passing other values of the virtual value system pertaining to international inter-state relationships, beginning with respect for the soldiers who died in battle, that is, burial of the fallen in times of war (31.34). Here Livy demonstrates how intentions of a ruler—"to secure the affection of his people and increase their readiness to encounter danger on his behalf"—were misinterpreted by his addressees, a phenomenon well known from modern democracies: "Nothing is as uncertain or unpredictable as the mental reaction of a crowd. What [Philip] thought would make them more ready to enter any conflict [a public exhibit and burial of the fallen], caused instead reluctance and fear" (watching the dreadful wounds of the victims).[28] Here affection and readiness to fight are juxtaposed with reluctance and fear of the army, and will be dealt with later in this chapter when the emotions of groups will be addressed. In this section Livy also adduces an example of two individuals who fail to reciprocate each other in the act of gifting, a matter that occurred frequently between states and caused not once or twice friction in inter-state relations.[29] Communal hatred and its expression in the policy/ritual of forgetting (*damnatio memoriae*) as a recurrent value in international affairs is described in an emotionally charged paragraph by Livy (31.44). The Athenians take revenge on Philip V due to his violent destruction of their holy sites and of the looting he performed in their fields (mentioned beforehand in the account). Livy describes the emotional process that led to the erasure of Philip's memory from Athenian public memorials:[30]

> The Athenian people, whose hatred for Philip had long been restrained by fear, in view of the prospect of aid at hand, gave full vent to their anger. Tongues ready to incite the mob are never lacking in that city; and this conduct is encouraged by popular applause, not only in free states generally, but especially in Athens, where oratory has greatest influence. (31.44.2-3)

The motion that the people passed was that all statues of Philip, all representations of him, their inscriptions, and also those of his ancestors, should be removed and eliminated. Also, that Philip, his children, and kingdom and "the whole race and name of the Macedonians" should often be cursed and despised during all the feast days,

---

[28] See also 31.34.2-3, a passage which is reminiscent of Judah's tactics. See 31.41, fear as motivation to flee into the mountains (Mattathias in 1 Maccabees), and a juxtaposition of fight in the plains and fight in the mountains—probably a well-known tactic in the Hellenistic period (compare to Bar-Kochva 1989).

[29] 31.43.5-7: Scopas, a famous Aetolian politician "who had not been generous with gifts to him."

[30] For memory and its erasure, see 1 Maccabees *passim*, where the Jews are afraid of physically being annihilated. On the other hand, the memory of their heroes is kept for future generations (3:8-9).

sacred observances, and priesthoods that had been formerly established in honor of the Macedonian dynasty. "It was added to the decree that if anyone thereafter made any proposal that had to do with bringing disgrace or ignominy on Philip, the Athenian people would adopt it in toto." Livy comments at the end of this chapter that "this was the Athenians' war against Philip, conducted by means of letters and words, which constitute their sole strength." This is corroborated by the following sentence: "Attalus and the Romans, putting in first at Piraeus after leaving Hermione, and tarrying there a few days and being loaded down with decrees as effusive in the praise of the allies as those others in condemnation of the enemy, sailed from Piraeus to Andros" (31.45.1-2). This entire description enhances the symbiosis between emotions of a group (army, body of citizens), such as boldness, fear, contempt, hatred and anger, and inter-state ethical conduct, namely, a system of values (*damnatio memoriae* as a means to erase bad and wayward deeds). Moreover, letters and other communicative means are the typical channels of expressing emotions and their relationship with values.

Talk during War

Four conferences will be tackled now, two in this section and two in the next one.

In the midst of the Second Macedonian War, Philip V was prevailed upon to discuss peace proposals through the mediation of the people of Epirus; hence a conference was convened on the banks of the Aous river (198 BCE).[31] This conference is one of a series of conferences whose aim was to try and avoid the continuation of the war. As already mentioned, avoidance of war and seeking either a truce or, preferably, peace was high up in the scale of rules of conduct during international deliberations. The dialogue between the Macedonian king and the Roman consul unveils some basic values/principles that yet again emphasize the presence of an inter-state value system with a political universal orientation.

The substance of the Roman consul's demands was this:

> The king should withdraw his garrisons from the cities; he should restore what property was recoverable to those whose lands and towns he had ravaged; a valuation should be made of the rest by an impartial board. Philip replied that the status of the several cities was not uniform: those which he had captured himself, he would set free; those which he had received from his forefathers he would not surrender his hereditary and lawful possession. If these states with which he had fought complained of any losses due to war, he would submit to arbiters chosen by them from nations with which both parties were at peace. The consul responded that for this purpose there was no need of any arbiter or umpire: for to whom was it not evident that he who had been the aggressor in war inflicted the injury, and that Philip, attacked by none, had first waged war on all? (32.10.3-6)

---

[31] Livy 32.10. For Livy Book 32 and its comparison to Polybius et al., see the detailed survey of Briscoe (1989: 166–247); Walbank (1967: 545–71).

When in the following the consul Titus Quinctius Flamininus mentioned Thessaly should be liberated, the king left the meeting in rage. The war goes on, but the dialogue enhances some ethical principles/values of the visual ethical inter-state code, such as respect for property which was hereditary and lawful, known as ancestral land; liberty, impartiality (neutrality), peace, justice (opposite of injury).

When later in the year ambassadors from the Roman army, King Attalus of Pergamum, Rhoads and King Philip were granted a hearing at the Achaean league's council, the Achaean participants, unlike their usual conduct (polemicizing) and their lively private arguments at home concerning leaving the Macedonian alliance and/or concluding one with Rome, remained silent.[32] Nobody dared to speak, apparently because of fear of the Macedonian representative who was present. Yet Aristaenus who was one of the leaders of the pro-Roman faction at the Achaean league's assembly mentions during his vehement speech some of the most important universal values of the Greek inter-state scene. His speech is in many respects an eye-opener for the study of the embedded moral codes of international relations in the leadership of states in the Hellenistic world.

His main argument is based on the preliminary assumption that when a choice has to be made by a state between assisting one side in a war, with whom the state had already a long-standing alliance which was taken under oath (the Macedonians), and an adversary with whom there is no alliance, special circumstances should be taken into consideration when the state comes forward with a decision (decision-making, I remind the reader, is a characteristic in my model explained above). But is a breach of contract made between states acceptable? Our speaker has a clear-cut view on this issue, saying that even if the Achaean league was in alliance with Macedonia which had been taken under oath, the league could nevertheless opt for the Roman side. The reason for that is that Macedonia has neglected her ally in the past on several occasions and does not show that it has the intention and military power to assist her at present. Macedonia could even become a "harsher master after the war." In contradistinction, the Romans were nearby with their fleet and army (and resources) and were interested in the Achaeans' friendship; hence, the Roman's offer should be grabbed since this golden opportunity would not recur in the future. Keeping neutral—in itself a well-known principle in inter-state relationships—was in this case "no course at all" (*ea non media, sed nulla via est*) and could turn against the Achaean league in due course. But how can all of this justify a breach of contract in particular when the Achaeans were bound to the Macedonians "by acts of kindness both old and new" (*beneficiis et veteris et recentibus obligati errant*)?[33] The answer given is that when loyalty (in particular under oath) is weighed against utility and benefit in international affairs, utility has the upper hand if special circumstances require and/or justify it. The Achaean speaker

---

[32] Livy 32.19-23.3. For their home meetings, see in particular Aristaenus, the praetor of the Achaeans' speech: "Where are those rivalries of feeling, Achaeans, which cause you hardly to refrain from blows, when mention is made of Philip and the Romans at your dinners and social gatherings? Now, in a council called for this one purpose ... you are silent" (32.20.3-4).

[33] In Part II we will discover yet again that breach of alliances was commonplace when the Maccabees were involved in inter-state war and politics (cf. for a treaty between Rome and Kibyra Sherk 1984: 24–5).

has made the role of utilitarianism crystal clear when he juxtaposed values (loyalty) with bad conduct (apathy) of one of the parties to an inter-state treaty. Hence, the Macedonians were, according to this view, the first ones to have breached the alliance. Within this context, it should be added, Aristaenus makes a clear distinction between a wayward ruler and the (good) state. He emphasizes the corrupt, cruel, and unjustified rulership of Philip V (as opposed to the one of Antigonus, his predecessor) who was viewed by the Achaeans, his allies, with suspicion since he violated "all human and divine justice"; as already mentioned, they even feared that he "would be a harsher master after the war." This distinction is crucial since those who might still have had a moral problem with the breach of treaty and disloyalty in inter-state relations get here a sophisticated answer: When a government is corrupt, and since the breach is of a contract concluded with ruler rather than with state, it is quite natural, and even justified, to breach this very contract in favor of another, a more beneficial one, which grants general welfare by a state and not an occasional leader (*salutis communis*), profit for the community (*quae nobis censerent utilia esse*), public interest (*commune consultum*), security, and protection: a new ally on whom you can *rely* at all times. Utility is yet again brought forward as a value imbued in the ethical inter-state system but should be balanced when it clashed with other values such as loyalty and friendship. Utility falls into the category of "applied ethics" since "utilitarianism puts the emphasis always on *consequences,* not on first principles. Employing the criterion of the 'greatest happiness of the greatest number'—originally made famous by the philosopher Jeremy Bentham ...—as a criterion for judging public policy becomes the means for deciding whether a particular policy is good or bad."[34]

The end of this scene is illuminating from our perspective. The majority in the Achaean assembly approved the cessation of the Macedonian alliance in favor of the Roman one. When the decision was declared, the delegates from Dyme and Megalopolis and some of the Argives left the council before the motion was passed, "no one expressing either surprise or reproach." And here comes the reason for their departure (32.22.8-12):

For within the memory of their forefathers, the Megalopolitani defeated by the Spartans, had been restored to their homes by Antigonus [the Macedonian king of the past][35], and to the Dymaei, who had recently been captured and plundered by the Romans, Philip had restored both liberty and their homes, having ordered them to be ransomed wherever they were enslaved; many of the Argives, too, besides believing that the kings of Macedon derived from them, were bound to Philip by personal ties as well and by private friendship.[36]

These were the reasons for their withdrawal from a council which was about to vote in favor of an alliance with Rome. "Indulgence was granted them for withdrawing,

---

[34] Bell (2010: 79–81).
[35] Antigonus Doson. Cf. Briscoe (1989: 208).
[36] Herman (1987) for ritual friendship.

bound as they were by great and recent acts of kindness" (*excesserunt, veniaque iis huius secessionis fuit et magnis et recentibus obligatis beneficiis*) (32.22.12).

Three points are in order. First, an attempt to reconcile between the right inter-state value system and utilitarian ideas is brilliantly exhibited in the speech of Aristaenus. He speaks in favor of a violation of a pact for another more beneficial one. Yet the three states that thought otherwise were exempt from voting in the assembly. They opted for staying with the Macedonian alliance because they were of the opinion that loyalty to a past ally should be preferred to benefits, favors, and utility granted at present. Loyalty is presented by them in one of its most elevated forms, namely, gratefulness to another state for its assistance in the past. Second, indulgence and tolerance were considered as institutional values of individual states which were applied, as we realize here, to inter-state relationships. Respect, forgiveness, and understanding expressed by a majority of the voting members toward the minority are quite astonishing at a time when modern democracies ignore and/or despise these very values.[37] By and large, the democratic procedure of a federal state remained a key mechanism for the public to express the states' stance concerning the value system adopted by all other states. Third, liberation here simply means freeing one state from its subjugation to another. This aspect will be discussed later on in our survey.

Good Faith, True Courage, and Wisdom

The narrative of the conference near Nicaea on the shore of the Malian gulf is fascinating (32.32-36). The participants were Macedonia, Rome, and her allies; it convened for three days ending nearby on the beach near Thronium. The conference, as Livy presents it, reveals some theatrical aspects in which the role given to the actors was probably designed in order to demonstrate how the art of performance was a strategy used in inter-state communications. For example, during the dialogue the king stayed in his boat floating on the water while the allies remained on the bank of the river, a graphic symbol, one of many, denoting a distance between the conflicting sides.[38] Another theatrical trick was a delay of the arrival of the hero while all other participants (and readers for that matter) were waiting for him in suspense. King Philip, instead of arriving at the set time, creates a theatrical tension by letting the other party wait for some hours, showing up at the very last moment before the meeting was dispersed. Then, he wished to speak with the Roman general tête-à-tête. In their ensuing meeting they agreed that the final decision would be made by the Roman senate. Be that as it may, the values that surface in this conference were first and foremost attentiveness to one's adversary during dialogue. Patient negotiations can clarify misunderstandings and avoid even war. Also, being flexible and giving in can be conducive to inter-state interactions. Although status quo ante was not yet a

---

[37] See for this minority 32.19-23.3. Among Philip's crimes (32.21.23), a political murder mentioned is reminiscent of the murder of Simeon in 1 Macc. 16:11-22.

[38] Later it will be Nabis who arrives with his whole army to a conference. See in Part II the conference of Judah with Nicanor, p. 162.

familiar and defined judicial term for inter-state relations in antiquity, it is what the Roman representative demands from Philip, yet Philip agrees only partially; when the case was later brought before the Roman senate his representatives leave with great disappointment. The Macedonian arguments were rejected by the house and the war resumed. Let us delve into the details that will shed light on our efforts to reconstruct the inter-state ethical code that emerged during the Second Macedonian War. But let us return to the conference.

Philip is asked by the Roman general Titus Quinctius Flamininus and the other participants to do the following (32.33): If the king really wants to have peace, he should withdraw his garrisons from all the cities in Greece and give up the captives and fugitives to the allies of the Roman people. He should also return to the Romans the parts of Illyricum that he had occupied subsequent to the peace that had been made at the end of the First Macedonian War in Epirus (205 BCE). The cities that he had occupied since the death of Ptolemy Philopator should be restored to King Ptolemy of Egypt. The ambassador of King Attalus required Philip to return the prisoners and ships that were confiscated in the naval battle off Chios, and "that the Nicephorium and the temple of Venus which he had despoiled and destroyed should be restored to their former state." The Rhodians also had a list of demands, namely, that the district of Peraea, "a district on the mainland opposite their island, and under their ancient control," should be given back to them. They also insisted that Philip's garrisons should be withdrawn from several cities that are specifically named: Iasus and Bargyliae and the city of the Euromenses, as well as Sestus and Abydus. Perinthus "should be given back to the Byzantines and permitted to enjoy its ancient rights (*et Perinthum Byzantiis in antiqui formulam iuris restitui*), and that all the markets and ports of Asia should be made free." The Achaeans adduced their own demands, namely, the restoration to the league of Corinth and Argos. Then the praetor of the Aetolians "having made practically the same demands as the Romans, [required] that Greece should be evacuated, and that the cities which had formerly been under the control and sway of the Aetolians should be returned to them" (Judah Maccabee was not the only one who was a champion for complete liberty of a state). Here comes a speech of an Aetolian noble, Alexander, who discusses conduct of states during war, proper and negative. But before dealing with this, I should mention Philip's reaction to the demands put by the allies. The Macedonian king began to complain that the Aetolians, like the Romans, ordered him to withdraw from Greece, although they were unable to define in which boundaries Greece lay:

> For in Aetolia itself, the Agraei, the Apodoti, the Amphilochi, who comprise a great part of the country, were not in Greece. "Or," he said, "do they have just ground for complaint that I have not kept my hands off their allies, when they themselves have long observed this custom as an established practice." (and here comes an example, 32.34. 4-7)

Further on Philip says that he did not capture Abydus, but that he aided his ally and friend Prusias during its siege. Moreover, he rescued Lysimachia from the Thracians, but "because necessity diverted me from guarding it to this war, the Thracians hold it." This was his reaction to the complaints of the Aetolians. Yet, he adds that he owed nothing to King Attalus of Pergamum nor to the Rhodians since they started the war, not he. And here comes a gesture on Philip's behalf when he says that

> to do honor to the Romans, I shall restore Peraea to the Rhodians and to Attalus the ships and such prisoners as can be found. Now, as to the restoration of the Nicephorium and the temple of Venus. … I shall take upon myself the responsibility and cost of planting—since this is the sort of thing that kings are pleased to ask and reply to one another. (32.34.8-10)

The rest of his speech was directed at the Achaeans, in which he reminded them of the services of Antigonus and himself to the people and asked

> that their decrees be read, which included all honors, divine and human, and taunted them with their most recent decree, in which they repudiated the alliance with him; after violently assailing their perfidy, he said that he would nevertheless return Argos to them; regarding Corinth, he would confer with the Roman commander and ascertain from him at the same time whether he thought it proper that he evacuate those cities which he himself had captured and which he held by right of conquest, or those also which he had inherited from his sires. (32.34.11-13)

I quoted part of this long dialogue in the participants' words because it brings to light some important segments of the code of conduct in a situation that was quite common in Classical and Hellenistic Greek history. That is, a dialogue between enemies during war that was meant to stop its continuation.[39] The notion of status quo ante bellum (which became a legal term in modern history) constitutes the framework of the conference. The idea that emerges yet again from this dialogue is that there were certain unwritten universal rules and values that all sides involved in a conflict were aware of, and that could be referred to and discussed, such as stubbornness as opposed to relinquishing, rights of conquest as opposed to unjust annexation of territory belonging to others, respect for ancestral inheritance of territories, the letting go and evacuation of conquered territories as a concession to one's enemy, a bunch of values associated with peace, and even the acknowledgment of the notion of borders of other states. A broader meaning can also be found in the above discourse, namely, the linkage between power and value. The negotiations just described reveal the effects of power in international relations manifested sometimes by a clash with an ethical set of values and at other times through their enforcement either by the use of violence or by persuasion. These "familiar contrasts between coercion and consent, between domination and hegemony, between hard power and soft power" are different forms of power that are differently utilized in different contexts.[40]

---

[39] We know this already from Thucydides in his account of the Peloponnesian war (Thucydides *passim* and Price 2001).
[40] Geuss quoted by Gamble in Bell (2010: 83).

When we return for a moment to the speech of Alexander the Aetolian, we discover a manual of conduct mainly through the presentation of its breach, that is, Alexander's reference to the negative behavior of Philip. Alexander said that

> Philip ... had never kept peace with good faith or waged war with true courage (*nec de pace cum fide Philippum agere nec bella vera virtute umquam gessisse*). In conference he plotted and tried to entrap his opponents; in battle he would not engage in the open field or fight hand to hand, but instead would retreat, burn and rob cities and, though conquered, destroy the prizes of the conquerors. The Macedonian kings of old did not conduct matters in the same manner, but were used to fight in battle array and to spare the cities, so far as they could, that they might have a richer empire. For what sort of wisdom was it to destroy the things for the possession of which you fight, and leave yourself nothing but the fighting? Philip had, during the preceding campaign, wasted more friendly cities in Thessaly than all the enemies Thessaly had ever had. (32.33.10-14)

Here three important ethical principles are enhanced, good faith, true courage, and wisdom. The latter value refers once again to the idea of the right balance between the use of excessive force and its benefits. Utility is a legitimate value in the arsenal of rules of the right conduct in inter-state relationships, provided it is used with wisdom.[41]

Trust in Inter-state Relations (*Fiducia*)

The following chapters in Livy and particularly the ones that end Book 32 of the *Ab Urbe Condita* are focused on the value of trust in inter-state relations. Philip, aware of the fact that the war with Rome and her allies will be continued after the winter of 197 BCE, and equipped with information that the senate has already rejected his proposals toward peace, decided to "commit Argos on deposit (*fiducia*) ... to Nabis, the tyrant of the Lacedaemonians. With the provision that he would restore it to him if victorious, but that Nabis himself should keep it if misfortune should come" (32.38). The legal procedure of fiducia in relations between individuals is familiar from Roman Law and Livy probably applied its terminology to the inter-state sphere. Then something quite surprising happens. Philip writes to Philocles, his representative in charge of Corinth and Argos, that he should meet the tyrant. Hellenistic rulers loved royal etiquette and Livy was eager to portray the details of official meetings: Philocles, apart from the fact that he was already arriving with gifts, added a pledge of future friendship between the king and the tyrant. He wished to unite his daughters in marriage with the sons of Nabis. The tyrant was reluctant to accept the city on any other terms but an invitation extended by the Argives themselves to assist it. Later when he heard that the Argives were against him (mentioning him in their assembly with "scorn and even cursing"), he took the city at night by deceit and immediately enacted a cancellation of debts and

---

[41] And, some further words on etiquette (and this refers directly to the conference with Nicanor described in 2 Maccabees, p. 162 Part II).

a distribution of land to individuals (in line with Sparta's "socialist" policies), "thus lighting two torches with which revolutions could inflame the commons against the nobility," a comment that shows how critical the socioeconomic gap between the haves and have-nots in Greece was.[42] This gap should be taken into account when we speak of an inter-state code of the right rules of conduct. The masses in contradistinction to the well-to-do had different preferences concerning the value system of the individual state, as well as the one pertaining to inter-state relations. Nabis, forgetting from "whom and in what terms he had received the city" changed sides and approached the Romans asking for a conference. Up to this point, the name of the game according to Livy was deception in an inter-state relationship. That is, Nabis was offered to be a trustee of the state of Sparta by a representative of the king who trusted him, received gifts and an offer to marry his sons to Philip's daughters; yet the tyrant took advantage of this generous offer of the king, learned about the weak position of Argos, and acted treacherously in order to become the city's permanent owner rather than just its trustee.[43] From the outset of this affair, Philip trusted the Spartan tyrant whereas Nabis paid back by using his power to gain the city by deceit.[44] The poor behavior of Nabis is a clear lesson concerning its ideal opposite, trustworthiness in inter-state conduct.

The Romans agreed to a conference with Nabis. Here we have again a good example of talk during war and the meticulous use of etiquette as a framework, this time at the conference at Mycenica. Here again the theatrical staging comes to the fore. First and foremost, the question arose who of the leaders comes to whom, Nabis to Flamininus or vice versa. Flamininus arrived unarmed whereas Nabis was fully armed accompanied by his whole army (to me it looks like a comic moment in inter-state relations). The Spartan tyrant apologized, explaining his fear of the Argive exiles who escaped the city after he had seized it. As a result of the dialogue between the Roman general and the Spartan tyrant, the latter was granted peace in exchange for certain requirements that he fulfilled only partially. King Attalus of Pergamum, who also attended the conference, demanded a free assembly of the Argives to prove that the citizens out of free will welcomed the occupation of their city by the tyrant. The tyrant agreed to send soldiers to fight alongside the Romans but refused to let the Argive assembly vote freely without a watch of a Spartan garrison. Attalus was the one who emphasized the betrayal of the city. He "charged Nabis with holding by force a city betrayed by the guile of Philocles" (*cum fraude*). Later it is alluded that Philocles himself was on the verge of betraying Philip V, his "boss" (32.40.5-7).

We should keep in mind three points before continuing with our survey. First, Polybius and Livy, our sources here, although being inspired by their cultural and

---

[42] Mendels (1998: 101–26).
[43] His offer to the Argives to receive him by consent was not just lip service but had a practical reason. The reason was probably that he knew that if he launches—what he after all did—a conquest of the city-state using force, he would instantly lose the support of the well-to-do who were against his "socialist" policy. Here again utility is juxtaposed with a value of consent in inter-state relations.
[44] We shall see in Part II of our book what trust meant for instance in 1 Maccabees—the Hassideans who were slaughtered by the Hellenistic general, Bacchides, going back on his promise, Chapter 7. See also the meeting and exchange of gifts between Jonathan and two kings in 1 Maccabees (Chapter 10:59-60), a pact between kings that was breached later.

political milieu, provide a portrayal of an inter-state ethical code that is quite accurate but related through their own lens. Second, when discussing dialogue and speeches in assemblies during wars and peace conferences, we should take into account that most of the views and moral statements uttered by representatives usually reflected the official views of states. This point will be demonstrated yet again in the following when the Boeotian and Acarnanian assemblies are tackled. Third, the term "freedom" that occurs now and again sometimes meant total liberty expressed by free will of the community.

Livy opens Book 33 of the *Ab Urbe Condita* with the narrative of events in the winter of 197 which lead to the final battle between Philip V and Rome and her allies at Cynoscephalae. Titus Flamininus encamps with a big Roman army near the walls of Boeotia, a league whose attitude had thus far been uncertain concerning which party to join in the war. With the cooperation of a Boeotian praetor who apparently betrayed the members of the Boeotian league, its assembly voted in favor of the Roman alliance.[45] A humane act of Flamininus is intertwined in the narrative as a short digression. Attalus the king of Pergamum collapsed during the assembly and the Roman consul remained in Thebes for as long as the sudden illness of the king required; when he somewhat recovered, Flamininus left him there to receive further necessary treatment and returned to Elatia (33.2). Humane treatment of rulers toward each other is a theme that recurs in our sources elsewhere,[46] hence it constitutes a symbolic act which cannot be dissociated from an expression of friendship and respect exhibited by one state toward another. From the Boeotian episode, we learn once more that assemblies and councils became significant frameworks for the exchange of ideas through speech, dialogue, and voting processes. Inter-state ethics was one of the main topics on the agenda of such conferences.[47] Be that as it may, after accepting the Boeotian league into the Roman alliance, Flamininus moved on to the Aetolian league's assembly while Philip who was short on manpower started to recruit additional forces from the Macedonian population from among the youngsters as early as the age of sixteen and even some of the veterans (33.3). It seems that Philip who "learned of the departure of the Romans from Elatia, and since he was in a situation where a contest for supreme power impended, he determined to encourage his troops." Hence, he "had repeated many oft-told stories of the brave deeds of their forefathers and also of the martial glory of the Macedonians,"[48] both themes will be discussed in Part II.

Still before the battle of Cynoscephalae took place, Philip again asked for a truce in order to talk to the Roman consul Flamininus. Yet before the conference with the king convened for the sake of concluding a truce, the Roman general was irritated about the "insatiable desire [of the Aetolians] for booty and their arrogance in claiming the glory

---

[45] See for another betrayal 33.5. For Livy 33 and its comparison to other sources (Polybius and the Annalists), see Briscoe (1989: 248–341). Cf. for definition of treachery Polybius 18.13-15.
[46] Cf. the story of Heliodorus' collapse in 2 Maccabees 3.
[47] The Jews at certain junctures also held assemblies for taking grand decisions in spite of the fact that the Hasmoneans were authoritarian (assembly at Mitzpeh 1 Macc. 3:46, assembly in 1 Maccabees 14).
[48] Livy 33.3.11-12: *Philippus cognita profectione ab Elatia Romanorum, ut cui de summa rerum, adesset certamen, adhortandos milites ratus, multa iam saepe memorata de maiorum virtutibus simul de militari laude Macedonum cum disseruisset.*

of the victory for themselves, while with their boasting they had offended the ears of everyone," and he also realized that if the power of the Macedonian kingdom would be weakened, the Aetolians might become the new masters of Greece. "For these reasons he deliberately took many steps to cause them to be and to seem of less moment and importance in the eyes of all men" (33.11.7-9). This means that arrogance and boasting (as opposed to modesty and humility) were considered as anti-values to be challenged on the inter-state level. The arrogance of the Aetolians was translated by the Roman consul into Realpolitik; it had its immediate expression, namely, to humiliate the Aetolians. The links that existed between power and a value system in inter-state relations came to the fore yet again, but in a positive way. Power and fear could in certain instances call to order wayward states that broke ethical inter-state rules. Thus, shortly before the crucial meeting with Philip, Flamininus held a preparatory conference with the allies among which were the Aetolians (33.12).

Flamininus presented before the allies his terms of peace that he was about to impose on the Macedonian king. Whereas one of the allies, Amynander the king of the Athamanes, proposed that the peace terms should result in an enduring peace and liberty that would hold even after the Romans leave Greece (*simul pacis libertatisque esset*), the Aetolians suggested that Philip will be eliminated altogether because if he remained on the scene—even if peace is achieved at present—he would be back soon. They said that Flamininus "was totally wrong if he thought that he would leave either assured peace to the Romans or liberty to the Greeks unless Philip were either killed or dethroned, either of which was easy if he were willing to follow up his good fortune."[49] The answer of Flamininus is interesting from our point of view since he claims that the Aetolians misrepresent the real goal of Rome in inter-state relations. Rome never waged a war of extermination:

> The Romans, in addition to observing since remote antiquity, their custom of sparing conquered peoples, had provided striking proof of their mercifulness in the peace granted to Hannibal and the Carthaginians; how many conferences had been held with Philip himself? Never was there any suggestion that he should give up his kingdom. Or, because he had been defeated in battle, did that make war an unpardonable offence? An armed enemy should be met in hostile mood; towards the conquered, the mildest possible attitude was the greatest thing. (33.12.6-9)

This mild stance in Roman imperialism—no doubt a major inter-state ethical rule—will later in the century have an echo in Judah Maccabee's speech in 1 Maccabeees 8. Obviously, in practice Rome's treatment of subjugated nations was not always in accordance with ethical rules, but the words of Flamininus here support our view that moral values were constantly on the agenda of speeches and dialogues, even if they remained just theoretical.[50] We frequently detected ethical conduct that was performed in practice, whereas at other times it looked good on paper. Against this background

---

[49] This is reminiscent of modern times: in the first war against Iraq (1990-1) the question arose whether to leave Saddam Hussein intact.
[50] For instance Rawls in Bell (2010: 74).

we can already deduce that the inter-state ethical code of values and rules of conduct were very much alive, even though some of it was not adhered to in the reality of international affairs. It is therefore not surprising that in this section Flamininus preached mainly for restraint and fair play, clemency toward the defeated, and war as a legitimate yet a last resort in the interaction between states. War should at any rate not be exploited for demolishing one's enemy. In the following Flamininus gets back to real life stating that the preservation of a Macedonian state is of great interest for the states in the region since a vacuum would cause others to invade Greece and become a menace to its liberty. All of that was said prior to the decisive battle at Cynoscephalae in 197 BCE and shows that the Second Macedonian War had as yet a limited goal on Rome's part, a goal which will be expressed even more clearly at the conference at Corinth once the war ended with a Macedonian defeat. Roman imperialism in the East was not the result of a planned strategy by Rome, but it evolved gradually, inter alia, by a clever use of an ethical code shared by a network of states that Rome created. Much of what Rome achieved at that juncture of her intervention was gained by dialogue combined with the use of force. Yet, we shall see in the following that her use of the inter-state ethical code became more and more cynical and cunning during the following thirty years. With hindsight, Rome had exploited for her own benefit the somewhat naïve belief of the Greeks in this code shared by all.

A Hearing Granted to Your Enemy

From my survey, so far, it becomes quite clear that by the end of the day, power, fear, interests, emotions, and Realpolitik were the factors that had the last word in inter-state relations during the Hellenistic era. In this respect not much has changed in inter-state affairs and conduct ever since. I will now go on with my survey.

A day after the abovementioned conference was adjourned, King Philip arrived at Tempe in order to get a hearing by "a full council of the Romans and allies" (33.13). According to Livy, "Philip behaved with great discretion, conceding voluntarily those points without which peace could not be obtained" (using *prudenter* and *voluntate*), and adds that "he accepted all the conditions commanded by the Romans or demanded by the allies in the previous conference, and would submit everything else to the judgment of the senate." Philip, who is portrayed above as a harsh, cruel, disloyal, and wayward king, is now presented as a humble and responsible leader who comes to talk and even agrees with his adversaries. Above all, this last observation proves that a manual of the right conduct agreed upon by states in the Hellenistic world had a significant presence. Namely, there were criteria for differentiating between good and bad leaders. It also shows yet again how natural it was to have civilized and cordial discussions between enemies alongside confrontational ones during war, even providing mutual courtesy and etiquette. Fierce enemies interrupted their war frequently for the sake of dialogue.[51] This was not because they had suddenly become friends, but because at

---

[51] See civil war in America and the Second World War.

certain junctures during a war when one side realized, for instance, that the enemy was stronger or had better chances to win, a break for exercising etiquette and conversation was considered as a perfect alternative for fighting—at least for a while. Sometimes the reason for such a pause was prosaic, namely, one side wished to spare the other side and to utilize the latter in the future.[52] At other times, dialogue was not a matter of diplomacy exploited to continue a war but rather an expression of pure Realpolitik. For instance, for creating a slight chance to avoid a continuous war for the benefit of one or more parties, or for gaining precious time for reorganizing one's resources and armed forces; meanwhile, also to learn what one's enemy had in mind concerning the near future. Many wars in history could certainly have been avoided had serious dialogue been initiated instead of bloody decisions on the battlefield. This common wisdom emerges frequently from Polybius and Livy's narratives.

Back to the conference. After Philip explained his position, the Aetolians insisted on receiving back territories that were formerly owned by them and were now in the hands of the king who promised to return them. The issues of status quo ante bellum and loyalty come to the fore once again. Concerning one of the cities that Philip agreed to return to Aetolia, there arose a dispute between the Roman consul and the Aetolian representative (33.13.6-14). Quinctius maintained that Phthiotic Thebes belonged to the Roman people by law (*iure belli*, meaning by conquest), because when the campaign started, the Aetolians were invited to become friends of the Romans; although they still had full power to break off relations with the king, they chose to remain in the alliance with the Macedonian king. The details of the dialogue in the following are of less importance for our main theme, but it should be mentioned that the two sides accused each other of breaching a contract that had formerly been signed. Be that as it may, the allies and the consul agreed to grant Philip a truce of four months in which he would send his delegates to the Roman senate, a procedure he was familiar with from the previous year. This time he was required to send his son Demetrius and some of his friends as hostages, to pay two hundred talents, and send ambassadors to Rome with "respect to other matters." This interim agreement assured the king of Macedonia that if the Roman senate would not conclude a peace, Philip would receive back the hostages and the money. Here comes an additional sentence referring to the Realpolitik of Rome: "It is said that nothing influenced the Roman commander more strongly to secure a speedy peace than the ascertained fact that Antiochus was planning war and an invasion of Europe" (33. 13.15). Yet an ultimatum is an ultimatum, and when the senate later did not ratify the agreement, the approaching final battle between the allies and Philip was unavoidable.

Still before the final battle at Cynoscephalae in 197, some minor battles were fought in mainland Greece, one of which occurred at the time of the conference (33.14-15). Lucius Quinctius had summoned to Corcyra the leading men of the Acarnanes, who held to the Macedonian alliance. According to Livy two principal causes had kept them loyal to the king: their "native habit of fidelity" and their "fear and hatred" of

---

[52] We find this stance in 2 Maccabees where a war was stopped since the enemy could be of benefit in the future. See Part II, pp. 154–6.

the Aetolians.⁵³ The Acarnanian assembly, misled by two leaders, passed an unofficial decree which favored an alliance with Rome. Outrage broke out against these two leaders within the Acarnanian league. Yet they became an example of courageous and civic behavior and the assembly of the league became an example of civic conduct in political affairs. Interaction between emotions of a group of citizens and the procedural of the individual state where a political inter-state decision was involved concerning a value (loyalty) is interesting for our discussion. Since the charge against the two persons who betrayed the state was treason, a common charge of disloyalty when inter-state affairs were dealt with points first and foremost that interpretation of an ethical code could differ among various groups of a state due to a socioeconomic and political gap. The final outcome of a debate of this nature had its impact on the relations with other states and the ruling power in the region. This will be clarified in the continuation of the narrative that portrays the rift in Acarnania concerning the issue of loyalty, and should be remembered when I will deal in Part II with the gap within the Hasmonean state at its beginning.

Livy tells us that during "this time of confusion in the state," Philip V sent two prominent Acarnanians who succeeded in abrogating the decree for a Roman alliance (33.16.4-9). They also managed to convict before the council on charges of treason Bianor and Archelaus, the two prominent men in public life, who had initially proposed the decree. Also, they proposed to remove the praetor from office because he had brought the pro-Roman motion to the assembly. The accused who were put in prison decided not to escape but "to throw themselves on the mercy of the assembly, and, by doing so, either mollify their wrath or endure what fortune had in store for them." They were welcomed by the crowded assembly with applause and admiration and then, due to respect for their former status and pity for their present condition, silence ensued. They were allowed to speak and "began like suppliants, but as their speech progressed and they reached the stage of defending themselves against the charges, they spoke with all the confidence that innocence gave them" and even criticized "the injustice and harshness of the treatment they received." The final result of the deliberations in the assembly was that the majority who were aroused by their feelings of pity voted against the decrees which were proposed against them yet rejected the alliance with Rome and decided to continue to observe the treaty with the Macedonians (33.16.10-11). The key words such as treason, pity, admiration, confidence, innocence, abiding by a treaty, and loyalty appeared frequently in inter-state exchanges. The episode shows first and foremost how orderly, democratic, and civilized decisions were taken in the individual states concerning inter-state relations and, second, how the embedded ethical awareness within state institutions (the big troublemakers, the Aetolians included) reflected on inter-state affairs and could not be dissociated from it. Later when the final war was over, the Acarnanians submitted to the Romans. By then they had no other choice.

During the preparations for the final battle at Cynoscephalae and during the war itself, Antiochus III who had already conquered Palestine in 200 BCE started the

---

⁵³ Livy 33.16.2: *Duae autem maxime causae eos tenuerant in amicitia regis, una fides insita genti, altera metus odiumque Aetolorum.*

conquest of more of Ptolemy's southern Asia Minor territories. Many of the cities there surrendered without resistance. The aggression of the Seleucid king alerted the Rhodians who were afraid that Antiochus and Philip might join forces against Rome and her allies. First their ambassadors were sent to Antiochus and he in turn promised to send ambassadors to Rhodes to renew the long-standing relations that existed between that state and himself as well as with his ancestors. He assured them that they should not fear the king's visit since "no fraud or mischief was planned either for them or for their allies; for he would not violate the friendship of the Romans, in evidence whereof he cited both his own recent embassy to them and the senate's complimentary decrees and replies to him." He adds that his ambassadors to Rome were treated "courteously" when the outcome of the war with Philip was "still in doubt." The Rhodians were relieved when during the assembly the news came of the decisive battle at Cynoscephalae in which Rome and her Greek allies crushed the Macedonians. Yet they still had a task to perform, namely, "maintaining the liberty of the cities allied with Ptolemy, which were threatened with war by Antiochus." Some they warned concerning the enemy's plans and others they helped with reinforcements. At any rate they were "responsible for preserving the liberty of the people" of several cities whose names are given (33.20.7-13). In this short narrative, we come across some of the familiar terms and expressions as well as patterns of behavior such as surrender without resistance, long-standing relationship that goes back to one's ancestors, fraud and mischief in inter-state relations and discourse (rhetoric), being loyal or breaching a pact between states, being courteous (etiquette). As we have already seen all the above are expressions of an inter-state value system that became the platform of a network of states during the period under discussion.

Hellenistic Kings and Their Universal Ethical Code

An integral part of both political inter-state ethics and etiquette in the Hellenistic world was the behavior of kings. Their good and bad conduct was measured inter alia by their generosity toward their allies and subjects in terms of concessions and gifts, that is, their *euergesia*.[54] Livy makes a short pause in his narrative to display an obituary on King Attalus who died in Pergamum, saying that he died at:

> his seventy-second year after he had been on the throne for forty-four years. Fortune had bestowed upon this man nothing but wealth to give him hope of royal power. By using this both wisely and splendidly he brought it about that he seemed worthy of the throne, first in his own eyes, then in those of others. Then when in a single battle he had conquered the Gauls, a people the more terrible to Asia by reason of their recent arrival, he assumed the title of king [reminiscent of Aristobulus I in 104/3 BCE], and henceforth his greatness of soul always matched the greatness of his distinction. He ruled his subjects with perfect justice, exhibited

---

[54] See Ma (1999), who tackles this issue extensively, dealing with epigraphical material.

remarkable fidelity to his allies, was courteous to his wife and sons—four survived him—and kind and generous to his friends; he left a kingdom so strong and well-established that possession of it was handed down to the third generation. (33.21.1-5)

Discussions concerning good and bad kings became a mantra in Hellenistic historiography and literary texts, hence it is also evident in the 1–2 books of Maccabees.[55] Most observations concerning the good and the bad conduct of governing institutions in the Hellenistic world reveal that the ethical awareness and its political praxis within states was crucial for the existence of an inter-state ethical code. The positive evaluation of King Attalus is juxtaposed with passing comments about Philip V who was frequently presented as the epitome of the bad king (who underwent, according to Polybius, a transition, *metabole*, from a good to a bad king). From views about the ideal behavior of kings, one can deduce that kings and other rulers who were heads of states which were endowed with enormous power, armies, and wealth, became the compass of good and bad governance in inter-state relations during the Hellenistic period. In fact, they were considered, as the "On Kingship" (*peri basileias*) documents demonstrate, as fine examples of written stately ethical codes. Here as in other cases discussed we can conclude that a linkage existed between ethical rules of conduct of states and patterns of inter-state relationships, both of which were frequently dictated by choices made by rulers and kings.

Reminder: Interaction between Values, Characteristics, and Emotions

I have already mentioned that an inter-state ethical system was embedded in the discourse of the international network of states but had to be activated from time to time by historical processes.

One of the most common patterns of conduct in inter-state relations during the Hellenistic period was the constant pressure to take decisions as to which of the empires (and their allies) the state should join in times of conflict. At certain junctures decisions concerning politics within individual states involved the choice of one set of values over others.[56] For instance, breaching a loyalty bond with one ruling power for the conclusion of a treaty with its foe could turn into rift and turmoil within the state itself when no consensus on this matter existed. Emotional outbursts occurred, causing tension between characteristics (decision-making, rifts), emotions, and values depicted in my triangle.[57] In extreme cases outbursts led to revolution (*stasis*) in individual states, which in turn brought to a change in the scale of values. This chain of events reflected on the ethical inter-state level of relationships. Let us now examine

---

[55] See Part II, Chapters 5–6.
[56] See in general for these issues Gamble (2010: 83).
[57] Mendels (2017).

the following example through the occurrences within the Boeotian league during the winter of 196 BCE.

Titus Flamininus with the Roman army was wintering at Elatia, when the Boeotian league asked him for permission to recover their countrymen who had served with Philip V, king of Macedonia (33.27.5-9). Flamininus granted this readily since he intended to win sympathy for the Roman people suspecting a future invasion of the Seleucid empire. Yet when these countrymen returned to Boeotia, "it at once became clear how little gratitude he had won from the Boeotians." Instead of thanking Flamininus, they sent ambassadors to Philip "thanking him for restoring their countrymen, just as if that boon had been granted to them and not to Quinctius and the Romans." Moreover, at the next election they chose as Boeotarch Brachyllas "for no other reason than having commanded the Boeotians who had served with the king, passing over Zeuxippus and Pisistratus and others who had sponsored the alliance with Rome." Before continuing with the story, we should pause for a moment and comment on what we just read. Flamininus acted kindly—in order to gain sympathy from the Greeks—and expected the Boeotians to repay him by formal etiquette which expresses gratitude. Not only did this not happen but an additional slap in the face of the Romans was dealt by the Boeotians who elected a pro-Macedonian leader. The expectations of the Roman general for reciprocity in itself demonstrate that a virtual code of ethics was regularly referred to during inter-state dialogue.

Events in the Boeotian league in central Greece serve as a good example for the tensions that brought about political decisions concerning which of the two empires should be joined during conflict, Rome or Macedonia. As we already learned from my survey, such difficult decisions were quite common in other states at that time. To return to the two abovementioned pro-Roman leaders, they were troubled and claimed that "since such things happened with the Roman army encamped almost at the gates, what in the world would become of them had the Romans retreated to Italy, and Philip, from his nearby kingdom, was aiding his friends and opposing those who had belonged to the other party?" (33.27.10-11). What do they do? They decided to murder Brachyllas, who was the main supporter of the Macedonian king. Thus, when the drunk Brachyllas returned home from participation in a crowded dinner accompanied by a group of "effeminate creatures" he was assassinated. Such political murders were quite common in the Hellenistic world (cf. death of Simeon the Hasmonean in Part II). The murder of the pro-Macedonian elected leader by the nonelected leaders of the pro-Roman party in the Boeotian assembly resulted in a chain of events in which the pro-Roman Zeuxippus fled to another city and Pisistratus and others were examined under torture and executed. But this is not the end of the story since the murder of Brachyllas "roused the Thebans and all the Boeotians to a frenzy of hatred against the Romans," for they assumed that a leading figure such as Zeuxippus has committed such a crime with the support of the Roman commander. Yet they could not initiate a rebellion since they had neither leader nor army.[58] Thus started a guerrilla war of brigandage and killing of Roman soldiers, while the Roman

---

[58] 33.28.1: *Ad rebellandum neque vires neque ducem habebant.*

army was in its winter cessation. In this short episode we have already encountered the arousal of several group emotions, such as sympathy, hatred, collective fear, revenge (for the murder of the pro-Macedonian leader),[59] which according to the historian ignited certain extreme actions, being on the verge of a rebellion. At the same time values were ignored as a result of the instability caused by the characteristic of *divide* within the individual state. The unsettled interaction between a set of emotions, a block of characteristics (divide, decision-making), and the value system had been ignited by one of the most burning issues of the day, that is, which of the fighting empires to join. When the casualties of the Romans grew and crimes of stealing became abundant, Quinctius Flamininus turned to the Achaean league and the Athenians asking them to be *witnesses* that his war against the Boeotians would be "a lawful and rightful war."[60] Yet, after a swift mediation of the Achaeans, peace was granted by the Romans and the siege on Thebes, capital of the Boeotian league, was discontinued.

Three interim conclusions can be drawn now. First, a wish of one state to have another state as witness for its lawful and rightful actions against a third party reveals yet again that a belief in a shared inter-state ethical code existed. Second, the characteristic of divide that had the potential of leading to revolution within the individual states was inherent in Hellenistic cities and states as a result of socioeconomic gaps, political confrontations, as well as religious tensions.[61] We learn that when confrontation and violence get the upper hand in the individual states, we can be sure that an inner and/ or outer trigger was in operation—be it an exploitation of socioeconomic distress by an outsider that ended in revolution or political distress and religious and cultural gaps that turned violent.[62] When inner struggle in a state, league, and kingdom was nourished by inter-state relationships, or just by an intervention of a dominant power, the inter-state ethical code of the network of states was affected. Let us view how the interaction of the angles within the triangle operated in the Boeotian case. When divide became an active characteristic in the Boeotian league, it triggered a belief that a decision to join the Roman alliance had been fraudulently reached by the majority in the Boeotian assembly. This aroused the group's emotions of hatred and revenge, which in turn accelerated the tension between the two parties in the Boeotian state (divide). In other words, the unhappy interaction between negative emotions that erupted in a section of the assembly and a destructive and dominant characteristic (divide) brought about a breach of certain basic values of the state's ethical code, values such as reciprocity and gratitude, loyalty and humaneness. This disharmonious interaction between the three angles within the Boeotian league had immediate repercussions on the inter-state scene. Yet, when a decision was at last made (to join the Roman alliance), and a peaceful relationship between state and empire ensued, the state did enjoy a certain degree of liberty, under "protection" (a common term used often as an excuse for imperialism), and even without a garrison put in its midst.

[59] Cf. Price (2001: 25): "revenge is closely related in Greek literature to *orge*, governs all political and even inter-personal relations" (refers to the classical period, with bibliography).
[60] 33.29.8: *Missis Athenas et in Achaiam legatis, qui testarentur socios iusto pioque se bello persecuturum Boeotos.*
[61] See Mendels (1998: 101–26).
[62] All of which I will discuss in Part II when I deal with the beginnings of the Hasmonean state.

Negotiating Inter-state Values—the Case of *Libertas*

The Second Macedonian War was over at the end of 197 BCE; terms of peace as well as numerous inter-state deliberations were initiated. Philip V king of Macedonia who was defeated in Cynoscephalae immediately sent a delegation to Rome that was received according to the rules of etiquette. At the same time ten Roman commissioners arrived in Greece. They declared the peace terms that included inter alia the following: that Philip should withdraw his garrisons from the cities that had been under his sway and give them to the Romans free of his troops; he may not wage war outside his realm without the consent of the Roman senate and pay an indemnity to the "Roman people" of a thousand talents "half at once and half in ten annual instalments" (33.30). So far, so good.

Whereas all the Greek cities approved this settlement, "only the Aetolians with secret grumblings criticized the decision of the ten commissioners who were sent to Greece by Rome: mere words had been trimmed up with the empty show of liberty." And here comes their argument which is important for our case since their urge for complete freedom and independence is perhaps the closest to Judah Maccabee's idea later in the century:

> Why were some cities delivered to the Romans without being named, others specified and ordered to be free without such delivery, unless the purpose was that those which were in Asia, being more secure due to their remoteness, should be set free, but those which were in Greece, not being named, should become Roman property, to wit, Corinth and Chalcis and Demetrias? The answer was that in the decree of the senate, under which the ten commissioners were sent from Rome, the other cities of Greece and Asia were beyond question set free, but regarding these three cities the commissioners were instructed to take such action as the public interest should have proved to demand, in accordance with the general good and their own sense of honor. (33.31.2-5)

This reservation of the Aetolians about the nature of *libertas* was taken seriously by the Roman commission and by Quinctius Flamininus, the victor of Cynoscephalae, who in a deliberation with the ten commissioners "urged repeatedly that the whole of Greece should be set free" in order to create genuine affection and respect for the Roman name and stop the complaints of the Aetolians (*si veram caritatem ac maiestatem apud omnes nominis Romani vellent esse*) and in particular to convey the message that they "had crossed the sea to liberate Greece and not to transfer dominion from Philip to themselves" (33.31.7-9). Genuine affection and respect were a pair consisting of an emotion and a value mentioned here in the context of inter-state relations. The other members of the delegation of commissioners agreed "as regards the freedom of the cities, but they assumed it safer for the Greeks themselves to remain for a while under the protection of Roman garrisons (*tutela praesidia Romani*) than to receive Antiochus as lord in place of Philip." The decision was reached: "Corinth should be given over to the Achaeans, a garrison, however, should be retained in Acrocorinthus; Chalcis and Demetrias should be held until the anxiety about Antiochus should have passed" (33.31.11). The Romans, at least partially, did accept the Aetolian reservation. This episode and others to follow reveal that liberty is a negotiable term since like many other values within the Hellenistic virtual inter-state ethical code, it had several connotations in different circumstances.[63] I will elaborate on this issue in Part II.

And now comes the climax of the whole story of the Second Macedonian War. I would even say that this last scene taking place at the Isthmian Games is the final act of the big theatrical play described by Livy in Books 32–33 of his *Ab Urbe Condita* in which the actors were presented as being larger-than-life. This does not mean that the narrative of the Second Macedonian War was an invention of Livy, but it shows that Livy looked at the reality as an impressive drama with powerful actors. This aspect is worth pursuing in the future by experts in Greek and Roman drama. In the meantime, let us examine the large assembly that was convened at the Isthmian Games of 196 BCE. The behavior of the crowd in this assembly reveals a symbiosis between values and emotions triggered by a significant external political act, reminiscent of a religiopolitical ritual: "The appointed time of the Isthmian Games was at hand, a spectacle always, even on other occasions, attended by crowds, on account of the fondness, native to the race (*stadium insitum genti*), for exhibitions in which there are trials of skill in every variety of art as well as of strength and swiftness of foot." But, Livy adds, that "this time they had assembled from all quarters not only for the usual purposes, but especially because they were consumed with wonder what thenceforth the state of Greece would be, and what their own condition." When everyone was seated a herald with a trumpeter "as is the custom" came in the midst of the arena and read the following decree: "The Roman senate and Titus Quinctius imperator, having conquered King Philip and the Macedonians, declare to be free, independent, and subject to their own laws, the Corinthians, the Phocians, all the Locrians." He had named all the states which had been subject to King Philip. When the herald's voice was heard "there was rejoicing greater than men could grasp in its entirety." Later it is emphasized that when the ground for the joy became certain "such a storm of applause began and was so often repeated that it was easily apparent that of all blessings none pleases a throng more than liberty ... joy alone had so completely replaced their perception of all other delightful things" (33.32). This decree of Rome included three elements: independence, liberty, and autonomy under one's laws. These three fundamental values which were separately mentioned in quite a few deliberations during the period under survey, alongside with the emotional outburst of joy they aroused, show yet again the tight linkage between values and emotions, here presented within an inter-state ethical discourse.[64]

---

[63] For its classical meaning, cf. Price (2001).
[64] This aspect will be discussed in Part II in connection with Jewish relationship with the Seleucids and alongside the narrative of ceremonies held after victories of the first Hasmoneans that ended with "great joy." And see Plutarch's wonderful description of the assembly in *Titus Flamininus* 10–11 (Gruen 1984:132–57).

The rejoicing continued for many days "in thoughts and expressions of gratitude" and here a eulogy of Rome as a benevolent empire is adduced, a passage which we should bear in mind when I discuss 1 Maccabees 8 which is reminiscent of the following (Part II). Livy says:

> There was one people in the world which would fight for others' liberties at its own cost, to its own peril and with its own toil, not limiting its guaranties of freedom to its neighbors, to men of the immediate vicinity or to countries that lay close at hand but ready to cross the sea that there might be no unjust empire anywhere and that everywhere justice, right, and law might prevail. By the single voice of a herald, they said, all the cities of Greece and Asia had been set free; to conceive hopes of any such thing as this required a bold mind; to bring it to pass was the proof of immense courage and good fortune (*virtutis et fortunae ingentis*). (33.33)

The passage speaks for itself and shows how a pro-Roman at that time thought of the role of Rome in the world, namely, to be a lighthouse for positive values. This stance will change later when Rome's imperialism becomes harsher, as we so clearly read in the speech of Mithridates in the first century BCE.

In the more detailed terms of the peace Quinctius and the ten commissioners warn the Seleucid representatives of Antiochus III that he should evacuate the cities in Asia which belonged to King Philip and to King Ptolemy and to keep them free whereas all the Greek cities everywhere must enjoy peace and liberty (adding here "peace" to independence, liberty and autonomy in the arena of one's own laws). In a council of cities and nations (*conventus civitatum gentiumque*—see the difference here), the Romans settled affairs with the states that were addressed "by name" individually. Territories were annexed to some, lands were taken from others and divided, and so on. One is mentioned as receiving back his own laws.[65] Territorial grants, return of one's own laws and territories, the grant of liberty and independence became pillars of inter-state patterns of relationship when the ruling empire was settling the affairs of a region. (Hence territorial grants by the Seleucids in Judaea were not alien to the conduct of Hellenistic rulers during most of the period.) Later each of the ten commissioners went to liberate cities in personally assigned territories. To Philip it was advised that he should conclude a treaty of alliance and friendship with Rome so that when Antiochus may arrive in Greece he will be associated with the Roman side, and the Aetolians were advised by the Romans during a full meeting of the states of Greece at Thermopylae (probably the Amphictyonic Council) "to abide resolutely and faithfully by the alliance with the Roman people" (*constanter et fideliter in amicitia poluli Romani permanerent*) (33.35). Resoluteness and faithfulness were values that occurred frequently, sometimes implicitly, when we dealt with the inter-state code of political ethics. Be that as it may, this last section shows clearly that Rome builds a network of states in Greece, herself included. The latter newly constructed network is

---

[65] 33.34, which means that his laws had been abrogated beforehand—see Part II; the relations with Judea concerning the ancestral laws, and liberty granted to several states. For the epigraphical evidence dealing with such issues, see Sherk (1984: 16–17, 25–6).

based not just on give and take between Rome and the Greek states but also on certain ethical rules shared by the members of the network on the one hand, and the exclusion of those states that did not participate in an already embedded inter-state platform of ethics on the other. I will come back to this issue later and show how all of this is relevant to the understanding of the relationship between the Hasmoneans with all other nations, including the ruling empires.

2

Two Zones of Influence—One Ethical System

Inter-state Ethics and the Territorial Component

Various territorial concepts were part and parcel of an inter-state ethical discourse. First and foremost, the notion that a territory belonged to a state because it was handed down by its ancestors was acknowledged in international relations yet frequently caused friction between claimants to the very same ancestral heritage. Second, quite popular was the claim of right of conquest that was high up in the inter-state ethical code.[1] Ownership of a territory by the right of might could, as it were, be relinquished in the context of an agreement between states.[2] It was also common for a state that claimed ownership of a conquered territory to lose it to another state during conflict and/or under agreement. Third, there were cases where one state consented to have another state rule its territories in exchange for safety, protection, and other benefits. Fourth, when a state was already subjugated by an empire, this same great power usually had the final word concerning the future of the territory of the former, for instance, either to be added wholly or partly to the territory of the conqueror, or granted to another state in the region. A territory/state can also be given in trust (*fiducia*) to another state based on an alliance concluded between the two. In Part II, I will discuss the territorial aspect in relation to territorial grants by the Seleucids to the Jews in Palestine. As we will see in the following, passion for the fatherland was common in the Hellenistic world. This frequently brought about conflicts between states that were solved by either persuasion or violence. Let us go back to our historical narrative.

Subsequent to the declaration of Corinth (196 BCE), when the Second Macedonian War was over, the Romans became quite concerned about the maneuvering of Antiochus III in Western Asia and Greece: "In the same year [196 BCE] King Antiochus, after wintering at Ephesus, tried to *coerce* all the cities of Asia into acknowledging the sovereignty which he once exercised over them" (*omnes Asiae civitates in antiquam imperii formulam redigere est conatus*) (33.38.1). And here follows the reaction of the city-states, a matter I will come back to in Part II when I deal with the Jewish Hellenists

---

[1] This is true until this day when states claim rights on a certain territory (Frederic the Great who for such a reason went to war against Austria in 1740). In practice it is accepted by other states and sometimes rejected.

[2] The issue of a state's power and its moral authority was discussed by Weber (2015).

who alerted the king to come and assist them, hence acting in line with many other Hellenistic states in similar situations, the king realized that states that were situated on level ground and/or did not trust their fighting men or their walls or their weapons would "readily accept his yoke" (33.38.3). Yet "Zmyrna and Lampasacus were contending for their *independence*, and there was danger that if they were admitted as they demanded, other cities in Aeolis and Ionia would follow the example of Zmyrna, those on the Hellespont, of Lampasacus."[3] Interestingly he used force to frighten the two states but also sent his agents that by courteous address and mild reproach would suppress their rashness and stubbornness [agents, emotions of the group and persuasion, like the scene at Modi'in], and "to create the hope that they would soon have what they desired, but only when it was clear both to them and to everyone else that their liberty had been granted by the king and not attained through mere grasping at opportunity" (33.38.5-6). This comment is interesting from our point of view since it shows what Hellenistic kings thought that only they were apt to grant liberty to cities and states, and that liberty could not be achieved by seizing opportunities by the states themselves, namely, by revolt. This is exactly the concept that we find in the grants of liberty to the Jews by the Seleucids later in the century (Part II), which the Jews according to 2 Maccabees were willing to accept; the book of 1 Maccabees portrays the second sort of liberty, namely, the complete freedom achieved by a fight against the Seleucids. In this line the Lampasacians claimed thirty years earlier "that Antiochus should be neither surprised nor angry if they were not inclined to submit with indifference to their hope of liberty being deferred" (33.38.7). Antiochus III then went against two other cities, one surrendered when they saw his army approaching and the other surrendered as well. There were not too many examples of fierce and stubborn fight against an empire when its forces started to move forward its engines to besiege a city. Antiochus decided to rebuild Lysimachia, a state that was destroyed and abandoned in the past, because it was "so famed and so advantageously situated." How did he act in such a situation? "He undertook everything at once." Namely, to rebuild the houses and walls, to ransom some of the Lysimacheans who were in slavery, to seek out and bring back some of them who were scattered in the Hellespont and Chersonesus, and to attract new colonists to settle in the city. He also made efforts to populate the city "in every possible manner"; at the same time, in order to remove the fears of the inhabitants of Lysimacheia of the Thracians, "he set out in person with half his forces to devastate the neighboring parts of Thrace, leaving the rest and all the naval allies engaged in the work of rebuilding the city" (33.38.14). In Part II, I will discuss the proposals for rebuilding and help against the background of the settlement in Lysimacheia and other states that were commonplace conduct of Hellenistic rulers (*beneficium, euergesia*) and had significant ethical overtones. Destruction of states or even harming them constituted only one aspect of Hellenistic rulers' attitude toward the subjugated states; building, construction, and rehabilitation of former hostile states the other.

---

[3] 33.38.2-3. This could have been also the fear of Antiochus IV, a well-known pattern in the relationship of a Hellenistic king with his subject states. Namely, that if he lets go of the Jews, others will imitate and demand the same. This is why he insisted on his tight hold of the citadel in Jerusalem.

Within this framework of claims on territories and the rebuilding of a capital city that was formerly destroyed, we can explain the following episode. In reacting to Roman claims about the territorial expansion of Antiochus III, which "was displeasing to the senate," the king refers to ethical principles of inter-state conduct. First, the king denies that he crossed into alien territory (Europe) and that he was acting from an "open declaration of war on the Romans." Namely, a war as we have already seen needs a formal declaration, according to common ethical conduct. This notion penetrated the international public sphere during the Hellenistic period and reflects an awareness of fair play and honesty. Second, Antiochus was "surprised that the Romans were making such diligent inquiry" into what he "should do or how far he should advance by land and sea, and that they did not see that Asia was no concern of theirs, and that they had no more right to ask what Antiochus was doing in Asia than Antiochus had to ask what the Roman people was doing in Italy" (33.40). A "natural" sphere of influence or ownership of certain territories is the concept that stands behind this statement (long before the Yalta conference in February 1945). Third, "all the country which had been the kingdom of Lysimachus [one of the heirs of Alexander the Great's realm] and which, on his defeat, had passed with his other possessions into the hands of Seleucus by right of conquest, he [Antiochus] considered his own."[4] Possession of some of these towns had been seized, first by Ptolemy, then by Philip, usurping the property rights of others [of Lysimachus]. Who could doubt, asked Antiochus, "that Lysimachus had been lord of the Chersonesus and the neighboring parts of Thrace which are around Lysimachia?" Antiochus claims that "he himself had come only to recover his ancient possessions and to found anew Lysimachia ... that his son Seleucus might make it the capital of his kingdom" (33.40.6). In the following Antiochus wishes even to inherit Ptolemaic Egypt when he heard a false rumor that Ptolemy, with whom he had a pact, was dead.[5] This means that after more than a hundred years since the death of Alexander the Great, kings in the region claimed to be the heirs of his kingdom and of the territories of his generals who ruled them after his death (hence Simeon's claim in 1 Macc. 15:33-35 to his ancestral land should not surprise us within this atmosphere). The mention of historical precedents turned to become clear expressions of the ethical principle of fairness and respect in international relations, namely, the acknowledgment of the legitimacy of others to owe or be in possession of a certain territory. However, this latter notion did not contradict the reality in which the activation of one's power in order to conquer others also became legitimate and was discussed frequently in inter-state conferences that dealt with moral and legal issues. The latter were not just ideas invented by the authors who wrote the historical narrative but an authentic expression of a virtual ethical code whose terminology was familiar to all participant representatives of states. This sort of discourse became a communication channel when diplomatic considerations played a role in inter-state relations. One such instance was when a super power wished to create an atmosphere of confidence, a recurrent value, namely, of reconciliation, sometimes just as a tactical

---

[4] Livy 33.40.4: *Quo victo omnia quae illius fuissent iure belli Seleuci facta sint*. This argument returns later in the book and was unacknowledged by the Romans (59).
[5] 33.40.3 and 33.41.

move. When Antiochus III wished to appease the Romans, they sent ambassadors to Quinctius to say, with a view to creating confidence, that the king would do nothing to modify their alliance.[6] On the other hand, value judgments uttered from time to time by representatives of cities and states enhanced the gap between values and their bad opposites in international relationships. When the Aetolians are depicted as unreliable in inter-state relationships and "a people both naturally restless and ill-disposed towards the Romans" (*cum ingenio inquietam tum iratam*),[7] and Nabis was defined as "a greater evil in Greece (*visceribus Graeciae ingens malum*)" and "equal in greed and cruelty of all tyrants known to fame" and Sparta will rule the whole of Greece if nothing will be done against her,[8] then their opposites, the good values, immediately spring to mind. They are: staying calm and stable, well-disposed and cooperative, virtuous and noble, and so on; those are presented as "advantage of the state" as against "not very great importance to the general interest of the state." In other words, against the evil intentions and behavior, Rome emerges as the champion of the components of good conduct, and as Livy expresses it works toward the advantages and interests of states in the international public sphere.

Once the Second Macedonian War was over, we discover how Rome perceived its own role as liberator and protector of Greece. First, the handling of Nabis, the tyrant of Sparta, should be mentioned. The Romans were reluctant to eliminate him for several reasons, one of which should be mentioned here: Sparta's so-called Lycurgan, ancient and well-respected constitution (and a typical written code of conduct),[9] whose restoration was linked to the liberation of Sparta. Flamininus says this very clearly: "while we were setting all Greece free, to restore Sparta as well as to its ancient liberty and its laws, which you have mentioned as if you were an imitator of Lycurgus" (34.32.4). Abrogating the ancient laws of a state, and their restoration later, was a common procedure in relationships between empire and its subject states; within this context one can better understand the later edict of Antiochus IV concerning the Jews and its abrogation and its restoration by Antiochus V (to be dealt with in Part II). For Hellenistic rulers, the restoration of laws of a city and/or a state, which had been taken from them, symbolized a significant part of their grant of liberty. Yet Quinctius Flamininus, who was given the authority by the senate to decide on war against Nabis, brings it to an assembly of Greek states (*koina*) in which Nabis is present. At first the assembly voted in favor of war but was then

---

[6] Livy 33.41.5: *Qui ad fidem faciendam nihil novaturum regem de societate agerent.*
[7] 33.44.7: Concerning the Aetolians, to use Edward Said's methodology in his *Orientalism*: "The term 'constitutive outside' describes the way in which a society takes a series of negative characteristics and projects them onto an excluded group, thereby reinforcing a sense of cultural identity. By representing the Orient [here the Aetolians] as irrational, sensual, and violent, Orientalism served to establish the superior rationality of the Occident." Polybius and Livy defined the Aetolians by "creating a stable depiction of its other, its constitutive outside." In other words, the Greeks (and Romans) found a way of characterizing themselves "by drawing a contrasting image or idea, based on a series of binary oppositions (rational/irrational, mind/body, order/chaos) that manage" their anxieties (see Kohn in Bell 2010: 203).
[8] Livy 33.45.3-4: *Quod e re publica censeret esse … non ita magni momenti ad summam rem publicam esset.*
[9] Xenophon, *The Constitution of the Lacedaemonians* (Moore 1975: 65-123).

persuaded by the Roman general that it was not worth the effort. Nevertheless, the war was then pursued because Nabis did not give in. But by the end of the day, he was left on the scene, reduced in power and without Argos that was returned to the Achaean league. Important for our case is the recurrent appearance of politicians and generals in assemblies where they respect voting procedures and decisions taken regarding inter-state matters. This method was not alien to Rome in its inner politics and rather familiar from the political scene in Greek states, both having a long tradition of democratic procedures. Dialogue was in the air all the time in informal gatherings (people in a party in the Achaean league) and during formal councils and assemblies, making the procedural a solid basis for decisions on inter-state moral behavior and political conduct. The discourse about ethics was quite popular and shared by all participants. Obviously, in a few cases the procedures were used as a cover to reach decisions that were made in advance (comparable to, for instance, 1 Macc. 10:46). This is a familiar trait to be found as well in modern democracies.

Among several tasks in the winter of 194 BCE in Greece, Flamininus took upon himself to "administer justice and undoing the arrangements in the cities which had been caused by the arbitrary conduct of Philip and his prefects, since by increasing the power of the men of their own faction they diminished the privilege and liberty of the rest" (34.48.2).[10] Apropos the description of the arrangements of the Romans in Greece during the aftermath of the war and their declaration of liberty, Livy expresses some ideas about the nature of liberty, or what the Romans meant by the concept. Here a basic principle that was shared by the Romans and the Hellenistic kingdoms is adduced, namely, that an active intervention in the inner balance of a state diminished the judicial status and liberty of all those who did not support the external intervening force. In the assembly of delegates of all the states, Flamininus refers to this latter point by enhancing the friendship that was instituted between Rome and the Greek people. Rome supports a balance within cities as part of her policy following the grant of liberty in 196 BCE. In his speech in the assembly, he recommends some of the states

> to judge their friends by their actions, not their words, and to reflect carefully on whom they should trust and against whom they should be on their guard. They should use their liberty with discretion (*libertate modice utantur*); controlled, it was salutary to individuals and to states; uncontrolled, it was both a burden to others and a source of impetuous and lawless action to its possessors. He advised the leaders in the states and the other orders to strive for harmony among themselves, and all the cities to take measures for the general good. Against men who acted in unison neither king nor tyrant would be strong enough to do harm; strife and dissension furnished every opportunity to plotters, since the party which was defeated in an internal struggle would rather join hands with a foreigner than yield to a countryman. (34.49.7-13)

---

[10] For a detailed commentary on Livy Book 34, see Briscoe (1981: 39–145).

He adds a useful comment:

> The liberty which had been gained by the arms of others and restored to them by the good faith of aliens, they should keep and guard by their own efforts, that the Roman people might know that liberty had been given to men who deserved it and that their gift had been well bestowed. (34.49.11)[11]

In other words, city-states should be balanced, keeping the harmony and unity among sections of the state—two cardinal values which imply the use of many other values such as mutual respect, reciprocity, restraint and mutual readiness to make concessions, and sticking to the truth (34.49.5): keeping all of those values in order to preserve the liberty they received as a gift from the ruling empire. This is a special kind of liberty, given by a super power as a gift, and should be distinguished from liberty that is achieved by fighting a super power. I will return to this issue later and in Part II where I will make an attempt to show yet again that in much of its basic political concepts concerning ethics the Jewish state is much in line with the Hellenistic world. Its Jewish framework is not hampered by this Hellenistic ethical background.

Then, after a burst of joy and various other strong feelings, Quinctius asked the assembly to free Roman slaves that were in their states and send them to him to Thessaly where he was heading to, adding that "it was unbecoming even for themselves that the liberators should be slaves in the land they had set free" (34.50.3). (Perhaps comparable to the freeing of Jews in the world, not just in Judea, in 1 Maccabees 10, mentioned in the letter of Demetrius.) At any rate, Quinctius lingers upon the Roman concept of liberty for Greece in order to demonstrate that at the end of the day the Greeks did not just change masters, when the Romans took over the protection instead of the Macedonians (34.49.6). These notions that the Romans used henceforward were probably a mixture of their views about liberty and those they adopted from the Greeks, who later applied it on the emerging Jewish state.[12]

Quinctius then went to Euboea reminding the council there "in what condition he had found them and in what he was leaving them," emphasizing the role of Rome as a stabilizer of political life in Greece. Stability, as an inter-state value, not only brought about calm and respectful discourse within the individual states but also affected more smoothly inter-state relationships. Moreover, a demonstration of gratitude and its etiquette was not absent. Escorted by all the citizens from Demetrias, Quinctius went to Thessaly:

> There were the states not only to be set free, but also to be brought into some reasonable condition of order after all the chaos and confusion. For they had been thrown into confusion not only by the faults of the times and the king's lawless and violent behavior, but also by the restless character of the people, which from

---

[11] This entire section about *stasis* and intervention should be kept in mind in Part II, where revolution in the Jewish state brought the intervention of foreign powers.

[12] These concepts, or part of them, were inherited by other more insignificant Hellenistic powers in the East, as we see so clearly in 1–2 Maccabees (Part II).

the earliest times down to the present day have never conducted a meeting or an assembly or a council without dissension and rioting. (34.51.4-5)

Such a denigrative language was probably also heard in the Seleucid court concerning Judah Maccabee and his supporters.[13] In other words, the inner political and economic stability of a state was a prerequisite for its suitability to be part of a civilized and balanced inter-state network with an ethical agreed upon code. Then, in order for Thessaly to become part of the network of an inter-state ethical code, the Romans did the following: Quinctius chose the senate of the Thessalians and their magistrates "mainly on the basis of property and strove to make that element in the community more influential which found it advantageous to have everything peaceful and quiet" (34.51.6). Gradually Rome's politicians painted the inter-state ethical code in aristocratic hues in which the powerful was also the one who made the decisions.

The agreements of Rome with states in Greece and with King Antiochus III had to be ratified by the senate. Thus, the embassies who have arrived from all Greece, parts of Asia, and from the kings were welcomed by the senate and received a courteous reception. The first speakers were the ambassadors of Antiochus III to whom Quinctius Flamininus was entrusted to make "such a reply ... as was consistent with the dignity and the interest of the Roman people" (*quae ex dignitate atque utilitate*) (34.57.5). Dignity and utility are mentioned quite frequently in our survey as values—sometimes opposing each other—in a value system of the Romans that they share with states with whom they had contacts in the East. For instance, equality of states within the network of inter-state relations could not always coexist with utility. I will get back to it later. And now comes an interesting passage from my point of view. The Seleucid ambassador presented the relationship of his country with that of the Romans as an easy matter since their embassy "had come merely to ask for friendship and conclude an alliance" and referred to some patterns of conduct relating to friendship in international relations:

There were three kinds of treaties ... by which states and kings concluded friendships: one, when in time of war terms were imposed upon the conquered; for when everything was surrendered to him who was the more powerful in arms, it is the victor's right and privilege to decide what of the conquered one's property he wishes to confiscate; the second, when states that are equally matched in war conclude peace and friendship on terms of equality; under these conditions demands for restitution are made and granted by mutual agreement, and if the ownership of any property has been rendered uncertain by the war, these questions are settled according to the rules of traditional law or the convenience of each party; the third exists when states that have never been at war come together to pledge mutual friendship in a treaty of alliance; neither party gives or accepts conditions; for that happens when a conquering and a conquered party meet. (34.57.7-9)

---

[13] This is heard by Ahasver in the book of Esther about the Jews.

The ambassador adds that since Antiochus belonged in the third class, why did the Romans "deem it right" to dictate terms that prescribed which city/state of Asia he was to leave "free and independent and what he was to make tributary to him, and what cities they forbade the king's armies and the king to enter? For in that way it was proper to make peace with Philip, an enemy, but not a treaty of alliance with Antiochus, a friend."[14] These three categories as far as I know were not adopted by the Hellenistic kingdom word by word but the spirit was there and we will encounter it when dealing with the relationship of the Hasmoneans with the Seleucids and Romans in Part II. The dialogue that follows, still in the Roman senate, concerns us even more since two principles are aired. One, by Quinctius Flamininus, who brings forward the political ethical principle of zones of influence—ethical, because it required a great deal of mutual respect and restraint on behalf of both sides, namely, the activation of the value of mutuality as a prerequisite for friendship between states; zones whose sovereignty should be honored by each other:

> If [Antiochus III] wishes us to have no interest in what concerns the cities of Asia, he too must himself keep entirely out of Europe. Second, that if he will not keep himself within the limits of Asia, but crosses into Europe, the Romans too shall have the right both to defend the existing friendships with the cities of Asia and to add new treaties of alliance. (34.58.2-3)

The ambassador of the king replies and adduces an argument we already met but should be emphasized yet again since it has a bearing on my discussion in Part II.

The king's ambassador says that "it was indeed monstrous even to listen to a proposal that Antiochus should be excluded from the cities of Thrace and Chersonesus, districts which his forefather Seleucus, when he had defeated King Lysimachus in war and slain him in battle, had most honorably gained and bequeathed to his successors" (34.58.4-5). He claims moreover that part of these territories had been reconquered "with equal glory" from the Thracians, "and when abandoned, like Lysimachia itself, he had repopulated by recalling the inhabitants, and which, when destroyed by calamities and fires, he had rebuilt at great expense" (34.58.4-7). He goes on asking

> what kind of analogy was there between the two cases, that Antiochus should be ousted from this possession, so acquired and so recovered, and that the Romans should keep out of Asia, which was never theirs? Antiochus is seeking the friendship of the Romans, but a friendship which, when obtained, will be a source of honor and not a cause for shame.

---

[14] Livy 34.57.10-11. The reader should pay attention to the different pacts Rome had with her allies which emerge from this passage: *Ex eo genere cum Antiochus esset, mirari se quod Romani aequum censeant leges ei dicere, quas Asiae urbium liberas et immunes, quas stipendiarias esse velint, quas intrare praesidia regia regemque vetent. Cum Philippo enim hoste pacem, non cum Antiocho amico societatis foedus ita sanciendum esse.* For the hierarchy of allies within the imperial system Rome created, see Badian (1958: 33–83) and Sherk (1984).

Honor and shame were two indispensable ingredients in inter-state ethical discourse, borrowed from the ethical code of conduct among individuals. This particular pair, like many other values on the list, contained some subcomponents to be discussed later. The dialogue continued with the reply of Quinctius Flamininus:

> Inasmuch as we are weighing the honorable, as it indeed ought to be considered either the only or at least the first object of concern to the foremost people of the world and to so great a king, which, pray, seems the more honorable, to wish all the cities of Greece which are found everywhere to be free, or to make them slaves and tributaries? If Antiochus believes it noble for him that the cities which his great-grandfather held by law of war, but which his grandfather and his father never treated as their property, be reduced to slavery, then the Roman people likewise considers it an obligation, imposed by its loyalty and consistency, not to abandon that championship of the liberty of the Greeks which it has taken upon itself. As it liberated Greece from Philip, so it intends to free from Antiochus the cities of Asia which are of the Greek race. (34.58.8-12)

Loyalty and consistency were familiar inter-state values that played a significant role during the events in which they were active (triangle). In this last passage we also see how liberty is juxtaposed with slavery of states, and it also acknowledges yet another version of the inter-state rights of conquest and possession of territory. Namely, when a state conquered another state, but later failed to treat it as its property (kind of desuetude), another nation (the Romans in our case) takes the opportunity and is, according to the Roman view, entitled to liberate the subjugated according to the international code of conduct The Seleucid ambassador adds that "it was more honorable to go out under the banner of liberty than of slavery" (34.59.1). The Roman argument is strengthened when Quinctius speaks the next day before all the delegates from Greece and Asia claiming that "with the same courage and the same fidelity with which the Roman people had won their *liberty* from Philip, they would win it from Antiochus if he did not retire from Europe" (*qua virtute quaque fide libertatem*) (34.59.4-5). Here liberty is clearly applied on the international scene, since a victory of one nation on another is perceived as gaining liberty from the defeated. I would not have lingered on the details here had they not been relevant for the discussions in Part II concerning in particular territorial arrangements, possession and rights on the land, ancestral and/or conquered, and their link to the issue of liberty (for instance, 1 Maccabees 15).

Talk about Liberty That Occurred between Two Major Wars

The two wars mentioned here are the Second Macedonian War (200–197/6 BCE) and the Roman-Syrian War (192–189/8 BCE). During the interval between the end of the former war and the final evacuation of Greece by Rome and the subsequent invasion of Antiochus III to Greece, a matter of two years at most, the slogan of liberty had become quite popular on both sides of the ensuing conflict between Rome and the Seleucid empire. The addressees on both sides were the Greek states in Greece and in Asia Minor.

Regardless its legal meaning in Roman law,[15] in line with Livy I look at it mainly from the viewpoint of the addressees. From the narrative of Livy *libertas* emerges as a loose term used by the two sides to the conflict in order to attract cities and states. The term was fairly flexible—namely, had several connotations—when used in persuasion, flattery, justification, and argumentation during dialogues and official letters (as will be seen in Part II). Both sides to the ensuing conflict shared the notion that the term was a precious asset as a tradable value just due to its variable meaning. Yet in any of its interpretations the liberty of a state was juxtaposed with its slavery.[16] In reality, regardless of the extent of intervention of empires, they loomed large at the historical background and the freedom they granted was limited to varying degrees. Sometimes the limitations on freedom were heavily disputed by the subjugated states themselves, while at other times they led to upheavals (to be remembered in Part II). At any rate, we should bear in mind that in spite of the generous grant of liberty by the Romans to states in Greece and beyond, when the masses were more influential such as in Aetolia, Boeotia and Demetrias the declaration of liberty at Corinth caused unrest. In these states the lower stratum of the society was quite sympathetic to the slogan of liberty announced by Antiochus III on the eve of his invasion into Greece and during the invasion itself. The Seleucid liberty seemed to the masses as being less limited than the one granted by the Romans that they now experienced for some years. The reality however showed that the freedom that Rome granted and the one the Seleucids promised were not always different from each other. In several instances the Seleucid rule was supported by the well-to-do—as we shall notice in Judea—whereas Rome occasionally received the backing of the lower classes (just to mention Judah Maccabee and his freedom fighters with whom Rome concluded an alliance thirty-five years later). In short, liberty as understood by the masses in Hellenistic states as well as by their rulers ranged between complete freedom to a restricted and limited one with different emphases and nuances. The inscriptions show as well that liberty as a universal value had various implications when translated into concessions: to just mention material grants and/or the extent of autonomy given to states by the ruling empire. This clarification concerning liberty has a bearing on our theme in Part II where we will deal with liberty (*eleutheria*) granted by the Seleucids to the Hasmoneans, each of whom interpreted the term somewhat differently. Moreover, liberty was usually coupled with other values taken from the virtual value system (code) such as peace, tolerance, reciprocity, mutuality, and nonviolence within the state and/or outside it. Let us now examine the evidence in line with what I have just said.

---

[15] Which I will not tackle here, and about which there are numerous studies, the most important of which still remains Wirszubski (1950), who deals with *libertas* as an inner concept in the Roman constitution yet sporadically alludes to the outer world beyond Rome. See his bibliography.

[16] For all the variants of liberty, see the following.

3

Hearings Granted to Enemies through Dialogue

The war with Antiochus was unavoidable very soon after Rome evacuated Greece in 194 BCE. I will not discuss here the political circumstances that led to Antiochus III's invasion into Greece, a subject that was discussed ad nauseam;[1] it will suffice to say here that too many in Greece and Asia wanted this war to happen, each for different reasons. For instance, King Eumenes of Pergamum feared the rising power of his neighbor the Seleucid empire, which he thought might use the existing uncomfortable peace to weaken the kingdom of Pergamum; Nabis and the Aetolians were dissatisfied with the Roman settlement of 196 BCE, whereas others were afraid of a Seleucid invasion that would bring to Greece a new master instead of Macedonia that had formerly been defeated. During the two years before the so-called Roman-Syrian War broke out, much inter-state dialogue and talk was taking place among the states of Greece, Rome, and Antiochus III. One such instance, actually the first meaningful one, occurred in Ephesus in 193 BCE and sheds light on our theme.

A meeting between the representative of Antiochus III and the Roman legate, Sulpicius, was arranged. The discussion between them was as follows: the representative of the king, Minnio says that

> I see, Romans, that you employ the plausible pretext of liberating Greek states, but your actions are inconsistent with your words, and you lay down one rule of conduct for Antiochus but yourselves follow another. Why are the people of Zmyrna and Lampsacus more Greek than the men of Naples or Rhegium or Tarentum, from whom you exact tribute, from whom you exact ships in accordance with treaty-stipulations? Why do Syracuse and other Greek cities of Sicily receive every year a praetor with the imperium and the rods and axes? Assuredly you make no other assertion than that you have imposed these conditions upon cities that have been conquered in battle. Learn from Antiochus that the case is the same with Zmyrna and Lampsacus and the cities which are in Ionia or Aeolis. Conquered in war by his forefathers and made tributaries and vassals, he restores them to their ancient status; I wish, therefore that he be answered on these points, if this is a discussion based on equity and not a search for a pretext for war. (35.16.2-6)

---

[1] See Mendels (1998: 211–22); Green (1990: 414–32).

Sulpicius replies:

> Antiochus has acted modestly, who, if there is nothing else to be said on his behalf, has preferred that anyone else should say this rather than he himself. What likeness is there in the status of the states which you have mentioned? From the people of Rhegium and Naples and Tarentum we demand that they owe in accordance with the treaty from the time they came under our sovereignty, with one unbroken continuity of right, always recognized, never interrupted. Pray, can you say that as those peoples have changed the treaty neither through themselves nor through anyone else, so the Asian cities, once they came into the possession of Antiochus' forefathers, have remained in the continuous possession of your empire, and that some have not passed under the power of Philip, some into the hands of Ptolemy, while some have enjoyed liberty with none to challenge them? For if the fact that they have once been slaves, constrained by the injustice of the times, is to confer the right of reasserting control and forcing them into slavery after so many generations, how does this differ from saying that our labors have been fruitless, in that we have freed Greece from Philip and that his descendants may again demand Corinth, Chalcis, Demetrias and the entire state of the Thessalians? But why do I plead the cause of these cities, which it is fairer that both we and the king should learn from their own pleadings? (35.16.7-13)[2]

After this dialogue, Sulpicius "ordered the embassies of the cities to be summoned … these embassies being admitted in great numbers, while each one brought in now its own complains, now its demands, and all mingled the just with the unjust, converted the meeting from an orderly debate into a wrangle" (35.17.1-2). Nothing was achieved but the phenomenon of assembly and dialogue is what matters here, the procedural. Then the king himself held a council regarding the Roman war. "There each tried to outdo the other in violence, since each thought that he would win greater favor in proportion to the severity of his attitude towards the Romans, while others assailed the insolence of their demands" (35.17.3-4). The somewhat ironic narration here points to the contrary, namely, the ideal orderly conduct required of a stately assembly. Two opinions that were heard in this council deserve our attention since they (and much of the following) confirm what I have said in the introduction to this section. The first opinion is uttered by others as a conclusion of their argument: "If liberty was not preferable to slavery (*servitus*), nevertheless, no existing situation was so attractive to anyone as the hope of a change of circumstances" (35.17.9). The second was put forward by Alexander the Acarnanian, who was present at the council. Livy introduces him as one who "once had been the friend of King Philip, but lately had left him and attached himself to the more flourishing court of Antiochus" and "was accepted as a member even of secret councils." He says (pleading for war): "even now, at the beginning, he would find the Aetolians, who dwelt in the naval of Greece, in arms, advanced troops ready for the utmost hardships" and adds that Nabis "would cause

---

[2] For a commentary to Book 35, see Briscoe (1981: 146–217).

universal confusion, trying to recover the city of the Argives" (35.18.1-5). Universal confusion was the opposite of orderly conduct in inter-state affairs, as the reader has already observed.[3]

The difference between the Roman version of *libertas* and the Seleucid interpretation of the term is enhanced in the following episode. Still before the Roman-Syrian War, a Roman delegation visited the cities of the allies, while the Achaean league was fighting Nabis the tyrant. Their aim was to check whether the allies stayed faithful to Rome or whether the Aetolians had managed to convince some of them to join Antiochus (35.31.1-2). The description of this tour gives us a glimpse of what the addressees of the Roman and Seleucid propaganda were like and how they related to the slogan of liberty. In Demetrias the leader and some members of the pro-Seleucid party (*factio*) were alarmed by a false rumor that Demetrias would be returned by the Romans to the king of Macedonia. This means that already at this early stage in the history of Roman imperialism in certain circles in Greece there was a belief that Rome could do in Greece whatever she wants. To prevent this, they wished that everything be thrown into confusion by Antiochus and the Aetolians. Against them some arguments were used such as:

> that not only all Greece was indebted to the Romans for the blessing of liberty, but this state especially; for not only had there been a Macedonian garrison there, but a royal palace had been built, that their master in person might always be held before their eyes; but their liberation would prove to have been in vain if the Aetolians should install Antiochus in the palace of Philip and if they should have a new unknown king in place of one who was old and tried. (35.31.8-10)

The speaker, a Magnetarch, who "was carried too far away in the passion of speaking, he threw out the remark that even then Demetrias was free in appearance, while in reality everything was done by the Romans' nod" (35.31.12). The crowd reacted with "a shout" (probably heard in the *synedrion*),[4] although in the council of the Magnetes some of the chiefs "were alienated from the Romans and wholly devoted to Antiochus and the Aetolians" (35.31.3-4). Some from among the crowd were

> expressing agreement, some indignation that he should have dared to say this; Quinctius, indeed, was so inflamed with wrath that raising his hands to heaven he implored the gods to witness the ungrateful and treacherous spirit of the Magnetes. All were terrified by these words, and Zeno, one of the leading citizens, and of great influence both because he pursued a seemly mode of life and because he had always indisputably belonged to the Roman party, with tears begged Quinctius and the other commissioners not to charge the insanity of one man against the community: each one was mad at his own peril; the Magnetes, he admitted,

---

[3] Hence anarchy, as Eckstein (2006) argued, was not an acceptable situation by most actors in the international scene at that time.
[4] See Larsen (1968: 295) (Magnesian confederacy). To me it seems that the *synedrion* is mentioned because of its pro-Roman stance (and not the *ekklesia* where the masses were mostly anti-Roman).

owed not merely their freedom but everything which man holds sacred and dear to Titus Quinctius and the Roman people; no man could pray to the immortal gods for anything which the Magnetes did not have from the Romans, and they would rather rage in madness against their own persons than violate the Roman friendship. (35.31.13-16)

His speech was followed by the prayers of the multitude, and Eurylochus left the council (*concilium*) and fled to Aetolia. Henceforward, quite clearly, the Aetolians were revealing their desertion (*defectionem nudabant*) (35.32.2). From this glimpse—in itself stimulating—into the conduct of the Magnesian league's institutions concerning the issue of *libertas*, we can deduce that the well-to-do were the ones who were satisfied with Roman liberty, whereas the masses were not, and explained their discontent by saying that Roman freedom was perhaps nominal but not real. But why did they think so? It is easy to guess: they were not happy with their quasi-oligarchic regime that was supported by Rome and that limited their daily freedom in many aspects of life. They hoped that Antiochus III would be their savior and that they would be fully liberated by him. Yet, those who wanted Antiochus to invade Greece, such as the Aetolians (whose popular segment was dominant), were seen by the pro-Romans as deserters (this is how the masses viewed the Judean aristocracy in Judea in the sixties of the second century BCE, see Part II).[5]

Later Quinctius and the Roman commissioners were present at the Aetolian assembly where a clear anti-Roman stance was aired (liberty of speech was still remarkable in those days). Quinctius thought that it would be advantageous for the council to be attended by representatives of the allies in order to remind the Aetolians of the Roman alliance and to freely address King Antiochus's ambassadors (35.32). Quinctius hence begged the Athenians to send delegates to the Panaetolian council because of the dignity of Athens and its ancient alliance with the Aetolians. Values, components of a virtual inter-state ethical code and their typical discourse, can be discerned here. For instance, comparable to an individual a state can be defined as being a deserter; the narrative yet again enhances the value of civilized and free dialogue during inter-state tensions and conflicts; the mantra that alliances should be honored regardless of tempting offers from states other than one's ally is again adduced; this means that loyalty was all along expected from states that were allies;[6] states, like individuals in a city, can be endowed with dignity (sometimes as a token of gratitude).[7] An ambassador of King Antiochus said in the assembly that

> it would have been best for all who lived in Greece and Asia if Antiochus could have intervened while Philip's [king of Macedonia] condition was unimpaired: each one

---

[5] And as opposing political parties are seen by other parties in modern democracies. This rhetoric has become nowadays a poison that affects some of the more advanced democracies.

[6] The mention of an ancient alliance between Athens and Aetolia, which is not known from other sources, is adduced here to show the value of loyalty when an alliance is kept and can be traced back to the past.

[7] Here, Fukuyama (2018) should be mentioned where the search for dignity of states is central and can be applied to ancient societies.

would have his own and everything would not have become subject to the nod and control of the Romans.⁸ "Even now," he said, "if only you steadfastly carry out to the end the plans which you have formed, by the grace of the gods and with the Aetolians as allies, Antiochus will be able to restore the affairs of Greece, however injured, to their former position But this rests on liberty, which exists by its own might and does not depend on another's will." (35.32.8-11)⁹

The recurrent necessity to interpret the term "liberty" shows yet again how loose the term was as used by the empires to gain supporters. Here we find an interesting variant to the term. The use of "restore" is of course somewhat vague: to restore what and to which period? But liberty is seen by the representative of a Hellenistic king as being an inner matter of the state or city and should not be enforced by a foreign power. It is the will of the citizens themselves as embodied by their own might, namely, by their constitution (*politeia*). By and large, this sounds like a comment of Livy himself who was thinking of the Roman Republic at its height, being an ironic hint to his own period, the Principate. The Athenian ambassador then gets the floor and emphatically says how crucial dialogues between states were: "before decisive action was taken, let them settle by words those matters which were in dispute rather than arm Asia and Europe for a fatal war." However, the Aetolian assembly showed that they did not follow his advice:

> The multitude was eager for a change and was all in favor of Antiochus, and they voted that the Romans should not even be admitted to the council; among the chiefs the elderly were particularly the ones who by their influence secured them audience before the council. When the Athenians reported this vote, it seemed best to Quinctius that he should go to Aetolia: he would either cause them some uncertainty or all men would be witnesses that the responsibility for the war would rest with the Aetolians and that the Romans would take up arms with justice and almost from necessity. (35.33.1-3)

When he arrived in the Aetolian assembly, Quinctius in the council mentioned first the origins of the alliance of the Aetolians with the Romans "and how often the faith imposed by the treaty had been broken by them," and then

> spoke briefly of the status of the cities about which there was debate: if, nevertheless, they considered that they had any just claim, how much better would it be to send ambassadors to Rome, whether they preferred to arbitrate or to appeal to the senate, than for the Roman people to go to war with Antiochus, the Aetolians being the matchmakers, not without great disturbance to mankind and the ruin of Greece. Nor would any experience the calamity of this war sooner than those who had caused it. (35.33.4-6)

---

⁸ 32.9: *Neque omnia sub nutum dicione*·*que Romanam perventura*.
⁹ Cf. Wirszubski (1950: 7-9).

The continuation of this shows how short tempered the Aetolians actually were, yet democratic in taking decisions on inter-state issues and full of eagerness to be totally independent: "Thoas then and others of the same party were heard with universal applause and succeeded in carrying a motion, without even adjourning the council or awaiting the departure of the Romans, and by this decree Antiochus was invited to liberate Greece and to arbitrate between the Aetolians and Romans."[10] This last paragraph points to what I have mentioned earlier. In spite of the fact that an inter-state value system was referred to time and again, it was sometimes open to interpretation. Here the rift between haves and have-nots in Greece and the various interpretations of the term "liberty" led to yet another comprehensive war (to remind the reader: the class struggle in Greece was, if we stick to Buzan and Little's definition of system, a major bond that was imbued in the inter-state system). Yet before this conflict started, we can still discern dialogue as a crucial phase before an armed conflict breaks out. At any rate, if dialogue was not successful a higher instance, the Roman senate, was approached in order to avoid war. States like individuals were endowed with a constant obligation toward a collective responsibility to keep the general order and to avoid inter-state war.[11] Livy adds a remark on the misconduct of the Aetolian praetor at the end of the assembly, misconduct that can be added to other cases where etiquette is not fulfilled or even breached (see Part II). He adduces the following episode commenting:

> To this so insolent vote a personal insult was added by their praetor Democritus: for when Quinctius asked for the actual decree, he, showing no respect for the high position of the man, replied that there was now a matter which was more pressing which he had to attend to; the decree and the answer he would presently deliver in Italy when his camp was pitched on the banks of the Tiber: such madness had at that time seized the Aetolian people and such their magistrates. (35.33.9-11)

The term "madness" made people think of its opposite, normality, that was expected in inter-state relations, meaning a right and sane conduct. From the following passage we get yet another glimpse of the inter-state value system (35.34). In order to reach a decision on which strategy to adopt concerning their relations with the Seleucid king Antiochus III, the Aetolians abstained from convening the assembly of the entire people subsequent to the dismissal of the Romans. Instead, they decided in their inner council (the apocletes being its members) to foment revolutions in the whole of Greece. "It was evident to all that in the cities the leading men and all the aristocracy were in favor of the Roman alliance and were pleased with the present state of affairs, while the multitude and those whose affairs were not in the best condition desired a complete change." It is added that the Aetolians "formed a plan not only bold but even shameless, both in its character and in its expectations, of seizing Demetrias, Chalcis and Lacedaemon" (35.34.3-4). Liberty here is not mentioned by the addressees

---

[10] 35.33.7-8: *Quo accerseretur Antiochus ad liberandam Graeciam disceptandumque inter Aetolos et Romanos.*
[11] In our modern democracies one of the cardinal issues is the relationship between authority and responsibility.

since their political and economic interests became the more important issue, whereas liberty was just a remote echo of only theoretical importance.

Ethical Dilemmas in Inter-state Relationships

In this section, two variants of an ethical dilemma will be tackled. The first, as described by Livy through the account of the events in Chalkis,[12] which similar to other cities and states in Greece was torn between the pro-Seleucid (and pro-Aetolian) faction and the pro-Roman one (the reader should bear in mind this situation when he later reads about split during the Hasmonean revolt). When the Aetolians tried to get hold of the city, the Roman faction claimed

> to pity their plight and respect the Roman alliance (*et Romanam societatem respicerent*) ; let them not permit Chalkis to become the property of the Aetolians; they would control Euboea once they controlled Chalkis; the Macedonians had been hard to endure as masters; the Aetolians would be far less easy to bear. Regard for the Romans had especial influence with the states, which had recently experienced both their valor in war and their justice and kindness in victory.[13]

Then the people of Chalkis sent ambassadors to the Aetolians

> to inquire what word or action on their part had brought allies and friends to attack them. Thoas, the Aetolian chieftain, replied that they were coming, not to besiege them, but to set them free from the Romans; now a more glittering chain, but a far heavier one, bound them than when they had a Macedonian garrison ... the Chalcidenses, however, denied that they were slaves to any man or that they needed the protection of anyone (*se vero negare Chalcidenses aut servire ulli aut praesidio cuiusquam egere*). (35.38.8-10)

Here we observe yet again how the term *libertas* was open to different interpretations, the Aetolians having the most radical view of it. Namely, that liberty means complete freedom from any intervention, military or legal, in the affairs of other states (probably the closest to the views of Judah Maccabee and the Hasmonean family when they fought the Seleucid empire). This did not deter the Aetolians from looting and subjugating others, at least this was the reputation they had in Greece at that time.[14] After this dialogue between the people of Chalkis and the Aetolians, the latter gave up the conquest of the city. Yet the Romans, to be on the safe side, sent five hundred soldiers belonging to their ally King Eumenes, to guard Chalkis.

---

[12] Livy 35.37-40.
[13] 35.38.4-6: *Graves fuisse Macedonas dominos; multo minus tolerabiles futuros Aetolos. Romanorum maxime respectus civitates movit, et virtutem nuper in bello et in victoria iustitiam benignitatemque expertas.*
[14] This phenomenon of liberal and democratic states that ruthlessly subjugate others without having any second thoughts is well known.

According to Quinctius the liberation of Chalkis would also have some effect on its neighbor Demetrias. He wanted to test the sentiments of the Demetrians (*ad temptandos animos*) "without any intention of attempting any action unless some portion of them was disposed to have regard for the former alliance" (35.39.4). Villius sailed up to the mouth of the harbor, and when all the people of the Magnetes (Magnesian league centered in Demetrias) arrived there, Villius asked them if they were Rome's friends or enemies. The Magnetarch replied that he came to friends but that he should leave the harbor and permit the Magnetes to live in harmony and liberty. Also, he should not stir up the populace under the pretense of a conference. A violent argument followed, "not a conversation," in which the Romans reproached the Magnetes for ingratitude—as against the value of *gratia* mentioned in another instance (35.35.2)—"and foretelling impending disaster, the crowd raising an uproar while accusing now the senate and now Quinctius. Without accomplishing anything Villius rejoined Quinctius" (35.39.7-8). This case is interesting from our point of view since first in Chalkis and then in Demetrias a threatening force of a super power in the region wished to intervene in order to liberate the cities but was turned down since it was claimed that the states were already liberated and did not need any further liberation and a garrison as a result. In the latter case it is made clear that a state can guard its harmony and liberty without physical presence in it of another state. The pro-Romans in Demetrias understood what real harmony and liberty were like, without the presence in the state of a foreign power. In both cases the loyalty to an alliance plays a role in states that were divided, and the choice made here was between letting the Romans in or rejecting their intervention for true liberty and harmony. The latter option prevailed and constitutes an excellent lesson in inter-state relations in the Hellenistic world. However, from the expressed fear of the Magnetes about the possibility that the masses would be stirred up against Rome one could already deduce that in reality the harmony was quite shaky; indeed, shortly thereafter a revolt of Demetrias from the Romans and shift to friendship with the Aetolians occurred. This caused King Antiochus III to rejoice and he "decided not to postpone longer his departure for Greece" (35.43.2-3). This piece of information is corroborated by another passage where it is stated that Thoas the Aetolian, "since everything in Greece had been thrown into confusion ... with lies like those about the king, with which, multiplying his forces in his harangues, he had roused the passions of many in Greece, he excited the hopes of the king also" (35.42.4-5). "Fake news" can be found here, but it was not anarchy, at least on the level of orderly procedures of decision-making and its rhetoric.

The inter-state scene becomes even more dramatic concerning ethical decisions and choices. Antiochus III by receiving the abovementioned information invaded Greece. Some states there supported him whereas he tried to convince others to remain neutral. The states in Greece which he had approached—as talk and dialogue before war was enhanced—were put in a serious dilemma. On the one hand, they were allies of Rome; on the other hand, they received a generous proposal from the Seleucid king to stay neutral without the need to abolish their alliances with Rome, which was to get an exemption from siding with the invading Seleucids and at the same time to be rewarded when the war is over and he the victor. In spite of the generous proposal of the king, the states opted for staying in the alliance with Rome (loyalty being the name of the game alongside interests to keep the status quo). Let us see how this mechanism of an ethical dilemma worked in inter-state relations.

King Antiochus III landed in Greece in 192 BCE and first went to Demetrias in Euboia, the Aetolians meanwhile called a council and confirmed the decree by which they had invited him. While this was happening Antiochus III left Demetrias through Phalara and arrived in Lamia. There he was "welcomed with great enthusiasm by the populace, with hand-clapping and shouts and the other demonstrations with which [says Livy] the unrestrained joy of a crowd is expressed" (35.43-44). Then he arrived and spoke at the Aetolian assembly and after he left, a discussion between the Aetolians concerning the future role of the Seleucid king in Greece was held. Some thought he should communicate with the Romans and avoid the war, while others thought that he would free Greece from the false liberty of the Romans. This in itself is interesting from our point of view concerning the exhibit of dialogue and dispute about values before a war is pursued. Yet the option of war prevailed in the Aetolian assembly (35.45).

Chalkis at that time was still pro-Roman. The king accompanied by the Aetolian chiefs met magistrates of Chalkis and the foremost citizens. A few from each side met for a conference outside the gate of the state. "The Aetolians urged them strongly while retaining the Roman friendship to take the king also as an ally and friend: for he had not come to Europe to make war but to free Greece, and to free it in reality, not in words and pretence, as the Romans had done" (35.46.5-6). They added that it was more useful for the Greek states to "embrace both friendships," the result of which would be that they "would always be guarded by the protection and good faith of the one from the injustice of the other" (35.46.7). Hearing this speech, one of the chiefs wondered

> for whose liberation Antiochus had left his own kingdom and crossed to Europe: for he knew no state in Greece which had a garrison or paid tribute to the Romans or suffered, under the compulsion of an unfair treaty, laws which it did not wish; therefore the people of Chalkis needed neither any champion of their liberty, since they were free, nor any protection, since by the kindness of the same Roman people they enjoyed peace along with liberty. (35.46.9-11)

The latter sentence means that liberty could exist without peace and vice versa (see Part II). He added that they neither reject the friendship of the Aetolians nor the one with the king. They were "determined not only not to admit them within the walls, but not to conclude any alliance even except in accordance with the authorization of the Romans" (35.46.13). What do we learn from this passage concerning our topic?

First, the proposal of neutrality adduced by the Aetolians jointly with the Seleucid king shows that the option of having two alliances at one and the same time with two states which are in conflict was a familiar phenomenon. This sheds light on the alliance the Hasmonean state concluded with the Romans in 161 BCE, and with Ptolemaic Egypt during the pact of the latter with the Seleucids while being under Seleucid rule. We will return to this in Part II.

Second, real and complete liberty usually included the grant of autonomy to live under the state's own laws (ancestral constitution), to be free of a garrison, and exemption from certain taxes and tribute. One would add that in certain cases the territorial borders of the subjugated state were either defined or corrected. Against this background the extent of liberty (*eleutheria*) given by the Seleucid kings to the Hasmoneans will be discussed (Part II).

Third, the proposal presented here before the people of Chalcis suggests a dilemma: either to accept a tempting proposal to remain neutral which was considered as an important value in the inter-state ethical system because of the components included in this term, such as inter-state friendship and loyalty, moderation, and responsibility. Or, to stick to the alliance they had joined beforehand to remain loyal to only one side of the conflict. The magistrates of Chalkis opted for keeping the alliance with Rome, a preference which meant a potential struggle henceforward for keeping the Roman kind of liberty and autonomy of laws, having no garrison and the enjoyment of an inner peace that was guaranteed under Roman rule.

After he was rejected by Chalkis, the Seleucid king consulted his allies, the Aetolians, who advised him to try the Achaean league, the Boeotians and King Aminander of the Athamanes, who agreed to their plan. The Achaean example is interesting for several reasons. They remain loyal to their alliance with Rome in spite of the proposal of King Antiochus III and the Aetolians to stay neutral without risk. They preferred war over peace in order not to breach a treaty that had been formerly concluded with the Romans. In the debate that was held at the Achaean assembly all opposing sides were heard. One theme in particular that sheds light on the subject of ethics is the one of *honesty* in inter-state relations. Wars could be caused by lies expressed, for example, in a public speech in an assembly. This comes so clearly to the fore in the narrative in which the representative of Antiochus who speaks at length in the assembly boasts about the size of the Seleucid army that would fight the Romans on Greek soil. Untruth (by modern terms "fake news") and truth are opposites that have a significant role when inter-state ethics is concerned. Let us elaborate a bit on this pair.

Livy reports that in Achaea a hearing before the council (*concilium*) was granted to the representatives of the Aetolians and the Seleucid king in the presence of Titus Quinctius in Aegium (35.48-49). The first speaker was the ambassador of King Antiochus, a "boaster, like most who are maintained by a king's power" who "filled seas and lands with the empty sound of words: an uncountable number of cavalry was crossing the Hellespont into Europe" (35.48.2-3). Yet although being the "mighty lord of all Asia and part of Europe" and arriving from "the farthest parts of the east to liberate Greece," he asked the Achaeans in the ensuing war not to side with either the Seleucids or the Romans with whom they had a tight and loyal alliance and friendship. "For he did not ask that they should take up arms on his side against the Romans, but that they should ally themselves with neither side. Let them wish peace for both parties as was befitting the friends of both; let them take no part in war." A similar request was made by the Aetolian ambassador who also preached for peace, "which was the easiest and safest course, and as onlookers at the war let them await the outcome of others' destinies without any risk to their own cause." Then he started to insult the Romans ("he was carried away by the vehemence of his tongue") (35.48.7-11). Quinctius replies at length saying that the Achaeans knew well that "the fierceness of the Aetolians consisted in words and not in actions, and was seen in councils and assemblies more than in battle." And adds a general truth:

> If anyone had been ignorant before what cause had brought Antiochus and the Aetolians together, it could now be clear from the speeches of their delegates that by an exchange of lies and of boasts of strength which they did not possess they filled one another's minds, and in turn were filled, with groundless hopes ... And would that I could, Achaeans, set before your eyes the frantic rush of the great king from Demetrias, now to Lamia for the council of the Aetolians, now to Chalkis; you would scarcely find the like of two poor legions of reduced strength in the camp of the king; you would see the king now almost begging food from the Aetolians to be distributed to his troops, now seeking the loan of funds on interest for their pay ... the less should you be deceived, but you should place your trust rather in the tried and known protection of the Romans. For as to what they say is best, that you should not take any part in the war, nothing, on the contrary, is so inconsistent with your interests; yes, disregarded and discredited you will be the prize of the conqueror. (35.49.1-13)

Here Quinctius highlights the significance of truth and the honesty in handling information as valuable assets in international affairs. Yet he does not forget to mention interests (utility) that are here discussed alongside values of honesty in speech. By now the reader should be convinced that the dialogues and speeches, fragments of which I adduce here in the words of the main actors, have a great deal in common with what is aired at present in the public sphere but certainly not less sophisticated.

Livy comments:

> Not without point did he appear to have answered both parties, and it was easy for his speech to be received with favoring ears by men who were on his side. For there was no debate or doubt that they would pronounce judgment that the people of the Achaeans would hold as enemies and friends the same whom the Roman people held as such, and that they would order war declared on Antiochus and the Aetolians. (35.50.1-2)

This passage would yet again be helpful in our interpretation of the alliance concluded between Judah Maccabee and the Romans in 161 BCE.[15] The continuation of the narrative demonstrates once again a case (in Athens) where a pro-Roman and a pro-Seleucid were in "a situation not much different from a rebellion" (35.50.4) where the Romans intervene and send their Athenian opponent into exile. This mechanism of *stasis* (revolution)—intervention of the empire and exile—will be tackled in Part II concerning the Hasmonean revolt.

---

[15] 1 Maccabees 8. See for this alliance in Part II, pp. 137–8.

The Roman-Syrian War

Antiochus III invaded Greece and stayed there for a relatively short time because he would soon be driven out by the Romans and their Greek allies; then he would be chased into Asia where at the final battle of Magnesia the Seleucid empire was defeated by Rome and heavily punished by the treaty of Apamea (189/8 BCE). The result of this war had a strong impact on the ancient Near East. Further on I will focus on the deliberations leading to the war which reflect an awareness of all parties of a virtual inter-state ethical code.

But first, how can we distinguish between inter-state anarchy and inter-state "orderly" conduct?[16] Anarchy is caused by the ignorance, disrespect, and shattering of the existing virtual oral ethical inter-state code or just of its agreed-upon scaling (by eliminating or disrespecting a certain value or values from within the ethical system). We can be sure that had such an inter-state ethical code not existed in the period under discussion, we would have seen quite a bit of inter-state political turbulence and anarchy. But this did not occur. The more orderly relationship between states required a certain degree of adherence to an agreed upon framework of values and other political patterns of conduct. Since a set of values was referred to in speeches, conferences, and other channels of communication, we may say for sure that a value system was active and became a kind of compass for inter-state good conduct. Interpretation of the value system could differ between parties and be argued, but by the end of the day all sides refer to the same value system provided they belong to the same society of states, called here a system. This at least is what Livy and his predecessors broadcast, as we encounter also in the following narrative where prominent values are exhibited, such as gifting (promised, given, and received), neutrality and its adjacent values, deceit and swap of allies (fidelity), utilitarianism, inter-state *parrhesia*, and the value of free discussion, loyalty, surrender and repentance, compassion, and so on.[17] I should emphasize yet again that talk (rhetoric) and discussion concerning political ethics before, during, and after wars were considered as values in themselves, which at certain junctures influenced the course of events.

At the beginning of the Roman-Syrian War, as in other wars that the Romans fought in the Hellenistic east, the issue of its declaration and the formal etiquette of its beginning became a major issue. When this was decided upon, and declaration was announced, war could formally start. It was decided that

> the friendship [with Antiochus] seemed to be already broken off since they had voted that restitution had not been made after ambassadors had so often demanded it nor fair satisfaction given; the Aetolians had taken the initiative in declaring war upon them when they had seized Demetrias by violence, a city belonging to the allies, had proceeded to invest Chalkis by land and sea, and

---

[16] Apropos Eckstein's thesis (2006) that at that period everything in Greece and beyond was anarchical.
[17] When I mention adjacent values, I mean that most values have subvalues or "satellites." For instance, loyalty of one state to another includes open deliberation, neutrality agreed by all sides, frankness, reciprocity when needed.

had invited King Antiochus to Europe to make war upon the Roman people. (36.3.10-12)[18]

This formality was then settled and preparations for war started, accompanied by a procession of gift donors to Rome. Gifting was, as we have already noticed, an indispensable component in international relations that symbolized the obligation and friendship of one state to another. Both King Philip V of Macedonia and King Ptolemy of Egypt were loaded with gifts and proposed to assist the Romans in the ensuing war. Some of the gifts were given while others were just announced as pledges. Those that were promised or the ones that the Romans rejected cannot be considered as gifts since they did not change hands.[19] They may reveal good intentions but if the gift did not change hands the receiver could see it as an act of nongiving. In the following passage there is an element that we have to bear in mind when we later discuss the Jewish case where variants of gifting are mentioned (Part II). The following information is interesting from our point of view. Philip promised aid, money, and grain for the war; Ptolemy sent a thousand pounds of gold and twenty thousand pounds of silver. None of these gifts was accepted by the Romans, "only thanks were expressed, and when each of them promised to come with all his forces to Aetolia and participate in the war, Ptolemy was excused from this." From other allies as well promises and grants of gifts were given to the Romans (36.4). The Romans rejected some of the promises and grants due to pure strategic reasons which will not be tackled here. Just to mention the case of Ptolemy who was exempt from participation in the ensuing war because the Romans probably wished that he would stay alert against Antiochus III who posed as a threat to his borders since the year 200 BCE when he conquered Palestine from the Ptolemaic empire. This was also the reason why the Romans wanted him to keep the treasures that the king brought along in case the Ptolemies would need it for hiring mercenaries for the war with Antiochus on their border while the latter was fighting the Romans in Greece. Be that as it may, gifting was a ritual that expressed good conduct and was a litmus test for the nature of a relationship between states. Gifts had to change hands, from doner to receiver; if rejected for some reason or another by the receiver, thanks had to be uttered by the latter (as we shall see in Part II, Mattathias rejected gifts and concessions offered by the Seleucids, but did not thank them, and this was probably considered as an insult toward the king). The act of gifting in certain instances was also a token of the nature of the relationship and status of states within the system, namely, being equal, inferior, or superior in status within the hierarchy of nations. I will return to this point in Part II (concerning Antiochus VII and Simeon).

While this was happening in Rome, Antiochus III made attempts to further broaden his coalition. Hence, he continued the dialogue with Greek cities and states, focusing on the choices between staying neutral or fighting alongside one of the parties to the conflict. When Antiochus arrived in Chalkis "sometimes was himself stirring up the minds of the states by sending embassies, sometimes was receiving delegations

[18] For a detailed commentary on Livy Book 36, Briscoe (1981: 218-88).
[19] Mendels (2013: 94-104).

voluntarily sent to him, as, for instance, the Epirotes." The Epirotes were prepared to support him, but their proximity to Italy deterred them from doing so. "The embassy of the Epirotes showed no outspoken and plain inclination to either side; they were trying to curry favor with the king, meanwhile avoiding giving any offence to the Romans" (36.5.3). Yet,

> if [Antiochus] himself could stand guard over Epirus with his armies and fleets, all the Epirotes would eagerly receive him in cities and harbors alike; however, if he could not, they begged that he should not make them, naked and unarmed, bear the brunt of the Roman war. It was clear that the object of the embassy was that either, if, as they rather believed, be kept away from Epirus, they might not be committed to anything in the eyes of the Roman armies, though they had well established their position with the king, since they had been ready to receive him if he came, or, if he did come, that thus there would be the hope of *pardon* from the Romans because, not expecting from them aid which was so far away, they had yielded to the might of the king who was so close at hand. (36.5.5-7)

In other words, the loyalty of the state of the Epirotes was pending on inter-state power politics in which they were just pawns. This needs some clarification: the existence of an ethical inter-state code that became embedded within the inter-state system could be maintained by a powerful super power that managed and protected its very existence and continuity. One of the facets of maintenance was the physical proximity of the state to the ruling empire. This is the theme of the case under discussion here when a dialogue is pursued by the Epirotes who surely were aware that the Seleucid king had arrived in Greece with a much smaller army than he had promised, and could still be manipulated. The king decided to continue the dialogue and said "that he would send ambassadors to them to confer with them concerning the questions which pertained to them and himself alike" (36.5.8). Not very different was the outcome in the Boeotian league. The king "proceeded to Boeotia, which had as apparent causes for anger at the Romans" because of occurrences I mentioned above. Anger of a group was frequently mentioned as a reason for launching inter-state operations; in several instances this emotion led states to take revenge. Here it does not, mainly because of fear of retaliation by the Romans. Livy comments that the discipline in which the Boeotians were once eminent, in public and private affairs, "had for many years now been degenerating, and the condition of many was such that it could not last without a change of circumstances" (36.6.1-3). The latter remark points to the inclination of the Boeotian league toward Antiochus III, and the interaction between the inner political and social structure of the state and its activity on the inter-state scene. Hence "with the chiefs of Boeotia coming out in crowds to meet him, he arrived in Thebes. There in the council of the people" he gave the same speech that "he held beforehand in the first assembly at Chalkis and had delivered through his delegates."[20] "He asked that they make a treaty of friendship

---

[20] 35.36-38.

with him, not that they declare war on the Romans. No one was deceived as to what was going on; nevertheless, a decree was passed, under a cloak of mild verbiage, in favor of the king and against the Romans" (36.6.1-4). In short, so far by dialogue the Seleucid king won over two important states. The nature of argumentation in speeches and their rhetoric (directness, obscurity, etc.), as we learn here, was an influential factor in inter-state political discourse.

Antiochus III then summoned the chiefs of the Aetolians and King Amynander of Athamania to Demetrias to discuss the general policy concerning aspects of the ensuing war (*cum quibus de summa rerum deliberaret*). These deliberations are enlightening not so much because of their content but due to the mechanism of open speech in inter-state conferences, the procedural. Livy tells us that "the question for consideration had to be with the Thessalian people, whose intentions, as all who were present agreed, should be ascertained." In the discussion there were several opinions, some opted for immediate action, whereas others for its postponement "while some thought that ambassadors only should be sent and others that he should go with his entire force and terrorize them if they hesitated" (36.6.6-10).

The debate did not end here but went on with a speech of Hannibal, the famous Carthaginian general, who after his defeat by Rome became a consultant to Antiochus III. He delivers a long speech which I will not tackle here (36.7), but only mention a variant of disloyalty that he highlights. When an army of the empire is close by, loyalty could be challenged by both sides to a conflict (see later Bacchides' treatment of the sixty pietists, in Part II). Hannibal says apropos the threatening approach of Antiochus III to the Greek cities:

Before anything else, I vote that Philip and the Macedonians be drawn, in any possible way, into a military alliance. For as to Euboea and the Boeotians and the Thessalians, who doubts that they, possessing no strength of their own, are ever fawning upon those who are close at hand, and will use the same fearfulness which they display in the council as a means of winning pardon, and that, as soon as they see the Roman army in Greece, they will turn back to their accustomed masters and that they will suffer no harm because, when the Romans were far away, they were unwilling to test, face to face the strength of you and your army? How much greater priority and preference should we give to allying ourselves with Philip rather than with them? ... What cause, then, convinces me that Philip can be allied with us? First, the common profit, which is the firmest bond in an alliance; second ... that Philip was enraged and that he found it hard to bear the laws of slavery imposed upon him under the guise of peace. Indeed, in his speech he likened the king in his wrath to a wild beast chained or shut up and trying to break his bonds. (36.7.3-13)[21]

Hannibal here expresses universal ideas quite familiar from Hellenistic inter-state discourse. From this passage of his speech, we become acquainted with some values

---

[21] See also 35.18.6.

that played a role at the time: strength and valor as against loyalty to one's allies, fidelity which becomes volatile during periods when conflict is imminent. Pardon is on the agenda and should be activated in certain circumstances.[22] Also, an advice is adduced by Hannibal concerning the concluding of alliances. A state should join an alliance not with the weak but with those who are strong and potentially awaiting opportunities to take revenge on former foes (Philip against Rome who defeated him less than a decade before the speech of Antiochus was held). Another element that comes to the fore is the one of profit, which is "the firmest bond in an alliance" (*communis utilitas, quae societatis maximum vinculum est*) (36.7.11). This again brings to the fore the issue of balance between utility and value that preoccupies experts in the field until the present.

Hannibal continues with his argumentation concerning the proper management of the ensuing war. The people in the assembly who were polite (present) "applauded it for the moment rather than adopted it in actual decision; for nothing of these things was done" (36.8.1). Politeness was exhibited, an important value at that time (which perhaps looks a bit odd to the modern reader who has seen so much impoliteness in public deliberations at state institutions in recent years). Immediately after the conference was over, Hannibal's assumption of the volatility of loyalty and its expression was exhibited. "Ambassadors [of Antiochus III] were sent to Larisa to the council of the Thessalians, and a day was fixed for the Aetolians and [King] Amynander to hold the muster of the army at Pherae; the king also with his troops came with speed to the same place" (36.8.2). Now comes the story about the collecting of bones of victims that were left on the battlefield after the battle of Cynoscephalae. This ritual is important for our reconstruction of the value system during war and is yet another background story to the one where Judah Maccabee collects bones after a battle (Part II). I will not linger on this story here but go on with the narrative about the Thessalians. Livy informs us that while Antiochus III was in camp at Pherae, where he was joined by the Aetolians and Amynander, ambassadors from Larisa came asking for "what deed or word of the Thessalians he was assailing them with war, and likewise asking that he should withdraw his army and discuss with them through ambassadors whatever seemed to him worth considering" (36.9.1-2). He answered mildly that he "did not enter Thessaly to make war but to defend and assure the liberty of the Thessalians." A delegate was sent to conduct similar negotiations with the people of Pherae; giving him no answer, the Pheraeans themselves sent their chief magistrate Pausanias to the king.

> When he had with a good deal of vigor presented certain arguments not unlike those which, in a similar situation, had been used on behalf of the Chalcidians in the conference at the strait of Euripus,[23] the king, bidding them again to ponder and not to adopt any plan of which, while being too cautious and thoughtful for the future, they would at once repent, dismissed him. When this mission was reported at Pherae, they did not even for a brief period doubt that they should, for

---

[22] See my discussion on 2 Maccabees 12 (in Part II, Chapter 6).
[23] Probably the conference mentioned at 35.38.7-10.

the sake of their loyalty to the Romans, endure whatever the fortune of war might bring. (36.9.4-7)

Hence in spite of the armies around them they decided to stay loyal to the Romans and to go to war. Antiochus's pride was hurt and he decided to fight in order to be scorned and feared by the Thessalians. The city surrendered and he very well understood that "there was no question about it ... that he brought every form of terror to bear from all sides on the besieged." After fighting bravely, the city surrendered and so did another city, the city of Scotusa, also attacked by Antiochus. Yet Antiochus III, in line with some conventions of inter-state behavior known from the Hellenistic world, used the more lenient tactical mechanism of compassion. The latter value was activated from time to time in international affairs. Thus, he released all without injury "because this act, in the king's opinion would have great weight in winning the sympathies of the Larisaeans" (36.9.9-15). In other words, loyalty was seen by some as high up on the priority list of values; they were even prepared to fight for it regardless of the dangers involved. Yet repentance and pardon remained an option even when states decided to fight rather than to surrender. We also learn yet again that pardoning one's enemy was considered as an advantageous gesture on behalf of the victor. (This may explain some obscure facets of the relationship of the Seleucids with the Jews later in the century.) However, Rome was already then considered a dominant power in the region and the Seleucids were aware of it. The value system was already affected by this awareness. When the Seleucids had encounters with the Jews two decades later, they had the role of being the dominant power in the ancient Near East.

The war in Greece lingered on for some more months and a decisive battle at Thermopylae in 190 BCE caused the retreat of Antiochus III to Ephesus. Within a decade the Greeks were left once more to the mercy of the counterinvasion of the Roman army. Livy's sarcastic remark reveals what he actually thought about the war: "[Antiochus], at last perceiving that he had gained nothing from Greece except a pleasant winter at Chalcis and a shameful marriage" (36.15.1). Already during this first stage of the Roman-Syrian War it became crystal clear that the Seleucids had made three fateful mistakes in their decisions. First, they built on the Greek promises to have an overall upheaval of the masses, which turned to be a wild exaggeration promoted by the Aetolians; second, they underestimated the power of Rome and her willingness to be the protector of Greece after 196; third, the loyalty to Rome and its settlements in the region was quite firm among most of the states. The Seleucids also did not realize that anarchy was out of the question for the Greek states and that the values and sociopolitical balance and harmony was what kept most of Greece—at least most aristocrats and many from among the masses—united against the invading Hellenistic king. Here loyalty and utility can be seen as an inseparable pair to be discussed later. By and large, Antiochus's final defeat in Asia Minor and the restrictions put on the Seleucid ruler by the treaty of Apamea (188 BCE) turned his territorial hopes of expansion into frustration. This somber mood of the king would have severe repercussions in inter-state ancient Near Eastern politics in general, and their relationship with Judea in particular.

Two outstanding incidents that occurred during the Roman counterinvasion of Greece should be mentioned. When the Roman army arrived in Boeotia,

> the citizens, conscious of their rebellion, were standing before the gates holding badges of supplication, in fear that they would be plundered like enemies. But during all these days the column marched just as if they were passing through a peaceful country, doing no injury to anyone, until they arrived at the territory of Coronea. There a statue of King Antiochus, set up in the temple of Athena Itonia, enkindled the consul's wrath, and the soldiers were permitted to devastate the land around the temple; then the thought came to his [the consul] mind that since the statue had been set up by a general decree of the Boeotians it was improper to vent his wrath on the territory of Coronea alone. The soldiers were at once recalled and an end put to the pillaging; the Boeotians received only a verbal reproof for their ingratitude to the Romans after such notable and recent acts of kindness. (36.20.1-4)

This is an interesting observation and sheds light on practices of the Seleucids in territories that they conquered. From this episode we can deduce that the Seleucid kings either put their images in temples directly or let the conquered themselves do it. It was just this consent which they probably could not get from the Jews later in the century when they asked them to put the statue of (probably) Antiochus IV in the Jerusalem Temple (*Shikkuz Meshomem*). For the Seleucids this was a common practice of manifesting their sovereignty. The behavior of the Jews was, as it were, unacceptable and interpreted by the Seleucids as lack of respect and even contempt toward their king (in a way, similar to the rejection of gifts). Interestingly, when the Roman consul discovered that the statue of King Antiochus III that caused his rage was erected by consent of a Greek state, the statue was respected and remained in place. Consent of a state was a precious value in inter-state encounters in particular when confrontation was on the agenda.

Second episode: During the retreat of the king to Ephesus in Asia Minor, the consul Acilius sent a delegation to the Aetolians at Heraclea hoping that they—having experienced the unreliability of the king—"might regain their senses, surrender Heraclea and take counsel about asking pardon from the senate for their madness or, if they preferred, their mistake" (36.22.1). This is an opening sentence for a short passage which underlines a few rules of conduct expected from a state in its relationship with other participant states in the ethical network. Namely, although one state has made a wrong decision because of its madness (emotion) and/or mistake (decision-making, a characteristic) in the eyes of the victor, a built-in mechanism existed in the inter-state value system for pardoning ingratitude and disloyalty (value). That pardon as a value with many of its adjacent components such as respect, potential reciprocity, repentance, and compassion, existed in the arsenal of values enabled every state to activate it in the changing circumstances. Further, Livy informs us that

> other states of Greece too in that war ... had revolted from the Romans who deserved so well of them, but because after the flight of the king, from confidence

in whom they had thrown off their allegiance, they had not added stubbornness to their fault, they had been received into alliance; the Aetolians also, though they had not followed the king but had summoned him, and had been the leaders in the war and not allies, if they could repent, could likewise be saved. When they gave no pacific reply to this, and it was evident that he must have recourse to arms, and that after the defeat of the king the Aetolian war remained as before, he moved camp from Thermopylae to Heraclea, and on the same day, to reconnoitre the site of the city, he rode on horseback around the walls on every side. (36.22.2-4)

This paragraph is a continuation of the narrative that exemplified the idea of pardon. Namely, if one state was disloyal and breached an alliance, yet did not add stubbornness to disloyalty—as for instance presenting additional conditions to an existing (breached) treaty or refusing conditions presented by the victor—then this state could be pardoned and returned to the former treaty. Moreover, even if a state has breached an alliance quite severely (as for instance summoning an enemy to fight the state with which one has concluded an alliance beforehand), only repentance would save it. Repentance seems to be high up in the inter-state value system. That pardon and repentance (with their adjacent values) were embedded within the value system of the Hellenistic inter-state scene will be discussed in the following.

Surrender, Giving In, and Talk

Antiochus III was gone and Greece lay open once more for the operations of Philip V and Rome, this time allies, during which Aetolia surrendered to the Roman forces. Rome, which had had quite a bad experience with the Aetolians, shows once more that diplomacy must be exploited before the use of power is pursued. She certainly could activate her army, as the consul says during the Roman-Aetolian dialogue, but prefers nonviolent action—in itself an important choice of a significant inter-state value, peace. Livy tells us that the capture of Heraclea broke the spirit of the Aetolians, and in spite of the fact that they sent ambassadors to Antiochus in order to summon him and renew the war,

> they laid aside their warlike designs and sent delegates to the consul to beg for peace. The consul broke in when they had begun to speak, saying that he had more important matters to attend to, and ordered them to return to Hypata, granting them a truce of ten days and sending Lucius Valerius Flaccus with them, telling them to state to him the matters they had planned to discuss with himself and anything they desired. (36.27.2-3)

When they reached Hypata the chiefs of the Aetolians conferred with Flaccus in what way they should argue with the consul:

> They were preparing to begin with their ancient treaty relations and their services to the Roman people, when Flaccus bade them cease to mention what

they had themselves violated and broken; a confession of wrongdoing would avail them more and a speech devoted entirely to prayers; for not on their own cause but on the clemency of the Roman people did their hopes of safety depend; he too would support them if they should plead like suppliants both before the consul and with the senate at Rome; for there too ambassadors should be sent.[24] This seemed to all of them the only way to safety (*ad salutem*), that they should entrust themselves to the good faith of the Romans; for that by so doing they would at once render the Romans ashamed to do violence to suppliants and themselves no less be absolutely free should fortune offer them anything better. (36.27.5-8)

In this passage we discover the (ideal) set of inter-state values which emerge when one state loses a war and is seen as the defeated party that should comply with conditions imposed by the victor. In this big drama the defeated gets the role of a suppliant that has to confess his past wrongdoings and pray so that the victor will show clemency and grant the expected safety. When the defeated confesses, although he initially has breached the alliance, the victor (the Roman Republic) might show its good faith and refrain from using violence toward the suppliants. If the Romans would act in such a manner, they would prevent their own shame within the international scene.

This dialogue was just the beginning. Now come the really tough words that show yet again that ethical systems were sometimes subject to the caprice of power politics but were not necessarily abolished. In the continuation of the narrative, we are told that

when they came before the consul, Phaeneas, the leader of the embassy, spoke at length and with manifold devices with which to soften the heart of the conqueror and concluded by saying that the Aetolians entrusted themselves and all their possessions to the good faith of the Roman people.[25] When the consul heard this he replied, "Consider again and again, Aetolians, whether you are submitting on these conditions." Then Phaeneas the Aetolian displayed the decree in which this was explicitly stated in writing.[26] "Since, then," the consul said, "you are submitting on these terms, I demand that Dicaearchus your fellow-citizen and Menestas of Epirus"—he had entered Naupactus with a garrison and compelled it to revolt— "and Amynander with the chiefs of the Athamanes, by whose advice you revolted from us, be delivered to me without delay."

He interrupted the speech of the Roman, saying: "We have not delivered ourselves into slavery but have entrusted ourselves to your good faith and I feel sure that you

---

[24] 36.27.6: *Confessionem iis culpae magis profuturam et totam in preces orationem versam; nec enim in causa ipsorum, sed in populi Romani clementia spem salutis positam esse.*

[25] 36. 28.1: *Se suaque omnia fidei populi Romani permittere.*

[26] The commentator in Loeb (vol. X, p. 238, note 1) says that "on the other hand, as Polybius (XX.IX) shows, the Aetolians did not understand that to the Romans *in fidem se permittere* meant complete and unconditional surrender. In consequence the two parties are at cross purposes in the following debate until the national definitions are made clear."

err from ignorance in giving us orders which are inconsistent with the customs of the Greeks." To this the consul reacted:

> Nor, by Hercules, do I care very much what the Aetolians regard as properly consistent with the customs of the Greeks, since I, in the Roman way, am delivering an order to men who a moment ago surrendered by their own decree and had previously been conquered by armed force; therefore, unless my order is immediately executed I shall at once order you to be put in chains. (36.28.2-6)

Before we go on with this fascinating story, we should note that this incident exemplifies a clash that is expressed in a dialogue between two states, one of which, the victor, threatens the use of force after a submission was agreed by the defeated party. The clash itself points to a hiccup in the mutual understanding that existed between Rome and the Greek world concerning the inter-state ethical code. This is yet again a clash which disrupted the more or less smooth discourse that existed within the system of inter-state relationships. We will come back to similar clashes in Part II when we discuss the conflict between the Seleucids and the Hasmoneans that occurred later in the century. However, this last passage of confrontative dialogue between victorious Rome and a defeated Greek state focused on inter-state ethical matters. The stubbornness (an emotion) of both sides brought about the following drama: The arrogant spirit of Phaeneas and other Aetolians was broken when the Roman consul directed the chains to be brought and the lictors to stand by. Phaeneas finally understood their situation and requested a truce of ten days in order to confirm the conditions of surrender in the council of the Aetolians. The council of the Aetolians (*apokletoi*) was convened and Phaeneas gave an account of what was happening. Livy adds that "the chiefs indeed groaned at their situation, yet recognized that they must obey their conqueror and that the Aetolians from all towns must be summoned to a council" (36.28.9). The assembly convened and when it heard the news,

> anger at the order and a sense of unjust treatment so inflamed their minds that, if they had been at peace, they would by that onset of passion have been provoked to war. Added to their wrath was also the difficulty of the orders (for how, in any case, could they possibly hand over King Amynander?) and the hope which by chance offered itself because just at that time Nicander, coming from King Antiochus, filled the multitude with the idle expectation that a great war was preparing on land and sea. (36.29.1-3)

The Aetolians who were depicted in Hellenistic historiography as fierce and warlike people are here portrayed as humble, quite peaceful, and orderly, adhering to their own long-standing democratic procedure meant to ratify a treaty with Rome. The Romans now bare their teeth and turn to the use of power (36.30). The use of power in inter-state relations seemed to be justified when one state was acting against the ethical code shared by all. This stance of ruling powers is familiar from the history henceforward.

Inter-state Order and Its Relationship to Utility and Consent

Throughout our survey we have drawn attention to the emphasis put by states in the Hellenistic era on continuous dialogue. A dialogue in itself expressed values such as mutual respect, reciprocal yielding, compromise, and listening with patience to each other. The art of listening to one's adversary—what we call today "hearing"—during a discussion in the Graeco-Roman world is remarkable, at least this is the impression we get from the sources. From the abundance of evidence that Livy adduces concerning this juncture of history, we will linger on one crucial value that is adduced here: order. In fact, Livy links between three significant values in the inter-state ethical code: order, utility, and consent. When these values cooperate (here through Roman arbitration), true order is achieved; in other words, a balance between order and utility requires consent of all sides to a conflict. Let us view this interaction in the following details of the relationship of Messene and the Achaean league in the aftermath of the Roman-Syrian War.

Livy tells us that the Achaeans besieged Messene because it had refused to join the Achaean league. Both Messene and Elis sympathized with the Aetolian league and hence remained "outside the Achaean council" (36.31). After Antiochus was driven away from Greece, he responded more moderately (*lenius responderant*) to the ambassadors of the Achaeans saying:

> if the royal garrison would be withdrawn, they would consider what they should do; the Messenians, on the other hand, had dismissed the ambassadors unanswered, and had begun war. Yet they were fearful for their cause when their crops were being burnt everywhere by a wide-ranging army and they saw the camp established near the city. They sent ambassadors to Chalkis to Titus Quinctius, the source of their liberty, to say that the Messenians were ready to open their gates and surrender their city to the Romans, not to the Achaeans. (36.31.3-5)

Quinctius listened to the ambassadors and sent to the praetor of the Achaean a message with an order to withdraw his army from Messene and report to him. Diophanes obeyed, lifted the siege, and traveled to see Quinctius.

> When he had explained the reason for the siege, Quinctius reproached him gently because he had undertaken so important a matter without his authorization [meaning probably authorization of the Roman army which was stationed in Greece],[27] and ordered him to disband his army and not to disturb the peace secured to the advantage of everyone. (36.31.8)

---

[27] Quinctius had no formal authority at that time but enjoyed an enormous prestige due to his fame as the liberator of Greece. In statues for him he is portrayed as "savior and benefactor," and excellent ("because of his excellence"). See Sherk (1984: 7-8). See in Part II, Chapter 5, the discussion on Hasmonean authority and its ethical values.

He also instructed the Messenians to join the council of the Achaeans and recall their exiles. "If they had any matters about which they wished to raise objections or to take precautions for themselves against future contingencies, they should come to him at Corinth; Diophanes he directed to give him an immediate opportunity to meet the Achaean council" (36 31.9-10). There he demanded that the island of Zacynthos should be restored to the Romans since it had been wrongly seized, having earlier been transferred to the Achaeans as a bargain. Now the Romans demanded it as a prize for their victory at Thermopylae in 190 BCE (32). The case of Zacynthos is presented here as a typical deal that could have been concluded also in a Greek market concerning a commodity or piece of land. This is the topic of the dialogue in which the Romans intervene in the conflict between the Achaeans and Messenians and prevent a war between the two, but fulfill the initial aim of the Achaeans by telling the Messenians to join the League ("recall their exiles and join the council of the Achaeans").[28] A quick procedure is conveyed for the maintenance of inter-state order backed by the consent of the confrontational sides to the conflict. As a result of their decision in favor of the Achaean league, the exchange was immediately required, namely, the transfer of the island of Zacynthos to the Romans. The dialogue then goes on with a quite surprising argumentation of Quinctius, which is important for our case here and reveals one aspect of territoriality. Utility as a value comes again to the fore and is presented here as cooperating with order and consent. Livy elaborates on this point by adducing the speech of Titus Quinctius concerning utility (36.32):

> If I believed that the possession of the island was useful to you (*si utilem ... possessionem eius insulae*), Achaeans, I should urge upon the senate and the Roman people that they permit you to keep it; but like a tortoise, which I see to be secure against all attacks when it has all its parts drawn up inside its shell, but when it sticks any part out it has that member which is exposed weak and open to injury, in no different fashion you, Achaeans, shut in on all sides by the sea, can both easily unite to yourselves anything within the boundaries of the Peloponnesus, and, when thus united, easily defend it, but as soon as in your desire for larger acquisitions you overstep those limits, I see that all the parts which lie outside are unprotected and vulnerable to every blow. (36.32.5-8)

Livy adds that "the whole council assenting and Diophanes not daring to struggle longer, Zacynthos was ceded to the Romans" (36.32.9). The speech of Quinctius in the council speaks for itself and reveals what Roman imperialism already at this stage—when Greece and the East were not yet Roman domain—meant for a Roman aristocrat. He promotes the idea of limited territorial acquisitions as one of the guarantees for order. In the wake of our imbued postcolonial cynicism, we sometimes address the issue of imperialism in general and the Roman one in particular as an

---

[28] 36.31.9. The exiles here are reminiscent of the letter of Antiochus VII to Simeon in 1 Maccabees 15 where he acknowledges the legitimacy of the ownership of the Jews on the region of Judea.

outlet of aggressive policies and exploitation of the conquered.[29] However, at this stage of Roman imperialism in the Greek East we can still detect a sincere will on behalf of the Romans to settle affairs and keep law and order by consent of most of their partners settled to their East; this notion developed during the seventies of the second century BCE into their strategy of playing the role of protectors of Greece. Not everyone was happy with their political settlements in Greece, as we have seen just now during the Roman-Syrian War, but on the inter-state level of encounters their set of values and exhibit of procedural ethics, they were still more or less on equal terms with many states in Greece and beyond. At any rate their conduct in Greece cannot yet be seen as an expression of their aggressiveness in reply to any kind of anarchy; on the contrary, they wished to settle affairs of inter-state relationships in Greece to achieve inter-state and stately harmony and stability. Moreover, they certainly were aware of the clash between utility and other values of the inter-state ethical code[30] but at certain junctures knew how to navigate wisely between these poles (this stance comes to the fore later in Judah's assessment of their imperialism, in 1 Maccabees 8). The Romans exploited their ability to manage and manipulate an ethical inter-state code shared by most Greek-speaking participants in a system ingeniously created by them. However, the urge for utility frequently jeopardized a perfect conduct that was dictated by the ethical code.

Tokens of Connectedness

Connectedness is defined by the Cambridge English Dictionary as follows: "structural connectedness is based on the idea that policy is made within a context of a network of actors and institutions" and according to the Cambridge English Corpus "the ensuing notion of connectedness extends the ancestor-descendant relation," and "higher and lower degrees of connectedness are indicated by the placement of communal facilities and shrines." In line with what I have said so far, I would like to add that a basic requirement for an inter-state value system to exist and be operational is a certain degree of connectedness between states that share the ethical inter-state network. This means that they operate in the same world of ideas and discourse that the framework of the inter-state ethical code provides. As we have already seen, when inter-state issues were discussed in assemblies, an agreement on terms of reference of an ethical code was always assumed in spite of sporadic divisions on interpretation. Thus, we can speak of "zones of connectedness" in certain regions of the Hellenistic world. For instance, the Hellenistic kingdoms, cities, and states whose language was Greek enjoyed such a built-in connectedness in every single sphere of life. Yet, at times they were fighting each other as a result of pure local power politics, not because they did not understand each other's basic rules of conduct and their shared universal scale of values. On the contrary, many of

---

[29] Harris (1979) (following the ideas of Montesquieu's *Considerations on the Causes of the Greatness of the Romans and their Decline*, 1734).
[30] Gamble (2010: 74–81).

the quarrels and wars between Hellenistic states were a result of what I call here "the ancestor-descendant relationship" (which I mentioned above, for instance, in the arguments of Antiochus III concerning Lysimachia). Ironically, through conflict one state enhances its own special identity, as every reader probably knows, but the basic features of connectedness still remained (similar to relationships in families and tribes). When the Romans intervened in the Greek world, although their language was Latin, the generals and ambassadors who were in touch with the Greeks were bilingual (the account of what I relate here does not mention translators). On the other hand, Greek systems of political conduct were not alien to the Romans (assemblies, voting, democratic mechanisms, etc.), and the Greeks who visited Rome met a similar political climate including the senate, assemblies, and deliberations; in short, the procedural was familiar to them. Hence the constant dialogue between the Romans and the Greek states and Hellenistic kingdoms—although confrontative at times—was from the outset of their encounter not a dialogue of the deaf. The encounter, as we learn from the sources, was quite natural and daily revealed a strong lingual, cultural, and sociopolitical connectedness, sometimes more intensively expressed and at other times less so. Let me now go on with my survey while emphasizing the tokens of connectedness and their effect on inter-state ethics.

Subsequent to Antiochus III's retreat from Greece, a section of his army remained in Greece. An episode related by Livy clarifies a gentlemen's relationship between two kings, Philip V and Antiochus III, who were formally still at war with each other (one should remember that Philip V, once a fierce enemy of Rome who was defeated by her in 197 BCE, was in the Roman-Syrian War fighting on her side against Antiochus III). The episode goes as follows:

> King Philip, as the consul was leaving for Naupactus, asked him whether he wished meanwhile to recover the cities that had abandoned the Roman alliance, and with his consent moved his troops towards Demetrias, well knowing what confusion reigned there. For abandoned by all hope, when they saw themselves deserted by Antiochus, with no prospect of help from the Aetolians, by day and night they looked for the arrival either of Philip, their enemy, or of the Romans, even more hostile in proportion to their juster cause for anger. (36.33.1-3)

The choice they had, as it were, to find someone who will help them to survive after being deserted by their ally, Antiochus, shows one important lesson: they felt as being left within the same political and cultural network that they shared with their allies and foes. They were not foreigners in this world and well-understood its vibes, as the continuation of the story reveals:

> There was in the city an undisciplined mob of the king's [Antiochus] soldiers, a few of whom had at first been left on guard, but afterwards more came, most of them unarmed, brought there in their flight after the defeat [of Thermopylae], nor did they have enough of either strength or courage to resist a siege; and so when agents were sent ahead by Philip, who showed them that the hope of pardon was attainable, they replied that the gates were open to the king. At his first entrance

some of the leading men left the city; Eurylochus committed suicide. The soldiers of Antiochus—for such was the agreement—were conducted by a Macedonian escort, that no one might injure them, through Macedonia and Thrace to Lysimachia. There were also a few ships at Demetrias under the command of Isidorus; they too with the prefect were sent home. After that he recovered Dolopia and Aperantia and certain cities of Perrhaebia. (36.33.4-7)

This is once more a typical example of tokens of connectedness. Agreement between Philip and the Roman consul concerning the condition of certain states is mentioned, and then the agreement between Philip and the deserted soldiers of Antiochus III who were at his mercy, and he well knew that they might serve later as soldiers of his enemy, King Antiochus. Nevertheless, he demonstrates what "pardon" is like and adheres to the agreement to save them. And they trust him and leave the gates open. I have already encountered the value of pardon and will return to it later. Subsequently one leader who knew what awaits him committed suicide.[31] And here we arrive at an additional episode which exemplifies a token of connectedness.

One aspect that I found quite intriguing is the fact that—unlike in many cases in our modern world—even enemies acknowledge each other's rights to exist as nations (active nationalism) or just as *ethne* (passive nationalism).[32] There were arguments about borders and territories and their aggrandizement that brought to many conflicts, but at the end of the day a certain respect for the other in inter-state relations existed. Let us examine the following story that is just one of many examples of this kind of behavior.

Livy tells the following episode:

While Philip was thus engaged, Titus Quinctius, after recovering Zacynthos from the Achaean council, crossed to Naupactus, which for two months now—and it was near destruction by this time—had been undergoing the siege, and if it were captured by force the whole name of the Aetolians there seemed destined to come to annihilation.[33] But though he was justly angry at the Aetolians because he remembered that they alone had cavilled at his glory when he was liberating Greece, and that they had not been moved by his influence when he warned them in advance, that that would happen which did actually occur, and tried to deter them from their mad purpose, yet, believing it to be his task to see that no people of the Greece which had received its freedom from him should be utterly destroyed, he began to walk around the walls, so that he was easily seen by the Aetolians. (36.34.1-4)

---

[31] This is reminiscent of a story of Eleazar who committed suicide in 2 Maccabees (Part II, Chapter 2, p. 149); the poor Hassidim in 1 Maccabees 7 naively thought that Bacchides as a Hellenistic general would keep a promise but they paid with their life for this belief.

[32] See my analysis in Mendels (2020: 564-70).

[33] The fear of physical annihilation as well as annihilation of one's name was a familiar motif in the Hellenistic world and is a leitmotif in 1 Maccabees. In contradistinction, the enhancement of a nation's name, namely, of its great achievements and valor, was also popular (for the Hellenistic side, see Eckstein 2006).

These considerations of Titus should be clarified. The Romans at that time were reluctant to annihilate their enemies in the West, even if the latter were fierce and caused a great deal of damage to them (Carthage only ten years earlier). This policy is usually explained, as far as I know, by political and economic interests of the Roman Republic and we hear some of it earlier in our survey (see above). Yet, the mention of annihilation of one's foe (or rather of his name) enhances the option of its opposite, compassion and mercy. And indeed, in the continuation of the episode, Livy elaborates on this aspect by saying that Titus Quinctius was immediately recognized by the soldiers and rumor spread that Quinctius was there. "Thus, there was a general rush from all quarters to the walls each stretching out his hands to him and with uniform cries calling upon Quinctius by name to come to their rescue and save them" (36.34.5). Titus Quinctius, who was then not the consul in power, was still endowed with unofficial yet significant authority in the eyes of the Greeks. He convinced the consul that the siege on the Aetolians was unnecessary now that Antiochus III had left Greece. Among other arguments, he says something that should interest scholars who are interested in the idea of ancient nationalism in antiquity:[34]

> Do you not see that you, after defeating Antiochus, are wasting time by besieging two cities, although now the year of your command is almost ended, but that Philip, who had not set eyes on the battle-line or the standards of the enemy, has already joined to himself, not cities alone, but so many nations—Athamania, Perrhaebia, Aperantia, Dolopia—and that as rewards for your victory you possess as yet not even two cities, while Philip has so many peoples (*gentes*) of Greece? Yet it is not so much to our interest that the power and strength of the Aetolians should be diminished as that Philip not grow beyond measure. (36.34.8-10)

This is a straightforward political consideration adduced to spare the Aetolian nation. Moreover, nationalism or ethnicity was a major trait of Greek states, since in spite of the fact that they shared the same language and cultural heritage, they kept for centuries their individual identities and even fought for it and other minutiae in many wars. Hence on the one hand we speak of connectedness in the Greek world which enabled to create an operative inter-state ethical code. On the other hand, an active sense of particularism can be discerned (namely, the division into states such as the Aetolians, Athenians, Acarnanians, etc.), both of which managed to coexist during 200–168 BCE. We should also bear in mind that nationalism (or ethnicity for that matter) was a shared inter-state value that surfaced time and again in speeches and dialogues held in the Hellenistic Greek sphere.

In the narrative that follows we discover Titus Quinctius as more of a promoter of inter-state moral values than just a shrewd Roman general. We hear that the consul agreed with the arguments of Titus Quinctius, "but shame (*sed pudor*), if he should withdraw before finishing what he had begun, came over him (implicit mention of the value of perseverance)" (36.35.1). The decision is then referred to Quinctius who went

---

[34] For ancient nationalism, cf. Mendels (1992).

back to the section of the walls where he had met the Aetolians somewhat earlier. With greater ardor they "begged him to have compassion on the Aetolian people, he ordered some of them to come out to him. Phaeneas himself and other chiefs at once came out. As they threw themselves at his feet, he said:

> Your plight makes me restrain both my wrath and my language. Those things have happened which I told you in the beginning would happen, and not even this is left to you, that they may seem to have happened to the undeserving; yet I, appointed by some destiny for the cherishing of Greece, shall not cease to do good even to ungrateful men. (36.35.2-4)

Then he suggests that they ask the consul for a truce in order for a delegation to be sent to the Roman senate where they could plead their case. Titus also suggests that he would be there with the consul to "support and defend" their cause. This is what they did and the consul did not reject their appeal. Here some inter-state values are mentioned such as compassion and pardon, civilized dialogue, respect, and fairness towards one's enemy, all being familiar tokens of connectedness within the framework of an ethical code shared by the participating states, enemies who share the basic principles of behavior—in itself a cultural asset—included. Here as elsewhere in Livy's story the interplay between inter-state values with shrewd interests of utility is emphasized.

Other tokens of connectedness in inter-state relations that express respect and honor in interactions between states were etiquette and ritual, which were already mentioned in our survey as channels for expressing mutuality in foreign affairs. The following examples will be tackled here. When the consul and Titus Quinctius arrived at the Achaean league there was a debate about "the Eleans and the restoration of the Spartan exiles; neither question was settled, because the Achaeans wished the case of the exiles left as a means of gaining favor for themselves; while the Eleans preferred that they be united with the Achaean league on their own initiative rather than under pressure from the Romans" (36.35.7). This remark is instructive: states had their own will regardless of the pressures put on them from a super power. Then "ambassadors from the Epirotes came to the consul; it was clear that they had not observed the treaty of alliance with true fidelity" (36.35.8), which means that there were variants of intensiveness to the adherence of certain values and their materialization on the ground. And now comes the explanation for true and untrue fidelity:

> Yet they had sent no troops to Antiochus; they were accused of having aided him with money; they did not even themselves deny that they had sent ambassadors to him.[35] When they asked that they be permitted to remain in their old status of friendship, the consul replied that he did not yet know whether to reckon them among enemies or among defeated foes; the senate would be the judge of that.

---

[35] See 36.5.3-8, above.

In Rome, later, the senate gave them a reply "from which they could seem to have obtained forgiveness, not to have established their case" (36.35.3-11). Yet King Philip their former foe and now their ally also sent ambassadors to Rome; this visit gives us an additional glimpse into the phenomenon of etiquette, which could be minimalistic in nature but here its maximalist manifestation comes to the fore and signifies a formal expression of connectedness between nations. Livy relates the following (36.35.12-13): "Ambassadors from King Philip also were at this time presented to the senate with congratulations on the victory [of Thermopylae]. Their request that they be allowed to sacrifice on the Capitoline and to deposit a gift of gold in the temple of Jupiter Optimus Maximus was granted by the senate." This was a mark of special honor, since foreigners had no share in Roman ritual,[36] and, I would add, a token of connectedness between the two states. "A golden crown of one hundred pounds weight was placed there. Not only was a gracious response given to the ambassadors of the king, but also Demetrius, the son of Philip, who was hostage at Rome was handed over to the ambassadors to be restored to his father." Although the war with Antiochus III came to an end in the camp of Antiochus III there were fears, expressed by Hannibal, that the war would continue in Asia since the Romans seek "dominion over the world" (36.41). Only thirty years later a similar view was attributed to Judah Maccabee when reality proved that Hannibal was right.

The Aetolians who were also sent to Rome were less lucky than Philip's ambassadors, and they received a much less friendly treatment. In a passage that enhances several values it is said:

The Aetolians, like men who reposed more hope in the mercy of the senate than in their own case, pleaded like suppliants, balancing former services against recent misdeeds. But not only while still present were they pursued by senatorial questionings from all sides, forcing from them confessions of guilt rather than replies, but when they were ordered to leave the senate-house they gave occasion to a violent conflict. Anger had greater weight in their case than the spirit of mercy, since the senators were incensed at them not as enemies but as an untamable and anti-social people. When the contest had continued for many days, it was finally decided that peace should be neither granted nor refused; two choices were placed before them; either they should entrust themselves to the free discretion of the senate, or they should pay one thousand talents and consider the same peoples as friends and enemies. When they tried to elicit a definite statement as to the extent to which the senate would exercise its discretion over them, no positive answer was given. So without any settlement they were ordered to leave the City that same day and Italy within fifteen days. (37.1.2-6)

The role of the senate as a regulator of international affairs and its procedural comes here to the fore. Moreover, in this passage inter-state modes of conduct and emotions are juxtaposed with their opposites. Former services (good deeds) are set against

---

[36] Loeb, Livy vol. X, p. 258, note 2.

bad actions, enforcement of confession of guilt is opposed to (free) reply, anger is set against spirit of mercy, enemies are juxtaposed with untamable and antisocial people (namely, in contradistinction with enemies they cannot be considered as part of the ethical network of states) and to be under free discretion of a super power as against paying indemnity and siding with the super power unconditionally. The mention of finding the "balance" between bad and good deeds implies a mechanism imbued in the value system for judgment and discretion when values adhered to outweigh bad conduct of a state or vice versa.[37] Last and not least, the Aetolians at the end of this episode are portrayed in negative hues by Livy but from our point of view they may seem quite positive.[38] The Aetolians did not want to lose the little liberty they could still entertain and wanted to be free from Roman dominance. In a way, they emerge as a symbol of nationalistic fighters of the Greek world.[39] Be that as it may, their hopes in mercy were shattered. This observation leads me to the next theme.

Roman Imperialism and the Inter-state Value System

The conclusion of the Roman-Syrian War on Asian soil is narrated by Livy in which several topics that have a bearing on our survey in Part II are narrated.[40] One of those themes mentioned by speakers is the Roman strive for world dominion and its implications on inter-state relations. The topic has already been alluded to in the above survey[41] but not elaborated upon. Here it becomes central. It seems that once the Romans invaded Asia, the inter-state value system gets a significant turn. No more endless dialogues between the warring parties and their allies during war, but more of a dictate against the main enemy, Antiochus III. It is emphasized that Rome has actually a role to play in the world of settling inter-state affairs and as the consul himself says, to the benefit of those who are her allies (in Part II we will meet a similar idea in the speech of Judah Maccabee, in 1 Maccabees 8). According to this view she gradually became the keeper of law and order in Greece. This view was already promoted with some variants by Polybius who himself experienced Roman expansion, and this led him to write his Histories. The view of Rome's role in the world had naturally a significant effect on perceptions of an inter-state value system. The Roman senate through its mediators, the Roman generals fighting in the Hellenistic east and the embassies, in addition to its role as regulator and mediator gradually became a sort of high court for inter-state conflicts by listening to, talking with, and deciding for the opposing parties. Since no formal international code of laws existed, the inter-state ethical system, shared by Rome and the Greeks, remained its virtual code of reference.

---

[37] Cf. the slander of the Hasmoneans against the Hellenizers, and the Qumran people against the Hasmoneans, and so on, taking a value system for granted but differing in its interpretation.

[38] See in general Mendels (1998: 127–38); Scholten (2000).

[39] If this is not a nationalistic stance, what is it then? Ethnicity and nationalism in extreme cases were imbued in the awareness of people at that time and they cared quite a bit (Mendels 1992, and see also in general Almagor and Skinner 2013).

[40] Book 37. See for a detailed commentary on Book 37 Briscoe (1981: 289–395).

[41] Hannibal's speech in Book 36, above.

By using an ethical terminology Rome made her way towards domination. But before discussing this process, let me just mention briefly several topics that relate to our theme, which cannot be discussed here because of the brevity required (but will be mentioned in Part II when needed). They are: various group emotions that energize political activity (panic, excitement, fear, hope, and terror and grief turned into anger, etc.), emphasis on values (kindness and generosity of states, the presentation of values by leaders, treachery and disloyalty as against fidelity and characteristics (divide of societies resulting from class struggle and foreign intervention [37.8]). Other topics should also be mentioned: etiquette in state relationships as an expression of certain values such as respect when one leader escorts his guest (37.7), dialogue during wars, innocence (37.17), lament of the hard plight of a city dominated by a royal garrison (37.17.7), peace granted only with authority of the powerful force in the region (37.19), contempt and carelessness (37.20), the familiar habit of plundering temples when opportunity arose (37.21).

A bold mention of Rome's role in the region comes from an envoy of Antiochus III who was eager to find allies in the region as a result of the Roman invasion into Asia Minor. It is told that Antiochus (37.25.4-7) "had sent ambassadors and letters to Prusias, king of Bithynia, in which he complained of the crossing of the Romans into Asia: they were coming to destroy all kingdoms, so that in the whole world there might be no empire save that of Rome"—reminiscent of modern ideology of certain super powers at present, as Henry Kissinger has shown so convincingly:[42]

> Philip, Nabis, had been defeated; he himself was the third to be attacked [the truth as we have seen was that he was the first to attack]; as each came next after the last destroyed, the fire, catching, so to speak, one after another in succession, would be everywhere; from himself their next step would be into Bithynia, since Eumenes had already given himself into voluntary slavery.

(Thirty years later Judah Maccabee would have a much more positive view on Roman imperialism based on the same data.) The Roman side, which diverted Prusias from such suspicions, was adduced by a letter of Scipio the consul,

> and more by the words of his brother Africanus, who, by citing the enduring tradition among the Roman people of increasing with every sign of honor the dignity of allied kings, and also, by giving examples from his personal experience, induced Prusias to merit his friendship; tribal chieftains, taken under his protection in Spain, he had left kings; Masinissa he had not only established on his ancestral throne but had placed on that of Syphax, by whom he had been driven out before; and he was both by far the richest of the kings of Africa and equal, whether in majesty or in power, to any king whatsoever in the whole world; Philip and Nabis, enemies, defeated, too, in war by Titus Quinctius, had yet been left in their kingdoms; Philip the year before, in fact, had had his tribute cancelled and

---

[42] Kissinger (2014).

his hostage-son restored, and had recovered certain cities outside of Macedonia with the consent of the Roman generals. Nabis too would have been in the same position of honor had not his own madness and then the treachery of the Aetolians destroyed him. (37.25.8-12)

Prusias was persuaded "how much surer were the Roman prospects of victory than those of Antiochus and how friendship with the Romans would be more respected and dependable" (Polybius 21.11). In other words, geographic closeness to an imperial strong army was conducive to the nature of a decision taken by an ally who speaks here of respect and dependability (meaning also durability). Here in a formal statement the Romans considered themselves as the keepers of order in the world by their view of justice and equality in inter-state relations. This excuse for keeping the world order as a mission endowed on a super power became a precedent for so many empires henceforward (Great Britain, the United States). However, this notion was rejected by the envoy of Antiochus.

In addition to terms for ending the war, the envoy of Antiochus III uttered the following remarks concerning Roman intervention in Asia:[43]

> The rest of his speech [after stating the terms for peace] was that mindful of human destiny, they should deal temperately with their own fortune and not hardly with that of others. Let them limit their empire to Europe, that even this was very large; that it was possible to conquer and gain it part by part more easily than to hold the whole; but if they wished to take some part of Asia too, provided they limited it by easily recognizable natural features, the king [Antiochus] would permit his own self-restraint to be overcome by Roman greed for the sake of peace and harmony.

Here the former stance of zones of influence is a bit altered by a Hellenistic king who promotes self-restraint for the sake of peace and harmony. The terms were rejected by the Romans arguing inter alia that "the king's garrisons should be withdrawn not only from Ionia and Aeolis, but just as all Greece had been liberated, so all the cities which were in Asia should be set free; this could not be accomplished otherwise than by the retirement of Antiochus from the occupation of Asia on this side of the Taurus mountains." This was in turn rejected by the envoy of the king. For our purpose I should emphasize here that a requirement to withdraw one's garrison can be equated to a demand from an empire to surrender unconditionally and lose its grip on a city or state it is holding. (Against this background I will later deal with the constant demands of the Jewish nation that the Seleucids should evacuate the citadel [Chakra] in Jerusalem that had become a symbol of Jewish servitude.) Then the Seleucid ambassador tried to convince Publius Scipio the consul, who replied to the former's overtures: "that you do not know the Romans as a race, that you do not know me, to whom you have been sent, I am less surprised to find since I see that you

---

[43] Given as a summary by Livy 37.35.5-10.

do not know the situation of the man from whom you come, [and here details about the reasons of the Roman invasion]." (37.36.3).

After the decisive battle of Magnesia and the final defeat of Antiochus III "ambassadors came ... from Tralles and from Magnesia on the Meander river and from Ephesus to surrender their cities." Other cities and states of Asia were likewise convinced by Rome's strength and her acquired role in the world so that they 'entrusted themselves to the good faith of the consul and the dominion of the Roman people" (37.45.1-3). Then, ambassadors from King Antiochus III arrived and were astonished to find King Eumenes being positive for peace:

> finding him more favorably disposed towards peace than either they or the king [Antiochus] had expected ... at their request they were received by a full council at which to announce their errand, and Zeuxis [one of the ambassadors sent by Antiochus] spoke thus: "We do not ourselves have anything to say so much as we ask of you, Romans, by what atonement we can expiate the error of the king and obtain peace and pardon from the conquerors. In your extreme generosity you have always pardoned defeated kings and peoples; with how much greater magnanimity and with inclinations how much more peaceful should you act in this victory which has made you masters of the world? Laying aside now quarrels with all mortals, you, like the gods, should consider and spare the human race." (37.45.6-9)

Livy comments that

> even before the ambassadors arrived, it had been decided what to reply. It was agreed that Africanus should answer. He is reported to have spoken to this effect: "Out of such things as were under control of the immortal gods, we Romans have those things which the gods have given us; but our souls, which are subjected to the will of our minds, we have kept and still keep unchanged in every kind of fortune, and neither has prosperity puffed them up nor has adversity depressed them. As proof of this to omit all else, I should cite to you your Hannibal as witness if I could not cite yourselves. After we crossed the Hellespont, before we set eyes on the king's camp or beheld his battle-line, when Mars was approachable to both sides and the outcome of the war undetermined, when you raised the question of terms of peace, we offered conditions, as equals to equals, and these same conditions we now propose as victors to vanquished: keep your hands off Europe; withdraw from all Asia on this side of the Taurus mountains. Then, for the expenses incurred in the war, you will pay fifteen thousand Euboean talents, five hundred now, twenty five hundred when the senate and the Roman people shall have ratified this treaty, then one thousand talents annually for twelve years ... when we have made this agreement, in order that we may hold it as certain that you will carry it out, there will be some guarantee if you give us twenty hostages of our selection ... it will be in a worse plight that the king will make peace because he makes it later than he could have done. If he delays now, let him know that the majesty of kings falls with

greater difficulty from the topmost point to the middle than it is hurled from the middle to the lowest point." (37.45.10-18)

The message throughout this passage is that when a decision has to be made by a state whether to accept terms of peace or go to war (and probably in other choices as well), wisdom, namely, the knowledge to read situations correctly, should be a lead to achieve the right decisions.

To conclude: During the Second Macedonian War and the Roman-Syrian War, most states that were involved in the conflicts were fighting for their release from the grip of a super power symbolized by foreign garrisons; many fought for restoring their old ways of life (their ancestral constitutions and laws); others were striving to get back their territories that they believed had belonged to them in the past and/or that they had inherited from their ancestors. Some states, and they were the majority, just wanted to be free so that they would be exempted from taxes and other duties. Certain states that suffered from chronic divide were sliding into revolution, in several cases one side to the conflict had been triggered and supported by one of the empires. I have also shown that the nature of the unit within the community of states, namely, the regime and its sociopolitical and economic condition (democracy, oligarchy, plutocracy), played a significant role in the stance of states toward the inter-state ethical system. The occasional abuse of this very ethical inter-state value system became more apparent during the following war, the Third Macedonian War (171–168 BCE).

4

The Use and Abuse of an Inter-state Ethical System—Rome's Slide into Dominance

The Inter-state Ethical Code in Trial before War

Perseus, Philip's son and king of Macedonia, almost twenty years after the Roman-Syrian War in which Macedonia fought with Rome against the Seleucids was over, started to prepare for yet another war, this time against Rome. I will not delve here into the issue of the preparations and overtures done before its outbreak[1] but remain in the subject of political ethics of states before war.

On the eve of the Third Macedonian War which lasted from 172/1 BCE to 168 BCE, the Romans had established their influence in Greece and the Greek western parts of Asia Minor. Liberty was still used as a popular slogan by her, but not necessarily seen as real freedom by many of her allies. I will discuss in the following how the notion of liberty was differently interpreted by the various segments of Greek societies. Two points have to be made within this context: One, the inter-state value system is enhanced in dialogues and etiquette before the outbreak of the war, and second, her settlement after the two preceding wars brought relative stability of inter-state relations in Greece and Asia Minor, but, as already mentioned, not necessarily to the satisfaction of everyone. Why then on the strict ethical level did her settlement break down in the seventies of the second century BCE?

The first signal for that was the rejection of etiquette which as we have already seen was frequently a bad omen for the continuity of good relations between states. Thus, when the Romans sent in 173 BCE ambassadors to Aetolia and Macedonia "an opportunity to interview King Perseus, since some pretended that he was away, some that he was ill (but both falsely), had not been given them. Nevertheless, they said, it had become easily apparent to them that preparations for war were being made and that Perseus would not further put off his resort to arms" (42.2.1-2) and here comes a list of prodigies that were clear signs for the Romans that war was pending. Their belief in gods who symbolize/represent values and virtues will be discussed later. Anyhow, rejection of an inter-state act of etiquette was considered a reason for

---

[1] See Mendels (1998: 158–78); de Ste. Croix (1981: 659–60); and Gruen (1984).

future tension and even conflict. In the continuation of the narrative, we read about Perseus's strategic decision to support the have-nots in Greece, quite familiar to us from the behavior of Antiochus III twenty years earlier. Livy criticizes the classes who supported Perseus instead of giving their support to another Hellenistic king, King Eumenes of Pergamum. This is interesting from our point of view. A wayward conduct in inner affairs of a state and the crushing of its basic values, such as justice and honesty, were factors to be taken into account when inter-state relationships were at stake. Let us go into some detail.

Already in the year 173 BCE ambassadors from Aetolia reported at Rome about the internal strife in their league whereas Thessalian envoys brought news of occurrences in Macedonia. Perseus, king of Macedonia, "was striving to win over to himself not only all the states of Greece but also the cities." He sent embassies and "making promises rather than carrying them out" (42.5.1-2). He probably was aware that the sympathies of a large proportion of the people were inclined to favor him rather than Eumenes. This, in spite of the acts of kindness and generosity of Eumenes which were granted to all of the cities of Greece and many important personages who as a result were under obligation to him. Moreover, "he so conducted himself in his kingdom that the cities which were under his control did not desire to exchange their condition for that of any free state" (42.5.3). This clarifies once more that liberty in the Hellenistic period was a fluid concept and had many variants. Here Livy adduces a distinction that is quite helpful. It was sometimes better to be under a benevolent king than being liberated by another, namely, enjoying something that is a far cry from complete freedom. One may speculate that since under Antiochus III the Jews were enjoying freedom under a benevolent king, they had no problem with the change of masters in the region (the Seleucids conquered Palestine from the Ptolemies in 200 BCE). In contradistinction, under Antiochus IV they wished at first to return to the status they received from Antiochus III. Moreover, we encounter here again that Hellenistic kings were not just intervening in the affairs of cities and states in their realm but were sometimes also expected to do so. (As we will see in Part II, the intervention of the Seleucids in Judea which was initiated by one section of the population can be explained against the background of this pattern of conduct in the Hellenistic world.) Reciprocity and loyalty (here breached) are yet again enhanced in this passage. Livy presents us with strong ideas about the effect of inner ethics withing the individual state on inner-state conduct and sets the standard by saying that

> there was the rumor that after his father's death Perseus had killed his wife with his own hand; that Apelles, once the agent of treachery in the murder of his brother, who for that reason had been sought out for punishment by Philip, he had recalled from exile, after the death of his father, with lavish offers of rewards for performing so splendid a deed, and then had secretly put to death.

The historian adds that a man

> made infamous by many other murders of citizens and aliens, and worthy of praise for no good quality whatever, was generally preferred by the states to a king so

devoted to his relatives, so just to his citizens, so generous to all men, whether because these states were predisposed, on account of the reputation and dignity of the Macedonian kings, to despise the origin of a kingdom recently formed, or because they were eager for a change in their condition, or because they did not wish all things to become completely subject to the Romans.[2]

A value system of the individual state, as we shall see in the following, had definite repercussions on its relationships with other states. In other words, what could one expect from a king who acts treacherously in his own state but to breach inter-state values and lead his country and all others into a fierce war?

In 173 BCE the Romans intervened as mediators in the class struggle in Aetolia, Perrhaebia, and Thessaly, and from there went to the Peloponnesus and called a meeting of the Achaeans. There, Marcellus "heartily praised" the people because they had steadfastly adhered to their old resolution "not to permit the kings of the Macedonians to enter their territory, he made conspicuous the hatred which the Romans felt for Perseus; that this hatred should break out betimes was the consequence of the arrival in Rome of King Eumenes" (42.6.2-3).

Eumenes, king of Pergamum, "was received [in Rome] with such honors as they believed not only due to the deserts but also commensurate with their own favors which had been heaped upon him in abundance." The king was introduced into the senate and there he said among other things, such as "his desire to see the gods and men by whose kindness he enjoyed a fortune beyond which he did not venture even to wish for anything," that he wished to give "public warning" to the senate that they should prepare against the designs of Perseus (42.11.2-3). This introduction given in the abridged words of Livy reveals more than meets the eye. First and foremost, it shows once more that a procedure to open a war was orderly, had some inner logic in it, and was not performed by sudden surprise attacks. Second, it reveals the utilitarian aspect in inter-state relationship in which reciprocity is a given. Third, the emphasis on seeing the gods (and men) is important since, although the specific gods are not mentioned here, many Greek and their equivalent Roman gods symbolized values such as mercy, justice and bravery, values that were actually "worshipped." We will discuss this aspect later since when some of the gods are mentioned by name, we already get a list of values (in fact some kind of an ethical code) which were universal and shared by the Romans and the Greeks (sometimes also by eastern Greeks and Hellenists).

Livy goes on with his description of Eumenes's appearance in the Roman senate in which he charges Macedonia and in particular her present king with the disruption of order in Greece and beyond, order that was established by Rome in 196 and 190 BCE, namely, a disruption of the international status quo. The reactions against it by certain states can be viewed as a result of an agreed upon ethical inter-state code. An ethical system was seen by many as a gatekeeper of order, stability, reciprocity, and mutual respect between states. Eumenes masterfully analyses the rise to power of a Hellenistic king

---

[2] Livy 42.5.4-6. For a commentary on Livy Book 42, Briscoe (2012: 151–385).

beginning with the plans of Philip [the father of Perseus and former king of Macedonia], he spoke of the death of Philip's son Demetrius … who had left his kingdom to the one who (he had seen) was most dangerous to the Romans. And so, Eumenes said, Perseus had long been preparing a war which had been left him as a legacy by his father and handed on to him along with the throne, and had been feeding and nursing it—it was now very close—by all possible schemes. Perseus, besides, was strong in the number of his young men, a generation which the long peace had brought forth, was strong in the resources of his kingdom, was strong too in his own youth. While he possessed strength and vigor of body, his mind too had been long trained in the theory and practice of war. Even from boyhood, in his fathers' tent, he had been made accustomed to wars with Rome, not merely to campaigns against their neighbors, and had been sent by his father on many and various expeditions. From the moment he had received the throne, Eumenes went on to say, he had gained, in a marvelous series of triumphs, many things which Philip had been unable to accomplish either by force or by craft, although he had left nothing untried. There had been added to his strength an influence which was usually acquired through a long period of time and by numerous and important services. (42.11.4-9)

Eumenes, by exhibiting strength of a state, emphasizes the aspects of gaining influence. Yet, influence is not gained just by having strength but by reciprocity, namely, impressing other states not only by one's strength but also by benefits and services that the super power grants to the influenced.

In the continuation of the speech Eumenes said that

all men in the cities of Greece and Asia revered his [Perseus] dignity. In consideration of what services or what generosity such respect was being paid him, Eumenes could not see, or say for certain whether this was happening by reason of a certain good luck or whether—and Eumenes feared to suggest this—the ill—will felt for the Romans won men over to his cause. Even among the kings he was great in influence and had married the daughter of [King] Seleucus, not having sought her but rather having been sought; he had given his sister to Prusias, who had begged and entreated for her; both marriages had been greeted with congratulations and gifts from countless embassies, and the nuptial processions were accompanied, as it were, by the noblest peoples as sponsors and attendants … but now a treaty with Perseus was engraved in three places, one at Thebes, the second at Delium in a most revered and celebrated temple, the third at Delphi [see end of 1 Maccabees 14 where the temple is mentioned but seen from the outside as a regular temple not necessarily the Temple in Jerusalem and a covenant put there]. In the Achaean council, moreover, if the action had not been prevented by a few men who threatened them with the Roman might, matters were almost brought to such a pass that access into Achaea was granted him. But by Hercules, the honors of Eumenes himself, of whose services to that people it could hardly be determined whether the public or the private were the greater, had partly been abandoned from disuse and neglect, partly abolished in hostility. Again, who, he asked, did not know that the Aetolians in their internal strife had sought aid, not from the Romans, but from Perseus? (42.12.1-7)

The rest of his speech was an exhortation (13) in which he, this time adduced in direct speech, blames Perseus for several misdeeds in Greece and elsewhere breaching the status quo with Rome, deeds that were interpreted by Eumenes and later the senators themselves that Perseus had warlike intentions.[3] Some of his misdeeds were a breach of international agreed upon values, for instance, political murders of those who disagreed with his policies, causing unrest in states for political advantages of Macedonia, disloyalty to some of the allies, and disregard of stately etiquette as exemplified earlier and later in the text. The attempt of the king of Macedonia to murder the king of Pergamum gets a special long treatment by Livy in the following. The emphasis of Eumenes at the beginning of his speech that the charges he adduces against Perseus are not founded on uncertain rumors and

> too eagerly accepted because I wish these charges against an enemy to be true, but as ascertained and discovered with as much accuracy as if I had been sent by you as a scout to investigate and were reporting what lay before my eyes; nor should I have left my kingdom, which you have made extensive and noble and crossed so great a sea, in order to diminish your confidence in me by bringing you an idle tale; I saw the most famed states of Asia and Greece daily laying bare their judgements more clearly, with the intention, if it were permitted, of proceeding as far presently that they would have no chance to draw back and repent. (42.13.1-3)

This statement of Eumenes takes into consideration some sort of agreed upon conduct that is expected from politicians and ambassadors of states, namely, to tell the truth. That this did not always happen does not mean that the truth as an asset in inter-state relations was not regarded as a crucial value and expected from states in international relations. In the following Eumenes explains how Perseus breached several rules of behavior. Whether all or part of his claims were based on reality does not matter for our survey here. In a moment I will explain why. Here they are in the words of a great Hellenistic head of state:

> I saw Perseus not limiting himself to the kingdom of Macedonia (trespass of political borders), seizing some places by arms, and by influence and kindness winning over others which could not be subdued by force; I saw how unjust was the fortune that caused you, while he was preparing war on you, to grant him the security of peace, although to me indeed he seemed to be, not preparing war, but almost waging it. Abrupolis, your ally and friend, he expelled from his kingdom; Arthetaurus, the Illyrian, also your ally and friend, because he had learned of some written communications from him to you he put to death; Eversa and Callicritus the Thebans, leading men of their state, because they had spoken too freely

---

[3] See Mendels (1998: 158–99).

against him in the Boeotian council and had declared that they would report to you what was going on, he caused to be done away with; he sent assistance to the Byzantines contrary to the treaty, he made war on Dolopia; he traversed Thessaly and Doris with his army, in order that he might in their civil war aid the worse cause and crush the better; he threw into confusion and turmoil everything in Thessaly and Perrhaebia by the prospect of abolition of debts, in order that with the band of debtors bound to him he might overthrow the nobility ... How safe or how honorable this is for you [since you remained passive and acquiescent] is for yourselves to consider. (42.13.4-11)

The question whether all these accusations had a factual basis is not relevant for our case here. Yet, when a list of charges of misbehavior is made by one head of state against another, the former has surely based the accusations on some kind of ethical system (the compass). In this respect the J'accuse uttered by Eumenes is an indispensable document of inter-state ethical discourse. The notion brought forward here by Livy is that a state that breaches an international order and its ethical code should be warned (most probably referring to talk and dialogue) before war is declared. But not everyone in Greece agreed with this negative portrayal of Perseus the king of Macedonia since certain sectors in Greece, especially the lower classes and some of the leaders, were not happy with the liberty that was granted by Rome in 196 BCE (and renewed later). Livy masterfully describes this situation (42.30), saying that after a mention of the

> feelings of the kings about the war, among the free groups and peoples (*in liberis gentibus populisque*), the commons everywhere were almost all, as usual, for the worse side, being inclined toward the king and the Macedonians; among the leading men one might notice conflicting interests. Some were so enraptured with the Romans as to undermine their own influence by their unrestrained partisanship; a few of them were attracted by the justice of Roman rule, most were moved by the thought that if they displayed some special service for the Romans, they would become powerful in their own states. Another group were toadies to the king; some because of debt and despair of their own fortunes if no change should occur, were driven headlong to the overturning of everything. Some were upset by their own windy instability of character, since the breeze of popular favor turned in Perseus' direction. A third group, which was also the worthiest and wisest, if merely a choice of a dominating superior were offered them, preferred to be under the Romans rather than under the king; but if they had a free choice of destiny in this respect, they wished neither side to become the more powerful through the downfall of the other, but rather that, the strength of both sides being unexhausted, peace on terms of equality should continue; thus the situation of the free states with respect to the two powers would be most advantageous, since one power would always protect the weak against wrongdoing by the other. (42.30.1-6)

This passage speaks for itself and sheds light on the nature of liberty and the position of the inter-state ethical code under Roman protection.

To summarize this passage in our own words we can say that most of the well-to-do in Greece supported the Roman kind of liberty, which of course was in their favor, whereas some of the aristocracy and the masses who had economic difficulties supported the kingdom of Macedonia. Yet the freedom to choose which side to support can only be explained by the fact that two powerful empires, Rome and Macedonia, were still visible on the scene. From the stance of the pro-Roman group one can deduce once more that the freedom that the Romans granted was limited. Only a few were attracted by the justice of Roman rule, namely, to their interpretation of the inter-state ethical code. All other pro-Romans, for different self-interest motivations, were supporting the Romans because they had no free choice to decide. But the group, the "worthiest and the wisest," wished for a balance of power, if free choice would have been given to them. They urged for a balance in which the two empires with equal power would coexist, resulting in (complete) freedom of the states that would live under the umbrella of two equal powers in the region. When one power would try to subject one of the weaker states, the other would automatically come to its aid. This wishful thinking was actually a partial reflection of the reality in Greece on the eve of the Third Macedonian War. A rejection of anarchy was central to the latter group who wished to be completely free.

As we already observed in the discussions in assemblies in Greek states the level of sophistication was quite remarkable.[4] The option of having the ability to make choices on the level of inter-state relationships was conducive to the perseverance of a value system in vogue. But it also caused splits between groups within the states because there were groups that felt more liberated than others under the influence of one empire or another. There are two reasons why I lingered on this passage. First, the segmentation of views in Greece as portrayed by Livy reflects a situation that occurred only four years before the outbreak of the Maccabean War in 168 BCE and has a bearing on our discussion. Second, the patterns of behavior toward the ruling empire related to the socioeconomic and political stance of the population is relevant to what happened in Palestine at that time. We will discuss this issue in Part II.

Etiquette and Diplomacy of Emotion

During the preparation for the Third Macedonian War an intensive diplomacy occurred between states, which entailed many acts of etiquette. References to a code of inter-state ethics occur time and again, yet seems to be more overtly abused by the ruling powers. Let us discuss the details.

The Roman envoys that were sent to Macedonia "to demand reparations and denounce the treaty of friendship with King Perseus" (172 BCE) came back to Rome. They "inflamed the hostility which the senate had felt of its own accord toward Perseus by telling, one after another, the things which they had seen and heard." They report about the preparations for war going forward "with the utmost vigor" through all

---

[4] 42.13.7: *Quia liberius adversus eum in concilio Boeotorum*, quoted above.

Macedonian cities. When they had arrived at the king's court, a meeting with the king was postponed for a long time and only when out of despair of "a conference" they departed, they were recalled from their journey and brought before the king (42.25.2-3). "The gist of their speech," says Livy,

> had been as follows: a treaty had been made with Philip, and renewed with Perseus himself after his father's death, in which he was explicitly forbidden to lead his army beyond his own territory, and also forbidden to assail in war the allies of the Roman people. Next the envoys had explained in detail the whole series of ascertained facts [as against fake facts] which the Fathers had recently heard Eumenes recount in the senate. Moreover, the king had held at Samothrace for many days a secret conference with embassies from the states of Asia. For these violations, the envoys informed the king, the senate thought it right that reparation be made, and that possessions which the king held contrary to the regulations of the treaty be returned to the Romans and their allies. The king had at first replied to these statements ungraciously, being inflamed with anger, had charged the Romans with greed and arrogance, and had yelled that embassies kept coming one after another to spy upon his words and actions, because they thought it right that he should do and say everything at their beck and call; finally, after shouting a long wordy harangue, he had ordered them to return the next day, since he wished to give them a reply in writing. Then the following written statement had been given them; the treaty made with Perseus' father was in no way binding on him; he had endured its renewal, not because he approved of it, but because immediately on assuming the kingship he had had to endure anything. If the Romans wished to make a new treaty with him, some agreement as to terms should first be reached; if they could bring themselves to make a treaty on terms of equality, he for his part would see what he should do and they for theirs, he supposed, would take care of the interests of their state. After delivering this message, Perseus had begun to hurry out, and the dismissal of everyone from the palace had begun. Thereupon the envoys had denounced the friendship and alliance. Angered at this utterance, Perseus had stopped and in a loud voice had enjoined upon them to leave the borders of his realm within three days. Accordingly, they had set out; no sign of hospitality or courtesy had been shown them during their stay or as they departed. (42.25.4-13)[5]

This episode demonstrates that first and foremost a treaty with Rome has to be renewed when succession occurs in a kingdom, actually reassuring the mutual loyalty, and this is the reason why the Hasmonean family renewed their treaty with Rome later in the century (Part II).[6] Second, we get here a lesson about etiquette and the value system. I have already mentioned above that etiquette contained universal rituals that accommodated and assured the relationships of states with each other. This included

---

[5] *Nec sibi aut manentibus aut abeuntibus quidquam hospitaliter aut benigne factum.*
[6] The conditions of Perseus to a renewal are reminiscent of the new claims of the Iranians at the moment Biden came to power.

gifts, receptions, sacrifice in temples, hospitality of various kinds, all of which were expressions of a handful of inter-state values, such as gratitude, reciprocity, respect (to a state's past and status at present), and dignity yet enhanced negative values in cases where one state was in conflict with another. In this passage we have also encountered a symbiosis between etiquette and the exhibition of emotion (hate and anger) and that etiquette can be upgraded or downgraded depending on the circumstances. For instance, an ally could be invited to participate in sacrifice to gods in temples where foreigners are not allowed in, which was a great honor bestowed on the ally. On the other hand, an ally could be denied festive welcome-rituals because of some tension that had arisen between the receiver and his ally.[7] Be that as it may, Perseus's reaction to the humiliation of the Roman delegation (when they ask for reparations and the finalization of their friendship) was answered by rudeness and disrespect (no courtesy or hospitality as well as banishment of the Roman delegation from Macedonia). The account of Livy concerning the breach of elementary rules of etiquette during the visit of Rome's delegation in Macedonia takes into consideration yet again the existence of a fixed inter-state protocol as well as an oral code of behavior among states. Livy later continues with the Roman-Macedonian relationship that went sour (42.36).

He tells us about the reaction in Rome to Perseus's insulting reception of her envoys earlier. During the same time envoys from King Perseus arrived. "It was decided not to admit them to the city, since the senate had decreed and the people had ordered war with their king and the Macedonians" (42.36.1). The envoys were then accepted at the temple of Bellona by the senate, and their speech shows yet again that the circumstances that led to the war were not a result of total anarchy.[8] On the contrary, a great deal of verbal and written dialogue preceded the outbreak of the Third Macedonian War. The Macedonian envoys spoke as follows: "King Perseus wondered why armies had been carried across to Macedonia; if he might persuade the senate to recall them, the king would make amends at the discretion of the senate for any wrongs done to their allies, of which they might complain" (42.36.2-3). The Romans did not accept this statement and others uttered by the envoys and sent them back to Macedonia with a warning that no further Macedonian delegations would be permitted into Italy.

That Rome early on created a pro-Roman network of states in the east is well-known, and that she assured the loyalty of states beyond Greece is also mentioned by the sources every now and again. Earlier Livy mentions that from Asia the envoys have returned and informed about their meetings with Eumenes at Aegina, Antiochus in Syria, and Ptolemy at Alexandria. "All had received overtures from the embassies of Perseus but remained nobly loyal and had promised to accomplish everything which the Roman people might command." Also, they found that the allied city-states were loyal except for Rhodes, "which was wavering and steeped in Perseus' plots." Although envoys of Rhodes arrived at Rome to clear that state of charges that "were generally being bandied about," the senate decided not to grant them a hearing until the new

---

[7] Hence the Seleucids who were not allowed into the Temple (or allowed into one of its sections) and were not permitted to sacrifice were naturally offended. This became a big issue in the relationship between Jerusalem and the Seleucids.
[8] As Eckstein wanted us to believe, in Eckstein (2006).

consuls should have entered their office (42.26.7-9). Later Livy returns to these contacts and reports about the stance of the kings in 171 BCE toward the ensuing war:

> In the consulship of Publius Licinius and Gaius Cassius, not only the city of Rome and the land of Italy, but also all kings and states both in Europe and in Asia (*omnes reges civitatesque*), had turned their minds to concern over the war between Macedonia and Rome. Eumenes was urged on by his former enmity and quite as much by his fresh anger, because through the king's crime he had been almost slaughtered like a beast for sacrifice in Delphi. Prusias, the king of Bithynia, had determined to refrain from arms and await the outcome [reasons given here] ... Ariarathes, the king of Cappadocia ... was from the time of his alliance in marriage with Eumenes in harmony with the latter in all plans for peace or war. (42.29.1-4)

It is added that Antiochus IV "was indeed threatening the kingdom of Egypt." He expected to have an excuse for waging war while the Romans were busy with their own war in Greece. Hence "for this war he had zealously promised everything to the senate through his envoys, and personally to the envoys of the senate." The guardians of King Ptolemy of Egypt, who were preparing war against Antiochus, "in order to clear their title to Hollow Syria, were promising the Romans everything for the war with Macedonia" (42.29.5-7). We will return to this later when we approach the year 168 BCE. The terms used here in diplomatic discourse—such as the king "wondered," "might persuade," "making amends at the discretion of," "wrongs done to allies," "complain" about "many wrongs done," "order to make no reply," "order to report," "giving satisfaction" as purpose of the king, "refrain from doing something," "charges against one state from others"—are interesting and assume a code of the right inter-state conduct and behavior that in this case was breached by the Macedonian king and his delegates.

While the Roman army invaded Greece, the dialogue continued with Macedonia, the main enemy, as well as with the allies of Rome. A sensitivity to the use of etiquette as an expression of negotiations to avoid a major war is enhanced here. In the following we hear that Lucius Decimius was sent to Gentius, king of the Illyrians, to convince him to become an ally of the Roman people (contradicting chapter 29.11 above). The Lentuli were sent to Cephallania to make a circuit in the coast of the westward sea in the Peloponnese, and Marcius and Atilius were sent to make the circuit of Epirus, Aetolia, and Thessaly, as well as Boeotia and Euboea, and then to cross to the Peloponnese and meet the Lentuli there. Before they left Corcyra, a letter from Perseus was brought to them. He wondered "what reason the Romans had for either sending troops over to Greece or garrisoning cities" (42.37.5). The answer was given to the messenger "not in writing" that "the Romans were acting for the protection of the cities themselves [this could be said also by the pro-Seleucid party in Judea, namely that the Chakra is a protective institution]." The Lentuli visited the cities of the Peloponnese, "exhorting all cities indiscriminately to aid the Romans against Perseus with the same good will and loyalty with which they had assisted them first in the war against Philip, then in that against Antiochus." Yet unfriendly murmur was aroused in the assemblies, because the Achaeans were angered that they, who had offered every assistance to the Romans from the first beginnings of war against Macedonia, should be placed on a level with the peoples of Messene and Elis who in the war with Philip the Macedonian had been enemies of the Romans and later had borne arms for Antiochus against the Roman people and, having been recently assigned to the Achaean league, were complaining that they were being handed over as spoils of war to the victorious Achaeans. (42.37.6-9)

From this passage it becomes clear yet again that a code of conduct in international affairs was on the agenda. What we learn from this passage is first and foremost that letters (and written speeches, as we have already seen) were sometimes more valid than the spoken word. This should be taken into consideration in Part II when we deal with the letters the Hasmonean brothers receive and their reaction to them. Second, "exhortation" was used once and again to persuade states to join or fight others. Third, "goodwill" and "loyalty" were ingredients of the recipe for political friendships between states. Fourth, "unfriendly murmur" in assemblies was a response to unfair and despising conduct of another state. Ethical standards in relationships between states were taken into consideration in such situations. I will come to that later.

Inter-state Remorse, Mercy, Breach of Contract, and the Ethical Code

The circuit of the Roman delegates on the eve of the Third Macedonian War continues. "Marcius and Atilius went up to Gitana, a town of Epirus, ten miles from the sea, called a conference of Epirotes, and were heard with great and universal approval" (42.38.1). At that time as against our modern times politicians and military leaders still had patience to listen to each other. From Epirus they went to Aetolia where a pro-Roman general was elected, and then to Thessaly.

There Acarnanian envoys and Boeotian exiles came to them. The Acarnanians were ordered to report that an opportunity had presented itself to them of making amends for the acts of hostility done by them against the Roman people, because they had been deceived by the king's promises, first at the war with Philip, then in that with Antiochus. If, when they had ill-deserved it, they had experienced the mercy of the Roman people, let them by deserving well experience the Romans' generosity. (42.38.3-4)[9]

The Boeotians placed the blame for entering into an alliance with Perseus on Ismenias, the leader of the opposite faction, "and said that certain cities had been drawn into the affair against their will" (42.38.5). Marcius replied that the individual cities should have

---

[9] Si male meriti clementiam populi Romani experti essent, bene merendo liberalitatem experirentur.

an opportunity to provide for their own welfare. A council of the Thessalians convened at Larisa.

> Both parties found there a pleasant opportunity to express their thanks, the Thessalians for the Romans' gift to them of freedom, and the Roman envoys for the vigorous help from the Thessalian confederacy, first in the war with Philip and again later in that of Antiochus. By this mutual recital of benefits the minds of the gathering were fired to vote everything which the Romans wished. (42.38.6-7)

This passage yet again enhances talk and dialogue as an important, if not the most important, way of inter-state communication, a prominent value on the list of the ethical code. The values of remorse, mercy, gratitude, forgiveness, admission of guilt, and so on come to the fore in this passage, which also shows that the notion of honoring the vote in assemblies that deal with inter-state relations was quite strongly adhered to in most instances.

Subsequent to this council envoys sent by King Perseus arrived, "relying especially on the personal guest-friendship (*hospitii fiducia*) which existed between his father and the father of Marcius" (42.38.8). This special relationship brought to a conference with the king. Livy tells us in detail about the etiquette before the conference and the speeches that were adduced at the conference itself (42.39). He relates that

> The royal retinue was large, a crowd, both of friends and attendants, thronging about him. With no less a train came the envoys, for many escorted them from Larisa, besides the embassies of certain cities which had assembled at Larisa and wanted to report home facts which they had heard. There was a desire, natural to mankind, to see the meeting of a famous king and the envoys of the people foremost in the whole world. When they stood in sight of each other, with the river between, there was a brief delay for exchange of messages, as to which party should cross over. The one group felt that some consideration was due to the dignity of the king, the other group, to the reputation of the Roman people, especially since Perseus had sought the conference. A jest from Marcius also influenced the undecided: "Let the younger," said he, "cross over to his elders, and"—for his own personal name was Philip—"the son to his father." ... The king thought it proper to cross with his entire suite; the envoys bade him either to come with three attendance, or, if he should bring over so large a train, to give hostages that there would be no treachery during the conference. He gave as hostages Hippias and Pantauchus, his leading friends, whom he had also sent as envoys. However, hostages were not desired so much as a pledge of good faith, as to show the allies that the king was meeting with the envoys on no terms of equality. The greetings were not like those of enemies, but welcoming and kindly, and when seats had been placed, they sat down (reminiscent of the conference of Judah with Nicanor some years later). (42.39.2-8)

This passage shows a behavior of respect and dignity that is based on a traditional contact that enabled a fine dialogue. The universal values that are mentioned here are: dignity, reputation and respect for certain family ties, and agreed upon etiquette, welcoming and kindly (even between enemies). The mere mention of such information by such a great narrator as Livy was also an important facet of inter-state relations at that time.

The following in Livy's narrative shows so wonderfully that *Ius gentium* is actually linked to what I call here a value system. It is certainly not a bunch of international laws but more of a code of conduct, unwritten but quite clear, that was practiced/breached and referred to all the time during the period under discussion. Moreover, in the following passage I also receive support for my observation in the introduction to the book that there was no international objective court to deal with complaints of states. Let me go into details. In a speech of Marcius addressed to the Macedonian king, he says:

> what is awaited, I suppose ... is a reply from us to your letter which you sent to Corcyra, in which you ask why we have come in this fashion as envoys with soldiers and are sending garrisons to the several cities. I hesitate to make no reply to this inquiry of yours, for fear of acting arrogantly, and also to reply truly, lest the reply seem to you, as you hear it, too harsh. But since one who breaks a treaty must be rebuked either with words or with arms, as on the one hand I should prefer war against you to be entrusted to some other rather than to me, so on the other hand I shall take upon myself the harshness of this speech to a guest-friend, however it may be, as physicians do in applying somewhat painful remedies for the sake of a cure. From the time when you attained the throne the senate believes you have done one thing which you should have done, in that you sent envoys to Rome to renew the treaty; yet even this, the senate considers, you should have failed to renew instead of breaking it after it had been renewed. Abrupolis, the ally and friend of the Roman people, you drove from his kingdom; the assassins of Arthetaurus you sheltered, so that it was obvious that you rejoiced, to say nothing more, in the crime of those who had killed the prince most faithful of all the Illyrians to Rome [here some additional accusations against the king are adduced]. ... Since you did inquire, we should have been more arrogant in keeping silence than we are in replying truthfully. Indeed, on account of our inherited guest-friendship, I am eager to hear what you have to say and hope that you will give me some foundation for pleading your cause before the senate. (42.40.1-11)

The accusations mentioned here so clearly allude to a certain standard of behavior expected in international relations. Yet since one side positions their standard of behavior—no standard is necessarily absolute—the other side can argue and relate their own interpretation to the matter, the ethical unwritten code being their reference. Neither are necessarily correct or ideal, but one thing is certain: both sides to the ensuing conflict were aware of the fact that inter-state relations were to be managed by rules of agreed upon conduct. This issue is clarified by the detailed answer of the king. The two conflicting parties listen to each other with patience and respect.

The king's answer demonstrates how one interpretation of the ethical code is not holy and can be argued. At present we are confronted daily by the use and abuse of standard ethical codes even in current democracies and by their opinion leaders. Hence, let us hear what the king has to say:

> A cause, which would be good if it were pled before impartial judges, I shall plead before men who are at once accusers and judges. However, of the charges made against me, some are such that I should perhaps boast of them, not such that I should blush to confess them, others are such that, since they are made in a word, it is enough to deny them in a word. For with what, if I should be a defendant to-day under your laws, could either the informer at Brundisium or Eumenes charge me, so that they might seem truly to accuse me rather than to revile me? (42.41.1-3)

Here he delves into many details that reveal his concerns about the right interpretation of the virtual inter-state value system:

> Even for the Thebans, who, it is known, perished by shipwreck, and for the murder of Arthetaurus I must give an accounting! In this latter case, however, no charge is brought against me except that his assassins went into exile in my kingdom. The unfairness of this situation I shall not protest, on condition that you too agree that whenever exiles betake themselves to Italy or Rome you will confess that you were sponsors of the crimes for which they have been condemned. If both you and all other peoples will protest against this, I too shall be among the others. (42.41.5-7)

Perseus here touches on a delicate issue that perhaps could shed light on the Judean leader who according to 2 Maccabees wandered as an exile from place to place and was rejected everywhere.[10] The chance that existed that one state would be accused because a criminal was hiding in its territory is actually yet another allusion to the concept of sovereignty of a state with defined borders. He goes on: "And, heavens, what use is there for exile to be allowed to anyone, if there is to be nowhere room for the fugitive? However, as soon as I had learned, on advice from you, that these men were in Macedonia, I had them searched out, ordered them to depart from my kingdom, and banished them forever from my territory," and goes on saying that

> the other charges are made as against a king, and are such as to involve interpretation of the treaty between you and me. For if it is written in the treaty that I may not be permitted to protect myself and my kingdom, even if someone attacks me, then I must confess that, inasmuch as I have defended myself with arms against Abrupolis, an ally of the Roman people, the treaty has been broken. But if, on the other hand, it is both permitted by the treaty and is arranged by the law of nations (*Ius gentium*) that arms may be beaten back by arms, what, pray, was it proper for me to do when Abrupolis devastated the confines of my kingdom even to Amphipolis, and carried off many free persons, a great abundance of

---

[10] See Part II, Chapter 6, p. 148.

slaves, and many thousand cattle? Should I have kept quiet and suffered, until he came armed to Pella and into my palace? But, you say, I proceeded against him in a just war indeed, but he should not have been conquered, nor have suffered the further consequences which befell the conquered; since I, who was assailed with arms, suffered the misfortune of like disasters, how can he who was the cause of the war complain that they happened to him? I will not use the same defense, Romans, for having checked the Dolopians with arms; since, even had they not deserved it, I acted within my rights (*etsi non merito eorum, iure feci meo*), since they were in my kingdom and under my sway, having been assigned by your decree to my father. Moreover, if it were proper for me to give an accounting, I could not seem, I will not say to you and your allies, but even to those who do not approve harsh and unjust exercise of authority even over slaves, to have exceeded justice and virtue in punishing them; inasmuch as they killed Euphranor, the governor placed over them by me, in such fashion that death would have been the lightest of vengeance for him. (42.41.7-14)

This passage reveals some important aspects. First and foremost, the notion of accountability in inter-state relations comes to the fore. Second, what we call today "area of jurisdiction" was known to states at that time (the king speaks of "your laws," etc.). Third, dialogue between states in conflict, as we have already seen all along, is not just civilized rhetoric but based on logical arguments and interpretation of custom and rules of conduct known to all participants of the system. Fourth, revenge and vengeance were part and parcel of ethical systems that are based inter alia on the notion of armed conflict in various degrees of reciprocity (from talk about it to real war).[11] Namely, if one state trespasses the other, a trespass done under the umbrella of a treaty with a third party, the attacked was allowed to act harshly within the rules of the current ethical behavior. This was in fact the interpretation of the king who saw his act against King Abrupolis as an act of self-defense, in itself an ethical principle with a few overtones. I would like to remind my reader that when the king refers to the "law of nations" he actually means a virtual ethical inter-state system and not to a written code of international law, as was explained in my introduction.

The king continues with his fascinating speech:

But when I proceed thence to see Larisa and Antronae and Ptelecn, by a way near which is Delphi, I went up to Delphi to offer sacrifice in order to pay vows long overdue. And to this charge—that the accusations may be greater—is added the further charge that I went with an army; as if indeed it was in order to seize cities, as I now am complaining of your doing, and to place garrisons in the citadels. Call to conference the cities of Greece through which I made my way, let any single person complain of injury from a soldier of mine; I shall not protest against being thought to have, by a pretence of sacrifice, sought ulterior ends. To the Aetolians and Byzantines we have sent military forces, and with the Boeotians we have made

---

[11] Buzan and Little (2000).

a treaty of friendship. These acts, such as they are, have been frequently not only announced but even defended by my envoys in your senate, where I usually found certain critics not as fair-minded as you, Quintus Marcius, a friend and guest by inheritance. But Eumenes had not as yet come to Rome as accuser, in order by slandering and distorting everything to arouse general suspicion and hatred and to try to persuade you that it is impossible for Greece to be free and to enjoy your bounty as long as the kingdom of Macedonia is intact. (42.42.1-5)

The king concludes his speech, saying:

Quintus Marcius and Aulus Atilius, that these charges which have either been made by you or answered by me are such as the ears and minds of the hearers are, and that it does not so much matter what I have done or with what intent as how you will receive the action. I am confident that I have done no wrong knowingly and that if I have done anything through an unintentional slip, I can be corrected and bettered by this rebuke. Certainly, I have done nothing irreparable, nor such that you should think it must be avenged by war and arms; or else the fame of your mercy and poise has been spread abroad among the nations all in vain, if for such causes, which are hardly worthy of complaint and protest, you rush to arms and declare war on your royal allies. (42.42.7-9)

This passage is full of information about the inter-state unwritten value system. For instance, an emphasis is put on cautious behavior expected from foreign armies when they move in territories that are under rule of peaceful others; slander and distortion that one state launches against another should not be tolerated since they cause suspicion and hatred. Liberty under one empire does not require the elimination of its adversary (Macedonia can be intact even if Greece is liberated by Rome); one state should be able to help other states but avoid helping others in their wars; acts of states on the international level should be announced (transparent, as it were). Mercy and poise should be exercised by the dominating power vis-à-vis other nations, and finally, there should be nothing that is irreparable in inter-state relationships. A bad relationship between states can be corrected by rebuke shown by dominant powers. In short, fulfilment of an agreed upon inter-state value system could and should avoid a resort to armed conflicts.

Another comment is in order. In his speech the king of Macedonia mentions Eumenes, king of Pergamum, and says, inter alia: "A far worse tyrant over Asia than Antiochus had been, exists in Eumenes; your allies cannot take their ease as long as the palace of Pergamum stands; that looms like a citadel over the heads of neighboring states."[12] This means that excessive architecture can be a symbolic feature of hubris and arrogance of a state with the inter-state sphere. We should bear this issue in mind when we deal with the Jerusalem Temple that should be "higher than other hills" (Part

---

[12] 42.42.6. Cf. Mendels (1992: 107–59, 277–331) (two chapters on the importance of temples and capitals in the Hellenistic Near East).

II). Was that not a signifier for Jews in the Hellenistic age that made them look, among other things, as being arrogant?

Truce as a Confirmation of the Adherence to an Inter-state Value System

The episode ends with the mention of applause for the king's speech (he was apparently still popular among many audiences). Marcius proposed that the king should send envoys to Rome:

> since the king believed that every recourse should be tried to the very last and no hope be overlooked, the rest of the conference was on means of safety for the envoy's journey. Although for this a request for a truce was clearly essential and Marcius was eager for it and was seeking for nothing else at the conference, he granted it grudgingly and as a great favor to the petitioner. (42.43.1-2)

This was—at least partly—a trick that was later interpreted as a calculated deception on the part of Rome that wanted to gain time for preparing the war. Yet, a truce in the Hellenistic warfare was first and foremost a familiar political strategy (which we will meet later in 1-2 Maccabees). For our case we have to emphasize the inherent values of a truce. Truces as well as peace pacts had clear overtones and meaning beyond their being technical and legal devices in inter-state relationships.[13] First, a truce was frequently an efficient mechanism for gaining time to be used for preparation of a war or for second thoughts on behalf of the confrontative parties before an armed conflict was started or continued. Sometimes it indeed led to peaceful solutions rather than to violent ones. Second, mutuality is required, namely, feelings of respect for one's enemy (as in the familiar "cease-fire" during the Olympic Games), instead of hostility and anger existing between warring states. Needless to say, the hiatus in an armed conflict that entails the obligation to keep it for a defined passage of time is yet another signifier of the shared compliance with an inter-state ethical framework of the system. Thus, deception in the context of a truce was seen as a breach of inter-state loyalty and faith, as the elders (who opposed the truce) in the Roman senate indeed thought and will be mentioned later in my survey.

Be that as it may, "from this conference the Roman envoys, relying on the truce as security, at once set out for Boeotia" (42.43.4). There the views were divided between Roman adherents and the Macedonian followers.[14] The disputes that became vehement and even violent were favorable in the eyes of the Romans. I will not delve here into the details but only state that the Romans preferred a weak Boeotian league than one that would join the forces of the Macedonians, hence the temporary support of their divide. Yet, whereas the Romans wanted a decisive war against Macedonia, the Greek

---

[13] See Buzan and Little (2001).
[14] See also Polybius 27.1-2; Walbank (1979: 290-4).

states were still striving for peace, which seemed to be very high up in their value system. It seems that the Romans were preparing for war whereas many Greek states and cities wished to avoid it. The Romans sent ambassadors to try and persuade the Greeks in Greece and Asia Minor to support their cause in the imminent war. Yet the hope for peace was still a dominant sentiment in the Greek east. Hope as we will see in Part II was an emotion that under certain circumstances became an independent value in inter-state politics of the Hellenistic era. Livy tells us about the Roman embassy that was sent to Asia Minor and among the islands. This is the place to mention how the very active territorial characteristic of the Romans clashed with the liberal value system of the Greek world that the former advertised in 196 BCE. Roman imperialism limited the choices of their allies in reference to their values and imposed as it were new priorities, peace not among the highest.

The dissonance that emerges on the eve of the Third Macedonian War between the passion of the Romans to be dominant over more territories and the urge of the Greeks to be free according to the Roman declaration at the conference of Corinth in 196 BCE comes to the fore in the following passage about the Roman ambassadors mentioned above who "went about exhorting the allies to undertake war against Perseus on the side of the Romans (42.45); and the richer any given city was the more painstakingly they negotiated there, because the lesser cities would follow the leadership of the greater" (42.45.1-2). In this remark of Livy, we encounter the characteristic of hierarchy in inter-state relations,[15] attached to which were subvalues such as appreciation, respect, awe, balance, and peace, a matter that will be discussed later on. Hegesilochus,

> who held the chief magistracy—their own title is *prytanis*—had by numerous speeches won over the Rhodians to give up the hope, which they had repeatedly discovered to be idle, of currying favor with kings, and to keep the alliance with Rome, the only alliance in the world at that time which was secure whether through power or trustworthiness. War with Perseus, said Hegesilochus, was imminent. (42.45.3-5)

Here again the value of speech and the persuasion of decision makers play an important role in inter-state relations. Values that are emphasized here and associated with the recognition of Rome as the supreme power in the world are security, power, and trustworthiness. This was a description of a situation that occurred four years before the Maccabean revolt started and ten years before the alliance of Judah Maccabee with the Romans was concluded. Against this background and Rome's proof of her supremacy by defeating Macedonia in 168 BCE, is it not natural that the Hasmoneans concluded a treaty with her while still under Seleucid rule?

But we go back to our story. When Perseus had returned to Macedonia from the conference with the Romans, envoys were sent by him to Rome concerning the terms of peace outlined with Marcius. He also sent letters to Rhodes and Byzantium and

---

[15] Cf. Buzan and Little (2001) for a hierarchy within a system in international relations, and Badian (1958) and Gruen (1984) concerning the formal and legal hierarchies. See also Mendels (2017).

probably to other states as well. He expressed his sentiments concerning the conference with the Romans saying that "what he had heard and what he had said had turned out to be such that he might seem to have had the better of the discussion" (42.46.2). To the Rhodians the envoys of the king said that he was sure that there would be peace and even more important,

> if the Romans continued to stir up war contrary to the treaty, then the Rhodians must strive with all their resources of friendly influence to bring peace again; if they did not succeed with their entreaties, they must act to prevent authority and power over everything coming into the hands of a single people. This was to the interest both of all states and especially of the Rhodians, in proportion as they were outstanding among other states in position and resources;[16] these blessings would be enslaved and in bondage, if there were no recourse to anyone but the Romans. The friendly hearing given to the letter and the words of the envoys was greater than the weight they had in changing the Rhodians' minds; the influence of the better party [in Polybius *tou beltionos*, the upper class] began to be the stronger. (42.46.3-5)

The decision of the Rhodians as voted was that the Rhodians hoped for peace. Yet, in case of war the Rhodians would not side with the king, a step which "would destroy between them and the Romans the ancient friendship, cemented by many great services in peace and war" (42.46.6). The passage reveals another view of Roman imperialism (a variant of which we have discussed above) that presents the idea of balance in the world rather than a supremacy of one single power. We also learn from this passage that letters, as we will also see later in Part II,[17] were a major vehicle for communicating ideas and shared values by Hellenistic kings to their allies and subjects. Some were answered and others not.

What happens in the following is intriguing from our point of view since some inter-state values and their opposites surface. They are communal will, desertion, restoration of exiles (recovery), deception, wisdom, honor versus advantage, betrayal, and injustice. Also, group emotions and manner of conduct are enhanced: anger, prejudice, insolence, harshness. As I said already in the above, these values cannot be dealt with if not shown within their historical contextual development. Let us then examine their appearance in our narrative:

> On the way back from Rhodes, the envoys also approached the cities of Boeotia, not only Thebes but also Coronea and Haliartus, for it was believed that their desertion of the alliance with the king and adhesion to the Romans had been forced upon them against their will. The Thebans were not at all moved, although, both for the condemnation of the chief men and the restoration of the exiles, they were angry with the Romans.

---

[16] Polybius 27.4-5, and Walbank (1979: 294-305).
[17] Letters of Hellenistic rulers are seldom adduced verbatim by Livy, in contradistinction with 1-2 Maccabees.

The peoples of Coronea and Haliartus, imbued with some inborn prejudice in favor of kings, sent envoys to Macedonia asking for a garrison, in order to protect themselves against the "reckless insolence of the Thebans" (42.46.7-9). (This shows yet again that garrisons were sometimes grasped as protectors and not necessarily as a menace to one's liberty; the Hellenists in Judea certainly felt secure with Seleucid troops, hence Jason being under the umbrella of the Seleucid forces should not surprise us [Part II].) To this embassy the king's reply was that he could not send a garrison since he had to adhere to the truce made with the Romans, "however, he advised them to protect themselves as best as they might against the injustice of the Thebans in such a way as not to offer the Romans an excuse for harshness against them" (42.46.10). The notion of the need for common will of a state during its inter-state relations has already been mentioned. Here it is said once more, namely, that action in inter-state relations requires a common will of the states involved (namely, at least a will of the majority). I would suggest that when a state was forced into an alliance, in particular a disadvantageous one, it was seen by the Greeks, or at least part of them, as a blow to their freedom.

Interestingly, the Macedonian king is presented as the one who sincerely wanted to keep the truce agreed upon. In contradistinction, the Romans are the ones who reflect deception. Their wish to use the truce for the preparations for war was not welcomed by some of the old senators who preached for transparency, honesty, and straightforwardness in inter-state relations in general and in war and its declaration in particular. However, their idea of honest wisdom was outvoted in the senate: "Thus the older men, who were less well pleased by the new and over-sly wisdom; however, that part of the senate to whom the pursuit of advantage was more important than that of honor, prevailed to the effect that the previous embassy of Marcius should be approved" (42.47.9), considerations of utility of the younger generation apparently prevail over honesty and trustworthiness of the older senators. But the Third Macedonian War started in spite of all the preceding talk about its avoidance.

Livy shares with us the thoughts of the crowd that participates in the ritual of leaving Rome for the war. This description is in itself illuminating, yet there is also a philosophy behind it, probably Livy's own. It is important for us, as we shall see in a moment. Livy says that the departure of a consul to war "in military dress" was always conducted

> with great solemnity and pomp; it particularly draws the eyes and minds of men when they escort a consul going against an enemy great and famous either for bravery or for good fortune. For not only care in paying their respects, but also eagerness for the spectacle brings crowds to see their leader, to whose command and wisdom they have entrusted the whole welfare of the state. Thereupon there steals over their minds a thought of the calamities of war, and how uncertain is the outcome of fortune and how impartial the god of war—a thought of reverses and successes, of what disasters have often occurred through the ignorance and rashness of leaders, of what gains, on the other hand, prudence and courage have produced. What mortal knows, men think, which kind of mind and fortune belongs to this consul whom we are sending to war? Shall it be a swift triumph, as

he climbs the Capitol with a conquering army toward those gods from whom he now takes his leave, that we shall see him, or are we to give that joy to the enemy? To King Perseus in particular, against whom the consul was going, fame had come from the brilliance of the Macedonian nation in war and from Philip, the king's father, whose reputation sprang from many successful achievements and, besides, even from the war with Rome. Then, too, Perseus' own name, because of the expectation of war with him, never from the time he mounted the throne had ceased to be on men's lips. With such thoughts, men of all classes escorted the departing consul. (42.49.1-7)

Then comes a description of the enemy, apparently the council of the committee of *philoi* of the king that was held in Macedonia's capital Pella. But before discussing the latter, we should pay attention to Livy's thoughts about the departure of the consul to his province. The characteristics of a leader going to war are reminiscent of the ones attributed to Simeon in 1 Maccabees 14 (and the praise of Judah in 1 Macc. 3:1-9),[18] not necessarily in their details but in the very notion that the leader in many ways represents the nation's values in its encounter with other states within the system, peaceful and warlike. Namely, bravery and good command, good fortune, command and wisdom, are entrusted with the welfare of the state (see Simeon), prudence and courage, fame and brilliance, being exceptional as against ignorance and rashness. In the Hellenistic period it seems that the features of the leader sometimes constituted a mirror of the ideal values of the state in its relationship with others.

And now we get to a description of the Hellenistic council of Perseus. Talking before and during wars is yet again seen as a tool to air ideas about the values of inter-state foreign affairs (42.50). In the Hellenistic world ideas and thoughts about the reality and its political ethics had to be shared in public and reach large audiences by speeches, deliberations in conferences, letters that were read openly, and with transparency (see in Part II examples of reading in public of letters by the Hasmoneans).

In the following we are brought directly into the inner advisory board of a Hellenistic king:

A few days before, after the envoys returning from Rome had cut off hope of peace, Perseus held a council. There a contest of opposing views took place for a time. There were those who thought that either a tribute should be paid, if it were imposed, or part of their territory yielded, if this form of fine were inflicted—or, finally, that anything else which must be endured for the sake of peace should not be rejected, nor should the king risk staking himself and his kingdom on a cast with so great a forfeit. If his hold on the kingdom remained quite undisputed, the passage of time might bring, they thought, many means not only of recouping his losses but of making him positively an object of fear to those whom he now feared. (42.50.1-3)

---

[18] See in the following pp. 139–40 (Part II) for this genre.

This opinion was rejected by the majority of the participants in the council, who held a "bolder opinion. No matter what he should have yielded, they declared, along with it he would immediately have to yield his kingdom. For the Romans were not in want of money or territory, but understood that not only all human affairs, but in particular the greatest of kingdoms and empires, were subject to many vicissitudes" (42.50.4-5). The conclusion was that "finally this discussion about peace and war was based on the universally accepted view that nothing is more disgraceful than to have yielded a kingdom without struggle, nor anything more glorious than to have made trial of fortune to the utmost in defense of rank and crown." Perseus says: "let us, then, wage war, since this seems best, with the kindly help of the gods." Then he himself, in regal style, offered a sacrifice of one hundred victims to Minerva whom they call "Defender of the Folk" (42.50.11-51.2). This passage shows once again a matter I have emphasized already, that is, that talk and dialogue during conflict point to everything but anarchy. On the contrary, war seems to have been a last resort while universal and humanistic values pop up all the time as a compass for the right and good inter-state conduct.

Let us now move to the king's speech in which the Hellenistic king airs his moralistic ideas about the situation and enhances the "treacherous conference" through which "by means of a pretence of reorganizing peace, the winter had been wasted, so that the Romans might have time for preparations" (42.52.8). He also emphasizes that "everything which, by the beneficence of the gods and by the prudence of the king, was to be made ready the Macedonians had in abundant plenty." Yet in addition they should be endowed with the "spirit which their ancestors had possessed" when they subdued all Europe and conquered Asia while opening up a whole world "unknown even to rumor." They had to cease their operations when they reached "the barrier of the Indian Ocean." But at present, Perseus continues,

> by Hercules, fortune had proclaimed a contest, not for the farthermost shores of India, but for the possession of Macedonia itself. When the Romans had been waging war with his father, they had held out the plausible pretext of the freedom of Greece; now openly they sought to enslave Macedonia, that there might be no king neighboring the Roman empire, that no people famed in war might keep its arms. All these things they must surrender to haughty masters, along with their king and kingdom, if they wished to cease waging war and do the bidding of others. (42.52.13-16)

The value of *parrhesia* comes here to the fore once more, namely, that many of the important decisions or declarations of the intentions in inter-state relations were aired in front of an audience. Secrecy was reserved for special occasion. Be that as it may, Livy informs us that after the speech of the king the audience was enthusiastic.[19] During the speech there "had been often enough outbursts of applause," and he put an end to his speech when an "outcry arose from those who were at once enraged and threatening, while some of them bade the king be of good cheer" (42.53.1). He ordered them to

---

[19] 42.53. See for publicity in political affairs in 1-2 Maccabees in Part II, Chapters 5-6.

prepare for a march and after dismissing the assembly embassies from the cities of Macedonia received a hearing. "These groups had come in order to promise funds for the war, each according to its ability, and grain. To all thanks were expressed and the offers refused" (42.53.1-4). In this passage, beyond the political argument (of a wish to keep a balance of power in the region), there emerges also a moralistic aspect, namely, to annihilate, or rather enslave your neighbor whatever your motives are, should be anathema and be defined as unfair and unjust in inter-state relations. Moreover, with hindsight the king approves of the "liberation of Greece" (using pretext) when it is granted during a period of coexistence with others in the region. Hence their wish to enslave the Macedonians looks as a dissonant and treacherous behavior on the part of Rome. Yet, this is an interesting comment adduced by a Hellenistic king. He assures us once again that a Hellenistic super power can grant liberty to a city or state under its rule, which affects the autonomy of the latter in which characteristics, values, and emotions are restricted in their free interaction. Hence living in peace restricts one's liberty up to a certain limit. The ruling power, as it were, wishes to balance certain characteristics so that they would be dormant whereas others are encouraged to be active (for instance, the empire suppresses territoriality but enhances divide where this characteristic exists and thus simplifies the intervention of the empire); it regulates emotions that might trigger a characteristic such as territoriality which would lead to insurrection, and keeps an eye on the value system of the state in order for it to be harmonized with the universal value system. We will see later that in the case of the Hasmonean family the super power did not manage to regulate the interactions between the three angles of the triangle, characteristics, emotions, and values, and the result was an unavoidable clash.

Later Livy adduces an interesting view on the mob during the war, saying:[20]

> The report of the cavalry battle, as it spread abroad throughout Greece, laid bare the inclinations of the inhabitants. For not only partisans of Macedonia but many who were indebted to the Romans for huge benefits, and some few who had felt the violence and tyranny of Perseus, received this news gladly, for no other reason than the morbid eagerness which the mob feels in athletic contests also—the eagerness to cheer on the worse and weaker party. (42.63.1-2)

Both examples to be discussed now enhance the emotional reactions of the people, the uneducated mob. In the latter case, the example given is of an illogical stance of the mob resulting from its unrestrained emotions (probably mercy).

Ethics Expected from Armies in Times of War

During the Third Macedonian War at a certain juncture, the Greeks complain about the misbehavior and unethical conduct of the Roman army during the war and bring

---

[20] Based on Polybius 27.9.

their case to what started to become the supreme court of inter-state affairs in the world, the Roman senate. That the Greeks paid attention and reacted fiercely to the wrong behavior of the Roman army stationed in their cities and states demonstrates their own built-in awareness of what should be the correct inter-state ethics. One should keep in mind that war was a typical interaction within a system that contained a conglomerate of states (units). Let us adduce here Livy's words about the matter that shed light on the behavior of the Seleucids toward the Jews in the Land of Israel later in the century: Those cities that had shut the Roman soldiers out were unharmed, but those that did not suffered from the soldiers of their allies. For instance,

> in Chalcis, temples had been stripped of all their ornaments and the loot of these profanations Gaius Lucretius had transported in his ships to Antium [to be remembered when we later deal with Antiochus IV's treatment of the Temple in Jerusalem in 170 BCE]; free persons had been rushed away to slavery; the possessions of allies of the Roman people had been plundered and daily were being plundered. For, according to the precedent set by Gaius Lucretius, Hortensius too was quartering his sailors, in summer no less than in winter, in private houses, and the homes of Chalcis were full of the mob from the fleet; at large among the Chalcideans and their wives and their children there were men utterly reckless in word and deed. (43.7.10-11)[21]

It should be emphasized that Rome reacted fast when this behavior occurred. "It was voted to summon Lucretius before the senate in order that he might plead in person and attempt to clear himself. However, when he appeared, he heard many more reproaches than had been hurled at him in his absence; and more influential and powerful accusers join in, namely, two tribunes of the people" (43.8.1-2). These not only accused him in the senate but also

> dragged him before an assembly, and after casting many reproaches at him, then set a day for his trial. By order of the senate Quintus Maenius the praetor replied to the envoys of Chalcis that, as to the services to the Roman people, both previously and in the war now being waged, which the envoys mentioned, the senate knew that they had spoken truly. (43.8.3-4)

As to their complaints about the wayward conduct of Roman soldiers, this was done "without the consent of the senate." The Romans, it was added, waged war first on Philip and then on his son Perseus with the aim "to preserve the freedom of Greece, and not to inflict on allies and friends such injuries from Roman officers." A letter was sent by the senate to the praetor Lucius Hortensius

> saying that the senate was displeased with those actions of which the people of Chalcis complained; that if any free persons had been sold into slavery, he should

---

[21] For Livy Book 43, see the commentary of Briscoe (2012: 387–464).

take steps at the first possible moment to search them out and restore them to freedom; that the senate deemed it just that none of the sailors, except the captains, should be quartered in private houses. (43.8.6-7)

The Romans take responsibility for this affair and send gifts to the Greek envoys of two thousand asses apiece, sent to Brundisium by carriages at "public expense." "As for Gaius Lucretius, on the day set for his trial, the tribunes accused him before the people and proposed a fine of one million asses. When the vote was taken, all the thirty-five tribes approved his condemnation" (43.8.8-10). This episode serves as a lesson for the recurrent value of accountability in inter-state relations. Rome admits and takes responsibility for the injustice done by her forces and bluntly and formally rejects such wayward behavior. By her response she adheres to ethical rules that were expected in the international scene during war. The procedural apparently worked well and international values honorably saved, for the moment at least.

Testimony and Secrecy

In our modern world we can find a variety of ethical codes of organizations, firms, communities, and states. The international ethical codes are available online (the UN ones, for instance). Most of such written codes abound with recurring terms such as identity, accountability, honesty, equality, loyalty, mutual respect, transparency, integrity, and secrecy. Although many of these latter terms changed their meaning during the many years that have elapsed since the Hellenistic era, it is still intriguing to realize how close the terminology of ancient ethical codes is to the modern ones. I will not delve here into a comparison but just highlight in addition to the abovementioned two of the recurrent components in modern ethical codes as they appear in our information about antiquity. The terms are[22] *Public Testimony* versus *secrecy*. Let us hear what Livy has to say concerning these matters in his narrative of the Third Macedonian War of 168 BCE (the year in which the Maccabean revolt started).[23]

> While these events were occurring in Italy, Perseus decided that since he had discovered that the Romans had entered the pass and that the final crisis of the war impended, he must no longer postpone the project which he could not bring himself to complete because expenditure of money was required—namely, gaining the adherence of Gentius, king of Illyria. (44.23.1-2)

Since Perseus had agreed to pay three hundred talents of silver for an exchange of hostages, he sent one of his most trusted friends, Pentauchus, to complete the agreement with Gentius. The two met and he received the king's oath and his hostages. In the following we encounter an orderly and civilized procedure when

---

[22] Koselleck (2004).
[23] For a commentary on Livy Book 44, Briscoe (2012: 465–608).

> Gentius too sent an envoy named Olympio to require the oath and the hostages of Perseus. Others were sent with him to receive the money; and, at Pantauchus' suggestion, Parmenio and Morcus were named as envoys to go with the Macedonians to Rhodes. To them instructions were given to set out for Rhodes only after the oath, the hostages, and the money had been received; it was thought that by the prestige of two kings at once the Rhodians could be induced to war with the Romans, and that once the kings were joined by the state to which belonged a unique reputation for sea-power, no hope on land or sea would be left the Romans. (44.23.3-6)

This dialogue between states occurred during the war and was an orderly procedure among the units (states) of the system. Then:

> On the arrival of the Illyrians, Perseus left his camp at the Elpeus River with all his cavalry and met them at Dium. There the terms agreed upon were executed in the presence of the surrounding column of cavalry, whom the king wished to be present at the ratification of the alliance with Gentius, thinking that it would somewhat raise their spirits. The hostages were also given and received in the sight of all, those who were to receive the money were sent to the royal treasury at Pella and those who were to accompany the Illyrian envoys to Rhodes were ordered to take ship at Thessalonica. (44.23.7-9)

I have already mentioned the principle or rather value of *parrhesia*, namely, of speaking openly before audiences and assemblies, and the obligation to have an open discussion. Here we yet again evidence a transparent procedure when testimony for a certain act is public ("in the sight of all"). The aim was twofold, to raise the moral of his soldiers and also to publicize his pact with the Illyrians and have a testimony thereof. In a way the whole section dealing with his pact with the Illyrians points to a wish for some sort of what we call transparency (knowing that secrecy in ancient diplomacy was dangerous since every side could deny a pact or an agreement cut beforehand). At the same time, identical messages were sent to both Eumenes and to Antiochus as follows:

> By nature a free state and a king were things hostile to each other; the Roman people attacked kings one by one; and—an unjust state of affairs—assailed kings with the help of kings; Perseus' father had been overcome with the aid of Attalus; with Eumenes helping, and to a certain extent Perseus' father Philip as well, Antiochus had been assailed; now both Eumenes and Prusias were in arms against Perseus; if the kingdom of Macedonia were out of the way, next would come Asia Minor, which the Romans had already made their own to some extent under pretext of freeing communities, and after Asia Minor, Syria. Already Prusias was being given a position above Eumenes, already Antiochus, though victorious, was being barred from Egypt, his prize of war. Perseus bade each king, on considering these facts, to take such steps that either he might force the Romans to make peace with Perseus, or if Rome persevered in an unjust war might regard the Romans as the common enemy of all kings. (44.24.1-6)

Republican Rome is here presented as a state that is contradictory to kingship but fights with some of them against others.

> The message to Antiochus was open; to Eumenes the envoy was sent under guise of ransoming prisoners, but in fact certain more secret matters were under discussion, which for the time being embarrassed Eumenes, who was already an object of hatred and suspicion to the Romans, with false and more serious charges; for he was already regarded as a traitor and almost an enemy, while the two kings with grasping hands vied with each other in guile and greed.[24]

Secrecy and betrayal will pop up again in Part II.

Concerning secrecy, we have yet another example:

> There was a Cretan, Cydas, one of Eumenes' henchmen. He had held conversations, first at Amphipolis with a certain Chimarus, a fellow-countryman who was serving in Perseus' army, then later at Demetrias, beneath the very walls of the city, once with a certain Menecrates and again with Antimachus, both of whom were officers of the king. Herophon also, who was then sent by Perseus, had similarly undertaken two previous missions to Eumenes. These conversations were *secret*, and the missions caused bad rumors, but there was no knowledge of what had been discussed or upon what the kings had agreed. (44.24.9-11)

The diplomatic encounters were sometimes conducted in complete secrecy, a value that was crucial in organizations in antiquity, and included in most ethical codes of organizations at present. I will not go here into the details of the following diplomatic encounters, but just adduce words from the summary to Book 44 of Livy concerning the end of these deliberations: "Although Perseus had urged Eumenes, king of Pergamum, and Gentius, king of Illyria, to help him, he was abandoned by them because he withheld the money which he had promised them." Promises in inter-state relationships as we will see later in the Jewish case were not always kept, but they show that there were rules in vogue.

Leadership and Authority and the Inter-state Value System

An inter-state value system is perhaps one of the strongest bonds that connects states that were members in the same ethical system. Values of authority were conducive to the identities which formed this network, but as I already emphasized (based on Buzan and Little) there were strong links between inner affairs of states and the system the state was part of. Thus, we will have a glimpse into authority within the state (which was also an important facet in the rule of the Hasmoneans as we will see in Part II).

---

[24] 44.24.7-8, and Polybius 29.7-8, and Walbank (1979: 368–9).

One of the most important values that had always a potential implication on the encounters between states was the existence within the individual states of a division of power between the different components of authority, such as kings, high priests, senate, assembly, army, financial management, judicial institutions. If the division of authority between institutions that managed a state was balanced, well-defined, and accepted by the majority of its citizens then their identity as a unit and their hierarchical status within the network of nations that shared one and the same ethical system was acknowledged. Let us take an example from the narrative of Livy who tells us about the last phases of the Third Macedonian War.

We start with the speech of the consul Lucius Aemilius in a public meeting in Rome defining the ideal general who has the sole authority to make decisions during war (and reflects the values of positive authority).[25] After a mention of the congratulations that were offered to him when he was assigned Macedonia as his province, he approaches the people of Rome in a cynical mode saying that

> for your part, see to it that you have confidence only in the reports I make to the senate and to you, and beware of nourishing by your credulity the gossip for which no sponsor will appear. For I have noticed that, as is commonly the case, so now especially in this war no one is so scornful of rumor that his spirit cannot be weakened. In all the clubs and even—God save us!—at dinner tables there are experts who lead armies to Macedonia, who know where camp should be pitched, what places should be held with garrisons, when or by what pass Macedonia should be invaded ... not only do they decide what should be done, but when anything is done contrary to their opinion, they accuse the consul as if he were in the dock. Such behavior is a great obstacle to the men in the field. For not everyone is as unwavering and as steadfast of spirit against hostile gossip as was Quintus Fabius, who preferred to have his independence of command lessened by popular folly rather than to neglect the best interests of the state for the sake of acclaim. I am not, fellow-citizens, one who believes that no advice may be given to leaders; nay rather I judge him to be not a sage, but haughty, who conducts everything according to his own opinion alone.

He continues with the more positive side asking:

> What therefore is my conclusion? Generals should receive advice, in the first place from the experts who are both specially skilled in military matters and have learned from experience; secondly, from those who are on the scene of action, who see the terrain, the enemy, the fitness of the occasion, who are shares in the danger, as it were aboard the same vessel. Thus, if there is anyone who is confident that he can advise me as to the best advantage of the state in this campaign which I am about to conduct, let him not refuse his services to the state, but come with

---

[25] 44.22. The issue of authority of generals comes to the fore in 1 Maccabees 5 when two generals take the role of the Hasmoneans without their consent (1 Macc. 5: 18-19, 55-62). For ideal leaders, see Eckstein (2006: 194–5).

me into Macedonia. I will furnish him with his sea-passage, with a horse, a tent, and even travel-funds. If anyone is reluctant to do this and prefers the leisure of the city to the hardships of campaigning, let him not steer the ship from on shore. The city itself provides enough subjects for conversation; let him confine his garrulity to these; and let him be aware that I shall be satisfied with the advice originating in camp. (44.22.6-15)[26]

This is a brilliant speech, still so relevant in modern times, the idea of which we encountered earlier in the narrative concerning the Achaean league.[27] The question remains: what does this have to do with our theme here? It is in fact part of the idea that Livy adduces here as to the authority and conduct of generals as related to politics in the state. In other words, the value that is promoted here is complete honesty and excellency in military leadership; this will result in full faith of leaders, soldiers, and citizens in the general who is one of those who interacts with the units (states) of the system through diplomacy and war. In the case of the military leader, he should have a great deal of freedom to take decisions during war. His authority derives from his experience, knowledge, and advice given by experts in military affairs and those who fight alongside him in the battlefield. One can deduce that the quality of the leaders who have a significant voice in inter-state discourse and relationships, including war, was crucial for the maintenance of the ethical code shared by all. This wonderful speech also demonstrates that politicians and generals were expected to be open minded and to listen to others who have the knowledge concerning the matters at stake.

Moreover, Livy adds another story that sheds light on decision-making during battle, a facet that has repercussions on the ethical system when a war is fought. Having in mind the narrative about the last battle of Judah Maccabee (1 Maccabees 9), the reader may be interested in the following: "the consul added a speech in the vein of his address in Rome: 'There should be a single general in an army who foresees and plans what should be done, sometimes by himself, sometimes with the advisers he calls into council. Those who are not called into council should not air their own views publicly or privately.'" A soldier should be as strong and as nimble as possible and care for the good condition of his weapons as well as for the readiness of his food supply

> for unexpected orders. For the rest, he should realize that the immortal gods and his general are taking care of him. In an army in which the soldiers deliberate and the general is led about by the gossip of the rank and file, conditions are utterly unsound. For my part, I shall do the duty of a general—that is, see to it that you have an opportunity for successful action.

He adds that the soldier should do his duty "when the signal is given" and not be bothered about "what is going to happen" (44.34.1-5) (this and the following should be remembered concerning the role of opportunity in 1 Maccabees 9). And now comes a passage that enhances the approval and support of the rank and file: "After these

---

[26] See Polybius 29.1(1a) and Walbank (1979: 361-3).
[27] See for futile political discussions in private parties Livy 32.20.3.

instructions, he dismissed the assembly, while throughout the army even the veterans admitted that they, like raw recruits, had for the first time learned how military matters should be handled" (44.34.6). There was an immediate response in action:

> Soon you could have seen no one idle in the whole camp; some were sharpening swords, others were polishing helmets and cheek-pieces, still other shields and coats of mail; some were fitting their armor to their bodies and trying the nimbleness of their bodies under arms, others were brandishing spears, others fencing with their swords and inspecting the point; so that anyone could easily see that as soon as an opportunity of joining battle with the enemy had been given, they would put an end to the war either by a glorious victory or by a death that would go down in history. (44.34.8-9)[28]

This adherence to a disciplinary manual within the army was part and parcel of the concept of ethical behavior and was impossible to achieve were there no comprehensive code of behavior of the system in operation. Later, reminiscent of the words of Judah in ch. 9, and before the decisive battle of Cynoscephalae that ends the Third Macedonian War, he adds:

> from many vicissitudes of war I have learned when to fight and when to refuse battle. There is no time to instruct you while you are standing-to for battle as to the reasons why it is better to be inactive today. You shall ask for my reasoning at another time; now you will be satisfied to take the word of an experienced general. (44.36.13)

And indeed, later the consul adduces a long explanation for his decision to postpone the battle. He says, in reaction to criticism behind his back that he lost the opportunity for battle (*pugnandi occasionem*),[29] that the

> excellent young man, Publius Nasica, alone among all those who favored fighting yesterday disclosed his opinion to me; he too kept silent later, so that he may have seemed to have exchanged his view for mine. Certain others thought it better to criticize their general behind his back rather than to advise him openly. Both to you, Publius Nasica, and to any others who less openly shared your opinion, I shall not hesitate to give an accounting for having postponed the battle. For I am so far from regretting our inactivity yesterday that I believe I saved the army by so planning. That none of you may believe me to hold this opinion groundlessly, come let each, if he pleases, review with me how many factors weighed for the enemy and against us. First of all, of their great superiority in numbers I am sure that you were all previously aware, and that you took notice of it on seeing the battle-line drawn up yesterday. (44.38.1-4)

---

[28] For defeatism as opposed to courage see 1 Macc. 9:9-10.
[29] Livy 44.37; cf. Plutarch, *Aemilius Paulus* 17.

He goes on to mention the advantage of having "the good help of the gods" and clever planning of his strategy ending the speech with an, as it were, general truth: "camp is the shelter of the conqueror, the refuge of the conquered. How many armies meeting with none too favorable fortune in battle, after being driven within their rampart, have in their own good time, sometimes after only a moment, sallied forth and routed the victorious enemy?" (44.39.3-4). I have lingered on this episode being a background to my reference later to 1 Maccabees 9.

Be that as it may, the battle of Pydna was fought in 168 BCE and ended in a decisive victory for Rome. A new era was dawning in the Greek east, used to be called for several years the protectorate of Rome. The speech of Aemilius Paulus the victor of Pydna quoted here was held, my readers should keep in mind, only eight years before the speech of Judah before the decisive battle in which he was killed. Here it will suffice to say that whereas the Roman general knew when the opportune time was to attack the enemy, that was apparently larger in numbers, Judah Maccabee did discuss the matter with his soldiers who were against the immediate fight and complained about the larger numbers of the enemy, quite reminiscent of Aemilius Paulus's speech here. Yet because of his trust in God (the good help of the gods, in Paulus's words), Judah risked a battle in which he found his death while the Seleucids were victorious. For our case here it is important to emphasize that authority and an orderly and disciplined army with a clear hierarchy was a value in itself and a visible component in the value system of the organization of states. Rome's message was to have law and order in her empire, but still to be somewhat humble in appearance and not to bother her subjugated allies too much, the ethical system being the mechanism of her slide into dominance.

Liberty in the Aftermath of the Third Macedonian War

The war was over, and the diplomatic action at its height. I will not delve into the details but focus on remarks adduced from several quarters about the notion of liberty. My first example refers to a speech held by the consul to King Perseus who was now a hostage in Rome. He says in Greek:[30]

> If you had received the kingdom as a young man, I should indeed be less surprised that you were unaware how powerful the Roman People is as a friend or as an enemy. As it is, since you had a part in the war which your father waged with us, and since you were aware of the peace that followed, which we observed with the utmost faithfulness toward him, what reasoning led you to prefer war rather than peace with men whose power in war, whose good faith in peace, you had alike tested? … however that may be, whether it has occurred through human mistake or chance or law of nature, be of good cheer. The misfortunes of many kings and of

---

[30] 45.8. For a commentary on Livy Book 45 see Briscoe (2012: 609–765).

many peoples have shown that the mercy of the Roman People offers you not only hope, but an almost positive assurance of safety. (45.8.3-5)

Then the consul continued, this time in Latin to his staff:

You see before you a notable example of the changefulness of human affairs. I say this especially for you, young men. Therefore, it is proper to offer no insult or violence to anyone, while one is in favorable circumstances, and not to trust to one's present fortune, since no one knows what evening will bring. He will be truly a man, in a word, whose spirit is neither deflected from its course by the breath of prosperity, no broken by misfortune. (45.8.6-7)[31]

In the following, Livy adduces some useful information concerning inter-state ethics:

Although men were being sent of sufficient caliber to justify the hope that by their advice the generals would establish nothing unworthy of either the mercy or the high position of the Roman People, yet discussions went on in the senate too as to general considerations, so that the commissioners might carry from home to the generals a full outline of policy. First of all, it was voted that the Macedonians and Illyrians should be given their independence, so that it should be clear to all nations that the forces of the Roman People brought not slavery to free peoples, but on the contrary, freedom to the enslaved. The senate wished nations, which were free to consider that their freedom was assured and lasting under the protection of the Roman People, and that those who lived under kings should feel for the time being that their rulers were milder and more just under the eye of the Roman People (*sub tutela populi Romani esse*) and if at any time their kings should make war on the Roman People, that the outcome of the war would bring victory to the Romans, but freedom to themselves. (45.17.7-18.2)

It was also voted among other things that

fearing that if there were a common legislator for the nation, some relentless demagogue would turn the freedom given in healthy moderation into the license which brings ruin, the senate voted to divide Macedonia into four sections, so that each might have its own legislature. It was further resolved that Macedonia should pay to the Roman People half the taxes which they had been accustomed to pay to their kings. (45.18.6-7)

---

[31] To switch for a moment to another region we hear that after Antiochus IV's withdrawal from Egypt, caused by an ultimatum issued by the Romans in 170/169 BCE, the senate's reaction was that Antiochus did the "right and proper thing in obeying the envoys, and that the Roman senate and people were pleased." To Ptolemy and Cleopatra, king and queen of Egypt, the senate conveyed that it "was very happy if by its agency something good and beneficial had come to pass," accentuating that "the greatest bulwark of their reign was founded on the good faith of the Roman people" (45.13).

The full speech, which is not quoted here, enhances values such as mercy, healthy moderation, to be mild and just, power in war as against good faith in peace, safety, good and beneficial behavior; emotions such as insult, violence, happiness, being pleased, and so on are mentioned as well. He lingers on the notion of liberty and freedom in the international sphere, maintaining that safety that is granted by a superpower compensates for the loss of part of one's liberty and freedom. Hence when the Seleucids in the following years offer liberty to the subjugated Jewish state, it was in line with the Hellenistic notions of liberty and freedom which are reminiscent of the peace of Pydna. As a rule, the states that were subjugated to a super power in the Hellenistic period and were liberated by them were nevertheless susceptible to further intervention in their inner affairs by restrictions of their autonomy, namely, appointing leaders, extracting taxes, and putting garrisons within their cities for the sake of protection and safety. In Judea, as we will see in Part II, a section of the leading priesthood came to terms with this concept of liberty, whereas Judah and the freedom fighters wanted to achieve complete freedom without any token of servitude. Another important element, as we learn from the above settlement with Macedonia, was the preference of the super power of "good faith in peace" on "power in war." The empire usually wanted to keep the stability in subjugated states rather than their turn to *stasis*, unless there was a benefit to be found in split and revolution within states.[32]

Among other embassies that arrived in Rome in the aftermath of the battle of Pydna, the Rhodians uttered the following speech in the senate, of which I adduce only the *ratio decidendi* (23):

> The rewards which we received from you after the conquest of Philip and of Antiochus were most abundant. If the good fortune which is now yours by the grace of the gods and because of your valor had fallen to Perseus, and we had come to Macedonia to seek a reward from the victorious king, what pray would we say? That we had aided him with money or with grain, with forces on land or on sea? What fortress had we held? Where had we fought either under his commanders or by ourselves? If he asked where there had been a soldier of ours, or where a ship, within his lines, what in the world would be our answer? Perhaps we should be defending ourselves before the conqueror, as now we are before you. For the result we obtained by sending envoys to both parties concerning peace was that we won no favor from either side, but incurred even accusation and danger from one of them. Yet Perseus might truly reproach us, as you cannot, gentlemen of the senate, because we sent to you at the beginning of the war envoys to promise you whatever was needed for the war; we would be ready, we said, as in the former wars, with ships, arms, and young men for every demand. The obstacle to our furnishing these things was of your making, since you for whatever reason spurned our aid at that time. Neither therefore have we in any way acted as enemies, nor have we failed in the duty of good allies, but we were prevented from performing that duty by you. (45.23.1-6)

---

[32] Schmitt (1969) unfortunately reaches only the year 200 BCE.

He goes on proposing "to separate the defence of the state from the guilt of private citizens" (45.23.7) and adds that there is no state which will not have only wicked citizens at certain times but an inexperienced commonalty always. He refers to a struggle within Rome, alluding most probably to the one between patricians and plebeians, saying: "even in your city I hear that there have been those who pursued ill-gotten gain by toadying to the mob, and that at certain times the commons seceded from you and you lost control of the commonwealth" (45.23.8-9). If, he says, this could happen in a disciplined state as Rome, no wonder that some individuals in Rhodes incited the people to support the Macedonians, whereas the "good element" of the leadership favored the Roman alliance (45.30.1, 23-24). However, the pro-Macedonians "wrought no harm beyond slackness in our loyalty as friends." As for the "serious charge" against Rhodes that the state sent embassies to negotiate peace to both warring states, Macedonia and Rome, "in spite of this error, whether it should be called arrogance or folly, was no different before you from what it was before Perseus." And now comes a general truth adduced by the Rhodian ambassador: "The character of states is like that of individual men; some nations are hot-tempered, some bold, some diffident, some over-indulgent in wine, others in sex. The people of Athens, report has it, is quick and bold beyond its strength in adventure, the Spartan hesitant and hardly undertaking matters of which it is sure" (45.23.10-15).[33] He continues saying that

> I would not deny that all the region of Asia breeds somewhat flighty temperaments, and that our rhetoric is rather inflated because we might seem to be outstanding among the states in our area—a position due precisely not to our own powers but to your favors and your choice of us. Enough punishment was meted out to the embassy on the spot and to their faces, when they were sent away with so grim an answer from you. But if at that time they paid too small a penalty of disgrace, certainly the present embassy, so pitiable and so humble, would be atonement [a sin-offering, as if to gods, Loeb, Livy vol. XIII, p. 324] great enough for an even more arrogant embassy than that other one was. Arrogance, especially of speech, is hated by the hot-tempered, but laughed at by the wise, especially if directed by an inferior against his superior; no one has ever thought it worthy of the death-penalty. There was danger, to be sure, that the Rhodians should despise the Romans! Even the gods are assailed by some with overbold language, but we have never heard that any one has on that account been struck by a thunderbolt. (45.23.16-19)

In the continuation of the speech of the Rhodian, some important inter-state values emerge, some of them I will mention now. After mentioning appraisals done by the senate concerning damages caused by the Rhodians he utters the following:

> Some believe, gentlemen of the senate, that we favored the king and preferred that he should win, and that therefore we should be punished by armed force; others

---

[33] Cf. Thucydides 1.70-71.

of you feel that we did, to be sure, have this desire, but that we should not on that account be punished by armed force, for, they say, there is no provision in the law, written or unwritten, of any state that he who desires the death of his enemy, but does nothing to bring it about, shall incur capital punishment. To these men who free us of the penalty, but not of the guilt, we are indeed grateful. (45.24.2-4)

At the end of this wonderful speech that would shed light on so many aspects of the relationship of the Hasmoneans with the active empires of the region, the Rhodian adduces the terms that the Rhodians set for themselves:

> If we all have willed that of which we are accused—we do not separate the will from the deed—let us all suffer the penalty; but if some of our leaders favored you, and others the king, I do not ask that because of us who sided with you the partisans of the king should be untouched; I merely beg that we may not perish because of them. You are no more hostile to them than is our state itself, and because they knew this, many of them have either fled or committed suicide; others who have been found guilty by us will be placed in your hands, gentlemen of the senate. The rest of us at Rhodes have no more deserved punishment during this war than we have deserved gratitude, either. Let the store of our previous helpful acts make good the present omission of service. (45.24.4-7)[34]

In this last speech we have received a high-resolution picture of a divide that did not turn into a revolution in any significant Hellenistic state. This divide was triggered by the issue of loyalty when a choice had to be made between two empires in conflict. Such divides were frequent and will be tackled in Part II when the rift in the rising Hasmonean state will be discussed. Rifts in subjugated states and cities affected the individual units of the system and their relationship with the leading empire. The passage just quoted is loaded with politically charged ethical terms and expressions that

---

[34] For those readers who are interested, here is the end of this important speech:

> As you have waged wars against three kings during these years; let not our slackness in one war be, to our hurt, of more importance than the fact that we fought on your side in two wars. Take account of Philip, Antiochus, and Perseus as if of the vote of three judges; two acquit us, the third is undecided: suppose that it is for our condemnation; even so, if the Kings were judging us, we should indeed lose our case, but your judgment, gentlemen of the senate, determines whether Rhodes shall exist on earth or shall be destroyed root and branch. For you are not deliberating about war, ... you can declare it, but you cannot wage it, for not a man of Rhodes will bear arms against you. If you will not abate your wrath, we shall ask of you time in which to report home on this fatal mission; every free person, every man and every woman of us in Rhodes will embark on ships with all our money and, abandoning our homes and our altars, will come to Rome; we will heap up in the assembly ground and in the entry of your senate-house all our gold and our silver, whether owned by the state or its citizens, and will put our persons and those of our wives and children in your power, that we may suffer here whatever we must suffer; far from our sight be the plundering and burning of our city. The Romans may judge that the Rhodians are enemies, but they cannot make them so. For we have also in us the power of passing judgment on ourselves, and we shall never adjudge ourselves your enemies, nor commit any act of hostility, though we suffer the utmost disaster. (45.24.8-14)

were part and parcel of our restored manual of the value system (and its adjacent anti-values). Since the passage is an easy read and speaks for itself, I will just mention some principles of conduct, such as inter-state faithfulness and loyalty, tolerance concerning errors made by states, mercy that offers hope, assurance of safety, wisdom endowed in a state which bypasses dangerous changes and bad omens, insult and violence as against trust of one's present fortune, wrong and right conduct in international affairs.[35] In short, the remark of the Rhodian speaker that states have characters similar to human beings actually manifests yet again that feelings and thoughts as well as values and characteristics as well as the interaction between them built in human beings should be applied to the relationships between states.[36]

Let us now move directly to the settlement that concluded the Third Macedonian War. Livy extensively adduces the terms, and those are important for our case since some of the components of the settlement can help us explain some of the concessions mentioned in letters in 1-2 Maccabees. Hellenistic rulers, through their contacts with Rome, apparently learned a great deal about inter-state affairs in general and their ethics in particular. Naturally, values in an inter-state virtual ethical code pop up in settlements between nations. The terms in our case were concocted with the advice of his council by the victor of Pydna, Aemilius Paulus who announced in Latin the decisions of the senate "as well as his own." The announcement was translated into Greek and "repeated by Gnaeus Octavius the praetor—for he too was present."

The relevant terms (for our discussion here) were the following: first and foremost, the Macedonians were given their freedom; they were to keep their own cities and lands,

---

[35] Some more: States have characters like individuals and can be apt to be pleased and happy (value of happiness), good faith of a state, compassion and high position of a state, independence, no slavery to free people but freedom to the enslaved, freedom assured under protection of a super power, kings being more just and milder under the eye of the empire (value of acceptance of one's authority on the international scene), economic intervention of empire hampers the freedom of an ally (this aspect is enhanced in 1 Maccabees in several instances), conspiracy and strife as anti-values in international relations (pending who is judging), healthy moderation in policy, abundancy of reward as payment for favors, grace of gods is good fortune, favors granted by states, to be prevented of performing a stately duty (namely in relations between states, omission as value), a state takes offence, separation of defense of the state from the guilt of private citizens of that state, wickedness of certain citizens (for instance, the mob) influences inter-state relations, in states with disciplined character the commons can be led astray (which has an effect on the state's encounters with other states; values of discipline as opposed to anti-values such as disorder and negligence in a state which has repercussions on its foreign policy), another anti-value: slackness of loyalty by some in a city can destroy a good relationship with super power (important for Part II in reference to the Maccabees), arrogance and folly as well as choices made by states are effective in inter-state relations, contempt is a characteristic of a state that hampers inter-state relationships, appraisal of damage made for unexpected desire (accountability on the international scene), guilt of state, grateful for favor and pardon.

[36] For yet another interpretation of liberty, namely, to be completely free in Asia, see Livy 45.25, who relates that:

> about the same time the Caunians revolted from them (Rhodes), and Mylassa seized the towns of the Euromenes. The spirit of Rhodes was not so broken that they did not perceive that if Lycia and Caria were taken away by the Romans, and the rest of their possessions either freed themselves by revolt or were seized by their neighbors, they would be hemmed in by the shores of a small island of infertile soil, which could by no means support the population of so large a city. Troops were therefore promptly sent and the Caunians compelled to accept their rule, even though forces of Cibyra were called in by the Caunians. (45.25.11-13)

to use their own laws, and to elect annual magistrates (comparable to the Seleucids who bargained with the Hasmoneans on liberty, autonomous law, and appointment of magistrates). They were to pay to the Roman people half the tax "which they had paid to their kings."[37] Macedonia was to be divided into four regions with four different capitals (*capita regionum*) where their assemblies were to meet. Moreover, "it had been decided that no one should be allowed the right of marriage or of trading in land or buildings outside the bounds of his own region." The mines of iron and copper were allowed to be used, whereas the ones of gold and silver were not. "The tax on those who worked the mines was set at half what they had paid to the king." The use of imported salt was banned (perhaps as a further ban on frequent communication between the regions). Aemilius Paulus also declared that "freedom was being given to all those who had been subjects of Perseus" (45.29.4-12). The latter refused them the region of Paeonia but granted them the right to import salt. While reading this passage my reader should bear in mind proposals and settlements of the Seleucids, for instance, the one adduced in 1 Maccabees 10. Furthermore, Paulus "ordered the third region [of the four regions of Macedonia] to carry salt to Stobi in Paeonia, and he set a price on it." In contradistinction, he forbade the Macedonians to cut ship-timbers or to permit others to do so. "The regions which bordered on barbarians—and this was true of all except the third—were allowed to have armed guards along their frontiers" (45.29.13-14). These arrangements which were announced on the first day of the gathering aroused mixed emotions:

> The unexpected grant of freedom cheered men, as well as the lightening of the annual taxation (compare for instance in 1 Maccabees 11-12, the letter of Demetrius II on cutting taxes); but to those who were cut off from trading between regions, their country seemed as mangled as an animal disjoined into parts, each of which needed the other; so unaware were the Macedonians themselves of the size of Macedonia, of how it lent itself to division, and of how self-sufficient each part was. (45.30.1-2)

Even in such circumstances the victor makes a settlement that is not devoid of ethical considerations. Not just Roman interests were at stake, but also the obligation that the Romans felt toward the Greeks with whom they still were partners in the very same ethical system. Later in the charter for Macedonia (45.31), Aemilius Paulus declared that "he would also lay down a law-code (*leges*)" since the Macedonians were to "use their own laws" (45.31.1 and above, 29.4). Then the Aetolians were summoned who "raised to an unbearable pitch of pride the spirits of those in all the states and peoples of Greece who sided with the Romans, and crushed helplessly under their feet any who were in some respect tainted by suspicion of having favored the king" (45.31.3). Livy finds here the opportunity to classify the leaders in Greece (31). This mention is important for our case since leaders, as I have already mentioned, were those who frequently were the chief communicators of foreign affairs; their characters

---

[37] See also Plutarch, *Aemilius Paulus* 28.

and position as well as their adherence to the international code of conduct reflected on the inter-state value system:

> There were three sorts of leaders in the states, two groups who by fawning upon the Roman power and the friendship of kings respectively gained personal wealth for themselves by tyrannizing over their cities; the middle group alone, opposing both the others, strove to guard independence and constitutionality. Their reward was greater affection from their own people, and less favor in foreign quarters. Carried along on the tide of Roman success, the members of the pro-Roman party were then alone occupying all magistracies and serving as envoys. These gathered in great numbers both from the Peloponnesus and Boeotia and the other leagues of Greece, and filled the ears of the ten commissioners, saying that not only those who out of vanity openly boasted themselves guests and friends of Perseus, but many more who kept under cover, had sided with the king, and under the guise of preserving independence they had turned the whole organization of the league meetings against the Roman interest; these peoples, said their representatives, would not maintain loyalty unless the spirit of the opposition was crushed and the prestige sustained and strengthened of those who had no object in view but the power of Rome. (45.31.4-8)[38]

For our case here it is sufficient to say that the middle-of-the-road party actually wished to have full independence of the state, its citizens, and constitution. We shall see that the Hellenists in Judea at approximately the same time can be compared to the pro-king group in the states of Greece and its leagues, whereas the group of Judah Maccabee can be equated with the group that wished to keep full independence. The Jews in Palestine were not very different from all others in the Hellenistic cities concerning their relations with the dominant powers of the region.

Rome managed to settle the affairs of Greece after the battle of Pydna in 168 BCE and a tight Roman protectorate on the Greek world started.[39] The remark of Livy concerning the settlement of the victorious Romans is enlightening: Aemilius Paulus "laid down laws for Macedonia with such care as to seem to be giving them not to conquered enemies, but to well-deserving allies—laws which not even experience over a long period, the one best amender of legislation, could prove faulty in actual use." With this assessment of a Roman general in mind, I will end Part I of my book, not before I comment on the last paragraph. In 168 BCE one of the two empires competing for influence and rule over the Greek world east of the Italian peninsula was crushed. This left the door open for the Roman protectorate. The ethical system which the Greeks experienced since 211 BCE would not be the same anymore. The ethical inter-state system that was the glue that connected Rome with the Greek states to her east

---

[38] Polybius 30.6 names three groups, but only of those accused of being anti-Roman; his first group, corresponding to Livy's third, or middle-of-the-road group, wanted the status quo undisturbed; the second wanted a decisive contest between Rome and Perseus, with victory for Perseus; the third group shared the sentiments of the second, and in addition was able to draw their states into open alliance with Perseus (see note in Loeb vol. XIII, pp. 354–5).

[39] Polybius 30.13 (10) and Walbank (1979: 434–7); Livy 45.31.

was abused through her own management; the system lost most of its validity until it finally crumbled when the total Roman conquest of Greece became a fait accompli in 146 BCE. Yet, if we regard all the passages quoted above as one block of knowledge, we can deduce that Livy memorialized a Hellenistic inter-state manual of conduct for generations to come.

Part II

Ethical Climate, Patterns of Behavior, and the Emergence of the Jewish State

Introduction

Several patterns of conduct and Graeco-Roman values imbued in inter-state relations have been portrayed in Part I. To mention only some: mutual respect between states, reciprocity of gifts and other commodities, loyalty between states and breach of faith, suicidal acts of citizens as a token of heroism during oppression, inter-state honor and etiquette, respect and honor given to ancestral territories, attempts to make peace and avoid war by dialogue and listening to one another's claims, respect and gratitude to gods who represent values of the international by all accepted value system, respect of war rules during conflicts and the obligation to declare wars, the collecting of the dead after battle, and the like. Also, tolerance and politeness toward the defeated in war (as against annihilation of states or part of them by an angry foe), keeping justice and fair play in inter-state relations, respect for a state's liberty and autonomy under its laws, taking responsibility for the state's aggression by the willingness to compensate and pay indemnities, respect for temples and gods of other states without trespassing their threshold with foreign deities and entering them against the will of the worshippers, and rulers of empires are expected to be benevolent toward their subject citizens in occupied states, namely the good king publicizes his own ethical code and as a result plays an important role in the inter-state relationships. Those and others will be discussed now with regard to the relationship of the Seleucids with the Hasmonean state. Whereas the book of 1 Maccabees emphasizes patterns of conduct, 2 Maccabees enhances the ethical.

In the following I will also touch upon the issue of the interactions between values, characteristics, and emotions, elsewhere defined as a triangle imbued in societies, states, and empires. Emotions that I mentioned above are, for instance, anger, frustration, love, affection, stubbornness. Characteristics that we came across in my survey in Part I are territoriality, divide, unity, imitation, and hierarchy, while the values that were mentioned are respect, compassion, responsibility, and so on. My first source is 1 Maccabees.

5

The Hasmonean State as a Test Case for Patterns of Relationship between Empire and Subject State—the Book of 1 Maccabees

I have written extensively on 1 Maccabees and will not delve here into the historiographic and political theology of this important book.[1] Yet I will briefly focus on an important theme that recurs throughout its narrative, namely, the relationship of the Seleucids with Judea, a subjugated state within the Seleucid empire in which a revolution broke out by one sector of the society. The conclusion that I will reach at the end of the chapter is that in terms of patterns of conduct in relationships between empire and subject state, Judea was treated in line with the familiar patterns of conduct pertaining in the Hellenistic world that I described in Part I. Let us summarize some of the more important patterns of inter-state relationship that I mentioned above and concentrate on Seleucid considerations when they tackled the Jewish problem.

1. Empires of the Hellenistic world as well as individual states (including Rome) strove for territorial acquisitions and conquered or just held territories with and/or without (legal or other) justifications.
2. Empires and individual subject states constantly exploited divides within other states and cities. Inner divisions helped subjugate and even conquer states and cities. Yet, naturally their interest was to rule as many states and cities that showed faithfulness with harmonious ancestral constitutions.
3. Empires in the Hellenistic world during the time span I discuss here ruled with the support of reliable leaders and privileged classes in the subject cities and states, and fought the wayward ones who did not accommodate with their rule.
4. All Hellenistic powers honored holy places and local temples up to a certain degree. They became confrontative concerning local temples when they had a roving eye for treasures deposited in the temples, in particular during war when they made frequent attempts to rob them.
5. Hellenistic rulers were reluctant to send whole armies to fight in local wars in their provinces. Usually only a section of the army was sent (except for the really big fights between whole armies such as the battles of Cynoscephalae and

---

[1] See Mendels (2013, 2021).

Raphiah). As said, these troops frequently invaded the subject city or state in order to support one (faithful) section against another.
6. Everywhere the Hellenistic powers created their networks in particular by etiquette, economic support, and value sharing (reciprocity in granting honor). Their interests were guarded by garrisons that they kept in subject cities and states, seen by many as guardians of the order, not necessarily of hostile intention of the ruling power. Even Romans had garrisons here and there, although this was not their overall strategy.
7. Hellenistic rulers did not hamper local institutions of self-rule, democratic or autocratic as long as those did not challenge their own rule; on the contrary, as long as there existed a harmonious relationship between empire and subject states, they supported and even encouraged their autonomy. Such a situation became the manifestation of the Hellenistic sort of liberty.
8. An important facet of the relationships between Hellenistic rulers and their subject states (the Roman Republic included) was the praise of the former's conduct. This was achieved through speeches, obituaries, and letters of the kings themselves. Comments of that nature concerning the good (and bad) king are not just propaganda of the kings themselves (who probably did not always need it) but a sincere way of thinking about rulers initiated by those who revered them.
9. Ruling empires including Rome were keen on achieving peace and harmony within their empire. Hence many territorial and other financial settlements were concluded between empire and subject state. This required usually good behavior on the part of the subject state or city.[2]

The attentive reader will discover in the following survey of my history of Seleucid conduct toward the Hasmoneans that the latter's patterns of conduct were not exceptional toward the Jews and were in line with their conduct toward their subjects elsewhere. I am not going to make here detailed comparisons that will cause a great deal of repetitions with the narrative of Part I. For the attentive reader the background portrayed in Part I will suffice when reading the survey here, where and how patterns of behavior emerge from our text. Also, my survey concerning Maccabees 1 will be concise since some of the issues that will be discussed I tackled elsewhere in detail.[3]

In the first section of the book of 1 Maccabees we learn that the Seleucids were the dominating power that ruled Judea. We also learn that Jewish society suffered at that time from a split caused by imitation of Greek customs mainly by the aristocracy of Judea, as against the resistance of its populace, to put it schematically. As we have already seen above, divisions of that sort (populace against the more well-to-do to the city/state) were common in the Hellenistic world and were exploited by the empires active

---

[2] As already mentioned, the Romans later even created a sophisticated hierarchy of cities and states (Badian 1958, Gruen 1984). The book of 1 Maccabees adduces several such settlements that consist of concessions, territorial and financial (tax relief and contribution of money to the Temple). I will not go into the, mostly technical, details of such concessions but refer to them as part and parcel of a common policy of Hellenistic empires, being common patterns of conduct.
[3] Mendels (2013).

in the region. When one power happened to support the aristocracy, the other hurried either to split the aristocracy or to support the lower classes, at least by the spread of "communistic" slogans. In the case of the Hasmoneans the Seleucids endorsed the upper level of the society, which showed a willingness to be Hellenized. The Hellenized leaders went back and forth to the king as did other leaders in the Hellenistic world who had contacts with central governments of empires. They smeared each other at court, a common habit among leaders at that time who wished to benefit from their connections, and accommodated with etiquette such as carrying gifts to the king and bribing his administration. On the other hand, when the Seleucid king went down to fight Egypt, he, on his way back, robbed the Jerusalem Temple, a regular procedure of Hellenistic kings who desperately needed money for their own maintenance and the many wars they fought. This warlike motivation was embedded in Hellenistic empires at that time. The eagerness for the collection of taxes as well as the putting of Seleucid soldiers in the citadel in Jerusalem—procedures well known from the Hellenistic world elsewhere—are described with dark hues by the narrator of 1 Maccabees. He also presents with emphasis an edict of the king which declared the abrogation of ancestral constitutions in his realm, Jews included. As a result of this, a conflict ensued between the subjugated state of Judea and the Seleucid empire. At first it was a fight on maintaining the ancestral constitution. To keep one's ancestral laws was usually a bonus given by Hellenistic rulers to support subject cities and states that show good behavior. The confrontation about this is described vividly by the author in chapter 1:41-64. The restrictions put on Jews to adhere to their ancestral constitution—a common procedure in the Hellenistic world—widened the gap between the two sections of Jewish society: "Many of the people, who were ready to forsake the Law, joined them and did evil in the land, and forced Israel into all the secret hiding-places of fugitives" (52–3). The erection of a statue in the Jerusalem Temple was not just a humiliating act that went against the Jewish ancestral laws but also problematic in terms of trespassing Jewish sovereignty, as we have already encountered in Part I. However painful these acts were for the Jews, seen from their point of view, the Seleucids could not put up with a situation in which a subject state whose ancestral laws were opposed to their own laws and habits would continue to adhere to these very laws. The issue of autonomy concerning a state's laws was high up on the agenda in the Hellenistic world as we have encountered in Part I. In short, seen from the perspective of the ruling empire, in this case the Seleucids, nothing unusual in its relationship with a subject state can be noticed. From the standpoint of the Seleucid ruler, it was not an anti-Jewish stance that brought about the conflict but the fact that the Jews continued to adhere to their ancestral constitution which was, like in many other places in the empire, abrogated by the empire (and could be restored only by the super power itself). Obviously enough, 1 Maccabees was broadcasting an interpretation of the events enhancing the stance of the more "orthodox" and nationalistic segment of the Jewish population. The more liberal streak comes to the fore during the narrative when the Hasmonean family itself relaxes its relationship with the surrounding world. Be that as it may, when we leave out many of the negative expressions and terms that were used by the narrator to promote the agony of the suffering Jews, the Seleucid behavior clearly emerges and is definitely in line with their conduct toward subject states elsewhere, and perhaps even more lenient since they agreed to a continuous dialogue between the Jewish leaders and themselves (unlike, for instance, the case of Abydus, in Part I).

Since the Seleucids realized that the local Jewish ancestral constitution had ordinances that the Jews would never give up under any circumstances, they exploited this for granting concessions from time to time in order to convince their subjects to stay loyal or to punish them with all kinds of partial bans. They definitely were not experts in Jewish law and knew that some of the Jews and especially some of their High Priests who were considered as their leaders endorsed Hellenic culture, and hence (wrongly) assumed that it would be easy to convert the other sector of adherent Jews as well. It has to be emphasized that the edict of the Seleucid king, according to the narrator of 1 Maccabees, demanded all the nations of the kingdom to relinquish their own laws but does not specify that everyone has to become Hellenized. So why did his representatives in Palestine force Mattathias, who was seen by them as a leader of the Jewish people, to sacrifice to a pagan god (perhaps to the bust of King Antiochus IV)? They even offered, as Hellenistic etiquette subscribed, to Mattathias and his sons gifts and offices at the Seleucid court. On the part of the Seleucids this was a measure for measure act, not driven by a religious motive. Namely, part of the Jews refused to accommodate with the order of the super power to abrogate their own laws, some of which prohibited them to worship statues and accept foreign deities. Hence the Seleucid representatives focused on this particular issue and behaved accordingly. The demands were bluntly rejected by Mattathias and if this was not enough, Mattathias killed a Jew who started to sacrifice to a foreign god.[4] This increased the tension and Mattathias and his followers became even more aggressive. We have encountered such a behavior against a ruling empire in Boeotia. The more the Romans pressed the Boeotians the more widespread and aggressive the latter's resistance became. Thus, the answer of Mattathias concerning the ancestral constitution of the city could have been uttered by any leader in the Hellenistic sphere:

> Though all the nations (*ethne*) within the bounds of the royal domain obey him, and each one forsake the worship of his fathers, and show preference for his commands, yet will I, my sons and my brothers walk in the covenant of our fathers (*diatheke pateron hemon*). Far be it from us to forsake the Law and the testaments. We will not listen to the decree of the king by going astray from our worship, either to the right or to the left. (1 Macc. 2:19-22)

As said, for the Seleucids a breach of the word of the king concerning a city's ancestral constitution constituted a justification to fight it.

The theme to be mentioned now is the communal suicide when facing a fierce enemy and its ethical background. As in the case of Abydus discussed in Part I, the choice between suicidal behavior of a group and fighting the enemy, the narrator of 1 Maccabees enhanced this topic as well. In face of the belligerent Seleucids, one group of Jews decided on a collective suicidal act whereas another group led by Mattathias

---

[4] Cf. Mendels (2013: 94–104).

the father of the Hasmonean family decided to fight back even on the Sabbath.[5] Some Jews, like citizens of Abydus during Macedonia's siege on their city, just escaped "to the nations to save themselves" (44). This reaction is defined by the narrator of 1 Maccabees as a war on "justice" and "judgment" (v. 29), terms used by speakers in various confrontations in the Hellenistic world discussed in Part I.

Then comes the deathbed speech of Mattathias that adduces a limited list of universal Hellenistic values that are meant to be a compass for the right behavior by his sons henceforward. The values mentioned are linked to the ancient heroes of the Jewish nation (linking of values and deeds to ancient heroes of nations was quite common in the Hellenistic era).[6] Some of these values will be followed later by the Hasmonean brothers, others will not. The values that are mentioned, familiar to us from the Hellenistic world, include zealousness for keeping the state's autonomous laws even in times of distress (Joseph), heroism, great glory and eternal renown, faithfulness and righteousness, and so on. These values, universalistic in nature, were the bread and butter of the Hellenistic inter-state code mentioned above. In the rest of the chapter Mattathias settles the succession of the leadership of the rebelling forces; this independent act of a rebellious sector of a state (as against the official rulers that were appointed and supported by the empire) was, as in many other cases examined in Part I, a good reason for the Seleucids to send forces to fight—what they understood— as a rebellion. The story here is told, as many of Livy's stories are, not with an attempt to be impartial but from the point of view of the rebels who fight against a hostile empire (which was not seen so by the ruling priestly sector of the Jewish population, who looked at their rivals as pure rebels). This reaction of the ruling empire was not exceptional and can be seen as a normal procedure in similar cases elsewhere in the empire. In the Jewish case the empire is a bit more patient than in other severe cases, such as the one of Abydus that I mentioned in Part I.

Three comments are in order: first, the army of the local rebel, Judah, is complaining: "How can we, so few in number, be able to fight against so great a multitude? Then too, we are faint, for we have had nothing to eat today" (3:17). Judah replied: "It is an easy thing for many to be hemmed in by the hands of a few. There is no difference in the sight of Heaven to save by many or by few. Victory in battle does not depend on the size of the enemy, but rather on strength that comes from Heaven" (18-20). The battle was fought and Judah and his army were victorious. Such a dialogue before and during battles between soldiers and leaders was typical also in the Hellenistic world. Second, a story is intertwined in the narrative about the unsuccessful attempt of the Seleucid king to rob the temple in Persia (6:1-4). Having in mind the robbery by the king's forces in the Temple of Jerusalem, this example of the failure in a temple in Persia shows how common this procedure was in the conduct of Hellenistic kings; in contradistinction, his attack on the Jerusalem temple was successful. Was this mention of the narrator some sort of criticism against the Hasmonean force who could not fight and/or avoid this robbery? Third, during the Seleucid invasion to suppress what was seen in Seleucid eyes as a common upheaval of a state in their realm, the Jews convened

---

[5] 1 Macc. 2:31-41; Mendels (2013).
[6] Sulimani (2011).

opposite their capital Jerusalem for a consultation. It seems that the conference at Mizpeh of the Jewish fighting forces was basically a religious affair with strong ritual hues as a result of the priests being sad and humiliated because of their temple being trodden down and profaned (3:50-51). These and other complaints correspond with similar complaints by other states at that time (Athens and the Acarnanians). It enhanced the motif of complete destruction of a nation (v. 52), a motif of fear that was quite common in the Hellenistic world during wars. Its frequent use points to a use of a topos, yet everybody in the Hellenistic world knew that the Seleucids could act quite fiercely against those who were mutinous. The conference ends with the sound of trumpets and shouts with a loud voice, probably to awaken God. But God does not react (part of the political theology of the book). As a follow-up of this conference Judah, the national leader, creates a local army of the rebels. An independent army of a sector within a subject state—without the permission given by the ruling empire—was anathema for its rulers. Hence the reaction of the Seleucid army came soon (4:1-35). The description of the battles henceforward is reminiscent of local battles with ruling empires elsewhere in the time span under discussion here. The fighting forces are defined as *ethne* (peoples or nations), quite a neutral term in narratives of that time. I should emphasize that tactical military actions of the Seleucids concerning Judea that they used elsewhere are beyond my expertise and will not be discussed. Yet some of the occasional references to ethical conduct will be mentioned. One that we find in ch. 4 is of particular interest.

Some values and patterns of behavior should be highlighted: Reminding the fighting forces of great events and heroes from the past was common in the Hellenistic world and not unique to the Jews (4:9); refraining from taking booty during a battle is one of those rules that can be found in the emerging virtual ethical code of the Hellenistic era (temperance as against greediness). Judah says to his army (4:17-18): "Do not be greedy for spoil, because there is a battle before us, … take your stand now against our enemy, and join battle with them and after that take the spoil without fear." The purification of the Jerusalem Temple in the second part of ch. 4 is in line with purity habits in other temples in the region. Here it is performed by Judah and his army without the support, financial and political, of the ruling empire, which was sometimes happy to grant support.[7] Financial support initiated by a Hellenistic king, as we encountered in the case of the Jerusalem Temple and other temples in the Hellenistic sphere, is not just help for the sake of help but a token that the ruling power dominates one's temple by supporting its building, renovation, and worship. This is why we see that the empire and its ruler, the king, have a great interest to do these beneficiary acts when temples are concerned. Temples and gifting have some elements of etiquette in common as we will see yet again in the following.

In local wars between nations and states within the empire, central governments did not usually show much interest unless it concerned their interests and safety. Hence in the war of the Jews in the Bashan and the Galilee it seems that neither

---

[7] Lysimachia, and as they did in the case of the Jerusalem Temple several times – see the edict of Antiochus III to the Jews in 200 BCE (mentioned by Josephus, *Ant.* 12.138-146, the same Antiochus who invaded Greece).

the *ethne* nor the Jews asked for or awaited Seleucid intervention (ch. 5). Another example: the Seleucid garrison in the Jerusalem Citadel as well as a section of the Seleucid army that was stationed in Jamnia hardly intervened in the local wars between the Jews and the local *ethne*. Yet when this same Seleucid garrison was challenged by the Jews later in the story it reacted fiercely and left two thousand Jews dead on the battlefield (5:58-68). I will examine here some of the examples of Hellenistic kings' intervention in local warfare and what their conduct was like. That the Jews have become an international factor in the region according to the narrator of 5:63-64 is interesting from our point of view. It was important to him to emphasize the participation and acknowledgment of the emerging Jewish entity among the states in the region: "This man Judah and his brothers were highly *esteemed* in all Israel and among all nations wherever their name was mentioned, and people gathered around them to extol them." This, perhaps wishful, comment of the narrator expresses the importance he saw in the valuable acknowledgment they received for their participation in inter-state relationships.

From the narratives that we have examined in Part I we could already conclude that Hellenistic kings were in many instances the driving force behind the keeping and/or abusing of the virtual inter-state ethical code. They are even the embodiment of the expectations that humans positioned in their leaders concerning stately and communal ethical behavior. From their deeds (good and bad), we can get a satisfactory picture about ethical codes of behavior. Hence the *peri basileias* compositions that described in detail the ethical behavior of the ideal king were quite popular. I have dealt with such documents in the past and mentioned them in Part I and will not repeat my ideas here.[8] This bring me to 1 Maccabees 6 where the dying Antiochus IV is depicted as a typical Hellenistic king who is punished for his hubris. On his deathbed he appoints his successor. Dying kings caused some awe among publics at that time and several examples concerning their death spring to mind (Attalus mentioned above). Antiochus IV is first and foremost presented as an example of a king's failure to rob a temple in Persia (seen as a bad habit of Hellenistic kings). In 6:5-8 we hear first about a normal procedure of Hellenistic kings in their treatment of subject territories. There is not much Jewish about it (the abomination we find elsewhere is differently told): When he still was in Persia

> someone came to announce to him in Persia that the expeditions that had marched into the land of Judah had been put to flight. That Lysias, heading a strong force, had been put to flight before them; that they had become strong because of the arms, material and much spoil which they took from the armies which they had destroyed; that they had pulled down the abomination which he had constructed on the altar in Jerusalem; and that they had surrounded the sanctuary with high walls, as it had been before, and also his city Beth Zur. When the king heard this news, he was struck with amazement and greatly shaken.

---

[8] See Mendels (1998: 324-33).

As a consequence, he is struck by an illness from which he does not recover. This passage is interesting from our point of view since the description shows a normal situation of retreat by a Seleucid general yet the king takes it to heart very seriously. He admits that his terrible physical and spiritual state was a result of robbing the Jerusalem Temple and sending forth to destroy the inhabitants of Judah "for no reason." In other words, we get here a lesson in universal inter-state ethics, namely, a Hellenistic king should refrain from robbing temples and destroying people for no reason. This entire passage that adduces the bad conduct of a king of an enormous empire who dies because of this can be seen as a sharp criticism on behalf of the narrator of the nonethical behavior of Hellenistic kings toward their subject states. This moral can be added to lessons of this sort that we have already encountered in the text of Livy.

We should now linger on a passage that tells us about occurrences that did happen and could happen time and again in relationships between empire and its subject state. It deals with one sector in a state that fights the garrison put there by the ruling empire, whereas the other party seeks peace. The latter even sends to the king of the empire to ask for help against their brethren. There is nothing Jewish in this passage and it reflects the conduct and reactions of the ruling empire that we have encountered elsewhere in Part I:

> Now the garrison in the citadel kept hemming Israel in around the sanctuary, seeking to do damage continually and lending support to the nations. Judah made up his mind to destroy them (this corresponds with the threat of annihilation that the Jews and other nations constantly feared), and he called all the people together to besiege them. They assembled and laid siege to it in the one hundred and fiftieth year, and he built batteries of warlike engines and missile throwers. Some of them escaped from the blockade, and some of the godless of Israel joined them. They went to the king, and complained: "How long will you neglect to do justice and avenge our brothers? We were content to serve your father, and to walk in accordance with his orders and to follow his commands. Because of this, our people have become estranged from us and have laid siege to the citadel. Besides, as many of us as they find they put to death, and seize our possessions. Not only have they stretched forth their hand against us, but also against all our borders. Why this very day they have besieged the citadel in Jerusalem, to take it over, and they have fortified the sanctuary and Beth Zur. Unless you stop them at once, they will do more than this, and you will not be able to check them." (6:18-27)

For the Seleucids this situation and these complaints by one sector of a subject nation against the other concerning their garrison was not new. If we drop the few names, Judah, Jerusalem, and Beth Zur, such an event was commonplace in the world full of empires. The real world is after all a world of topoi. "The king was very angry when he heard this" and ordered an army to retaliate in Palestine. After some hostilities that occurred between Jews and the Seleucid army the general in the field, Lysias, said (57-59):

We are growing weaker every day, our provisions are giving out, the place we are besieging is strong, and the affairs of the kingdom press upon us. Let us then extend the right hand to these men, and make peace with them, and with all their nation. Let us make a treaty with them so that they can follow their own laws, as heretofore, for because of their laws which we abolished they became angry and did all these things.

Is there any special Jewish idea here? We know that the laws were the laws of the Torah,[9] but when a pagan read it, namely, the Seleucid officers in place, he thought of so many other instances in which Hellenistic rulers toyed with the abolishment of ancestral constitutions entirely or partially (and their restoration when states deserved it by showing good behavior). The general gave an oath and breached it immediately thereafter, quite typical of the era (6 60-63).

The Seleucid general invades the wayward revolting state at the invitation of the sector of peace seekers and the ones who strove for stability even if liberty of the state was restricted. This pattern of conduct of a ruling empire is familiar to us from the cases I have discussed in Part I. Even more so, during war loyalty and faithfulness to agreements was becoming quite loose, or rather ignored and despised by the ruling power, which shows first and foremost that there was an awareness that agreements under oath were expected to be kept, and were a manifestation of certain values of the inter-state value system. Let us see how the military intervening force of the Seleucids behaved on the ground. They, as we will see in a moment, exploited the divide within Judea, a matter that was a standard reaction of empires to unrest in states within their domain.

The Seleucid court treated the Jewish state as it treated other states in the realm. Hence after a coup in the Seleucid court Demetrius eliminated both Antiochus and Lysias and "sat upon [the latter's] royal throne" (7:3-4). Then a delegation from Judea arrived with Alcimus as one of its members and who wanted to serve as High Priest (namely, leader of the Judean state). The narrator denigrates the delegation by describing its members as "all the lawless and irreligious men." They complain in the denigrative style of oppositional delegations that we already met in Hellenistic courts saying that "Judah and his brothers have killed off" all the friends of the king and have exiled them. Suffice it to examine the occurrences in Argos and Sparta mentioned above to discern the similarities. The delegation continues saying: "Now, therefore, send a man in whom you have confidence. Let him go and see all the damage that he has done to us and to the king's country. Let him punish them and all who help them" (7:5-7). Interestingly, they use here an expression that assures their faithfulness to the Seleucid king, namely, that Palestine is "the king's land" (ownership of territory was one of the main targets of the Roman Republic and the Hellenistic kings. Simeon's words later in ch. 15 demonstrate in contradistinction who the real owner was in Palestine). As in so many other instances that I discussed above, complaints of that sort usually triggered the ruling head of state (here the Seleucid king) to send forces

---

[9] Other states in the region also had "strange" customs and laws in the eyes of Greeks. Cf. in general Isaac (2004).

to the province where unrest was reported by influential locals. And indeed, he sends Bacchides, one of his *philoi*, to settle the affairs in Palestine. Alcimus, the leader of the Jewish opposition, is sent along with the Seleucid army and confirmed as High Priest (seen by the Seleucids as the leader of the state, like for instance the apocletes of the Aetolians). The narrator uses the term "revenge" for this expedition (v. 9). The intervention of the Seleucid army in the land of Israel caused a lot of havoc since it—what Rome and Hellenistic rulers used to do—wished to stabilize a state by replacing a competing anti-Seleucid sector (Judah and his group) with the pro-Seleucid ones that invited the army to intervene. As I have already mentioned above, there were instances where such a tactic succeeded and harmony was restored within the subject state, whereas in other places (Boeotia) and Judea it increased the inner unrest. In fact, the appointment of Alcimus and his pro-Seleucid group henceforward caused an unrest initiated by the opposition of Judah that "when Alcimus saw that Judah and his men were becoming strong, he perceived that he could not stand against them, so he returned to the king and brought evil accusations against them" (25). The king was convinced and sent Nicanor, a standard procedure when unrest perseveres in a subject state in spite of attempts to stabilize it. The Jewish narrator adds that Nicanor "hated and despised Israel, and [the king] ordered him to get rid of the people." The threat of annihilation was, as I have mentioned, quite common in particular when Hellenistic kings were outraged. Hence anti-Jewish feelings were not the trigger that drove Nicanor to act but the pattern of behavior so often used by the Roman and Hellenistic rulers to keep the imperial order.

Before going on with our story let us reflect for a moment on the occurrences during Bacchides's invasion from the standpoint of the Seleucid ruler. An incident that is not wholly clear occurred when one group of peace seekers came to Bacchides who was already in Palestine and

> spoke words of peace with them, and swore to them, saying, "We have no evil intentions either against you or your friends." They believed him, but he arrested sixty of them and slew them in one day … fear and dread of them [the Seleucids] fell upon the people, because they said, "There is neither truth nor justice in them. They transgressed the covenant and the oath which they swore."[10]

Before leaving and installing the opposition group led by Alcimus in power, Bacchides slew "many of the deserters who had been with him, as well as some of the army … casting them into the great cistern" (7:19). Did the Seleucid general do this in order to frighten and deter the liberation fighters of Judah from fighting the new government that he had installed? Be that as it may, when Bacchides spoke words of peace and swore, he was relying on the mutual awareness that a pact (called in v. 18 *stasis*) and an oath were values to be adhered to by all actors on the inter-state scene. Hence the anger about its breach in Jewish circles was quite understandable. It also enhances the ferocious conduct of Hellenistic kings and their generals during war in

---

[10] 7:15-18 (probably accusing both Bacchides and Alcimus, the Jewish leader who was in the Seleucid camp).

spite of the civilized dialogue they sometimes had before they showed their disrespect and scorn for the virtual inter-state ethical code. After all, the lack of a regulator similar to the Roman senate that dealt with international trespass and breach was felt daily at that time during Seleucid imperialism. But the inter-state value system was still on the agenda and referred to by all, as we will see in the following.

To return to the Seleucid general Nicanor who was sent to suppress the riot of the liberation fighters of Judah and the Hasmonean brothers, Nicanor adopts a measure that was frequently used to settle affairs that arose between states in the Hellenistic period, namely, a conference. In 7:29 we read that Nicanor "came to Judah, and they greeted each other peacefully; nevertheless, the enemy were prepared to kidnap Judah." But Judah discovered the plot and refused to meet the Seleucid general again. Thus, they met in battle at Caphar Salama. Then Nicanor—against all proper behavior and etiquette expected from the representatives of the ruling empire, Jewish and pagan— entered the Temple in Jerusalem and although

> some of the priests came out of the sanctuary along with some of the elders to greet him peaceably, and to show him the whole burnt offering that was being offered in honor of the king, he sneered at them and jeered at them and polluted them, and spoke disdainfully. He swore with rage, saying, "Unless Judah and his army are delivered into my hands right now, it shall come to pass when I return in peace, that I will burn down this house." (7:33-35)

Interestingly, Nicanor does not disdain God but the *hagia* (the holy place). This may have been an occasional utterance of the narrator whose God was shy and not too confrontative, at least explicitly, against the Seleucid enemy.[11] The Seleucid general went away in great rage. Yet he was defeated by the liberation fighters led by Judah; his head was cut off and so his right hand "which he had stretched out so arrogantly, and brought them and hanged them near Jerusalem" (7:47). He was punished because he so bluntly, being a representative of the ruling empire, breached one of the most important rules of the ethical code. He arrogantly trespassed a holy place of a subject state (in Persia his king, Antiochus IV, was punished as well when he desecrated a temple, as I have mentioned above). Several cases that I tackled in Part I have demonstrated that trespassing of holy places of others, be it by individuals or states, meant humiliation and disrespect for the "other" and usually aroused—as in this case here—outrage and even acts of revenge. Here it is specifically said: "Take revenge on this man and on his army. Let them fall by the sword. Be mindful of their blasphemies, and give them no peace" (v. 38). I will return to this issue later in the discussion.

A treaty between two states is one of many sources to examine a bilateral relationship in modern times, but also in antiquity this can be done. Judea was subject to the Seleucid empire, and yet concludes a peace treaty with the Roman Empire which thirty years beforehand defeated the Seleucids. Was it possible in the Hellenistic period for a subject state to conclude a treaty with other states without the need for consent of the

---

[11] Mendels (2013: 129–62).

ruling empire? As we have learned in Part I, it was the Seleucid king Antiochus III who during his invasion of Greece aired the notion that a state can be on friendly relations with both empires during a war between them, in other words, to remain neutral. Hence even if the Seleucids were aware of the pact concluded in 161 BCE between Judah and the Roman Empire they were not too surprised and probably ignored it, in particular because they had very bad memories of the clash with powerful Rome. The terms of this treaty point yet again to the existence of an inter-state ethical code. Before entering the issue of the treaty, I will examine the famous words attributed to Judah that deal with Roman imperialism in ethical terms (ch. 8). The Romans according to Judah were "favorably disposed toward all who joined them," and they "offered friendship to all who approached them." Yet, when he tells the story of Rome's expansion, he mentions only conquests and subjugation. This does not deter him, like at the beginning, to say "They had conquered kings both near and far, and all who heard of their fame were afraid of them. Whomsoever they wished to help and make kings became kings, and whomsoever they wished they deposed; and they were greatly exalted" (12-13). When we read this excursus, we are quite astonished at its simplistic view of Roman imperialism. This document was probably added long after Judah had been killed since it most probably mentions events that occurred in 146 BCE. The author of 1 Maccabees who had a dichotomic perception of the world, and judges conduct of states and individuals according to their good or bad behavior, actually juxtaposes in this description a good empire as opposed to the bad Macedonian one. By drawing the Roman Empire in mostly positive hues he is actually implicitly agreeing with the ethical code it represented in the world without adducing any special reservations.[12] And now to the treaty itself.

The treaty with Rome has some standard terms such as *philia* and *summachia*, which express friendship between states. The clause for mutual material assistance and reciprocity during wars is also well known from treaties of Rome with other states in the region and elsewhere. The treaty shows very clearly that contracts between states were operating as a formal channel of manifestation of the virtual inter-state ethical code.[13] The veto attached to the treaty against a Hellenistic king Demetrius (8:31-32) is interesting from our point of view since it enhances the possibility of a king acting against the international agreed upon terms of reference. Except for the value of friendship just mentioned, other values are also mentioned such as reciprocity, faith, and refraining from deceit and violation. Be that as it may, Demetrius in the next chapter continues the war against the Judean nationalistic group without taking notice of the Roman threat. The Romans were still far away from this part of the ancient Near East so that Demetrius could act freely in his domain.

Chapter 9 is yet again a description of a warlike relationship between the empire and the subjugated state in which the leader of the liberation army dies in battle.[14] The letters in ch. 10 are filled with promises of concessions to a subjugated state that

---

[12] Conquests by a super power are not necessarily bad according to the author of this chapter. See his description of a bad empire, namely, the Macedonian one, in ch. 1.
[13] Sherk (1984).
[14] For the following, see Mendels (2013; 2021).

are typical of relationships that we already encountered between empire and subject state (Part I), for instance, gifting and territorial arrangements as well as appointment of leaders (grant of the High Priesthood).[15] Chapter 11 shows what the Hasmonean family did in order to become part of the network of Hellenistic rulers in the region. In fact, one can argue that their participation in Hellenistic court etiquette does not necessarily point to their either rigorous or skin-deep Hellenization.[16] I have already emphasized that a distinction should be drawn between the acceptance of Hellenistic ethics, which is sometimes a deep process as we can learn from the later Hasmoneans, and the acceptance of etiquette which is a superficial stance toward Hellenistic culture. Hence so many scholars were misled by the portrayal of the Hasmonean family as becoming more Hellenistic based on their participation in Hellenistic etiquette. The letters of Hellenistic rulers to the Hasmoneans can be seen as official statements of the usual relationship of the ruling empire with its subject states and the meaning of liberty, which the Seleucids interpreted as partial liberty and the nationalistic Jews as full independence. It should be made clear that most, if not all, scholars who deal with the encounters of the Jewish state with the Seleucid empire and its various kings and claimants to the crown interpret it as being hostile but sometimes positive when concessions are proposed by the ruling empire. Scholars hence view the correspondence as a normal procedure within the Hellenistic inter-state relationships of empire with subjugated state. However, let me argue against this view. The correspondence points to a negotiation process between the ruling empire and the Jewish subjugated state. The negotiation, unlike many other cases of complete abrogation of the ancestral constitutions with other subjected states and cities, shows that the Jews received a much better treatment than most other nations. Negotiation during war—occurring in one-time conferences or multiple correspondence of letters—of a subject state with the ruling empire, in spite of the hostility of a sector of this state, shows the flexibility and non-arbitrary stance of the empire versus the Jews. I will address this attitude in the next chapter when dealing with the edicts of the kings. The reason behind this special attitude towards one nation or another is yet again not unique. Alongside complete abrogation of "ancestral constitutions" we found a few cases where negotiation with the subject state occurred (see Part I). The negotiation, concessions, participation in etiquette point to the adherence of both empire and its Jewish subject state to some sort of an ethical code of the right conduct prevalent in the world of Greek-speaking nations. This was also apparent during the frequent breaches of the ethical code that pointed always to what is the right conduct.

Chapters 14–15 of 1 Maccabees is yet another expression of the elements that make a nation at that time more or less free from the yoke of the ruling empire. The emphasis as we saw in Part I is on the ancestral land, autonomy of law and constitution and leaders that emanate from the nation itself and are the outcome of their independent will (namely, no leaders imposed by the ruling empire—we have seen in Part I that usually the ruling powers leaned on local leaders rather than on ones that were imposed, such as foreign generals, etc.). Since I have dealt elsewhere with the

---

[15] For details, see Mendels (2013: 94–104).
[16] Mendels (2021).

declaration of independence during Simeon's term as ruler (ch. 14), I will here adduce only the perhaps literary climax of 1 Maccabees. This is the ode to liberty, written by the narrator, or some poet, and attached in the text to the declaration of independence of the Jewish state. Why is this so important? The answer is quite simple. We hear a praise to true liberty in line and in correspondence with other poems of the same genre uttered by other nations at that time. The poem is of a universal nature using here and there biblical expressions (which strengthens its nationalistic nature) and exhibits yet another proof of the existence of an inter-state platform of the ethical system. Here is the poem in the words of its author:

> The land had rest all the days of Simeon. He sought the good of the nation; his rule was pleasing to them, as was the honor shown him, all his days. To crown all his honors he took Joppa for a harbor, and opened a way to the isles of the sea. He extended the borders of his nation, and gained full control of the country. He gathered a host of captives; he ruled over Gazara and Beth Zur and the citadel. And he removed its uncleanness from it; and there was none to oppose him. They tilled their land in peace; the ground gave its increase, and the trees of the plains their fruit. Old men set in the streets; they all talked together of good things, and the youths put on splendid military attire. He supplied the towns with food, and furnished them with the means of defense, until his renown spread to the ends of the earth. He established peace in the land, and Israel rejoiced with joy. All the people sat under their vines and fig trees. And there was none to make them afraid. No one was left in the land to fight them, and the kings were crushed in those days. He gave help to all the humble among his people; he sought out the law, and did away with all the renegades and outlaws. He made the sanctuary glorious, and added to the vessels of the sanctuary. (14:4-15)

The description of the (ideal) state which is fully liberated enhances some of the values that I discussed in Part I and in this chapter. The value of sovereignty (without hampering enemies within the land and outside it), safe and broad borders, rule of law, harmony within the state (no conflicting factions), good, abundance, safety, peace, glorious sanctuary, no fear, renown of a state in the world, an independent army, honor of the leader, and free trade with the world around. This poem in praise of Simeon (and Judah in 3:1-9) corresponds with similar praises of leaders and states in the Classical and Hellenistic world where the broadening of borders and the enlargement of one's fatherland are seen as good acts alongside the increase of the states' power (*auksesis*).[17]

The anticlimax of the book is the death of the local leader Simeon that is portrayed like cases of political murder which we have encountered in Part I.

Although 1 Maccabees is a Jewish composition with all its typical Jewish fears and yearning, it reveals one main important point: The Jews, in the first thirty years of their strive for religious autonomy and then even for complete independence from the ruling power, were treated by the latter in the same way as it treated so many other

---

[17] Eckstein (2006: 192–3) has assembled some of these references in inscriptions and the literary sources.

states and cities under its rule, and probably even better. This book deals inter alia with patterns of conduct between empire and a subject state. We will see now that if the book of 1 Maccabees was concentrated on patterns of conduct and etiquette, the book of 2 Maccabees was focused on a relationship with the ruling empire but from a different perspective altogether: it enhanced the close link between ancestral constitution and the ruling empire on the basis of a mutual Hellenistic ethical code that I mapped in Part I. The very existence of an ethical system and its management is what interests me in the next chapter.

6

The Subject State Corresponds and Reacts to the Hellenistic Inter-state Ethical System—the Book of 2 Maccabees

In Part I we followed the history of the creation of an inter-state ethical code in the Hellenistic world (200–168 BCE). Within thirty years the newly created inter-state ethical code was abused by the dominant empire and exploited as a tool to expand eastward. After 168 BCE when Rome had proved yet again her powerful dominance in regions outside Italy, much of this code persevered in the form of remnants of a (free) inter-state ethical system. Against this background attentive readers will immediately find themselves at home when they read the following narrative of this chapter; he/she will realize that 2 Maccabees shows a strong correspondence with the ethical system/s prevalent in the Hellenistic world in the second century BCE. Let us start with the survey of what we still find in the ethical system of the Hasmoneans during the thirty years of their conflict with the super power, the Seleucid empire.

One of the cardinal issues concerning the relationship of a subject state to the empire, as we have seen in Part I, was the one of "ancestral constitution." When the empire wished, it was fully or partly abrogated (arbitrarily or because of the wayward behavior of the subject state), and in certain circumstances, when the right opportunity arose, the empire agreed to return the ancestral law/constitution to the subject state. Elsewhere I have argued in detail that 2 Maccabees presents the Jewish *patrios politeias* in a typical Greek style and shows that even a partial abrogation of it brought about conflict with the ruling empire, the Seleucids.[1] This stance is shared by the two books of Maccabees. Yet whereas 1 Maccabees accentuates all along the Hasmonean conflict with the ruling empire on the level of patterns of conduct on both sides to the conflict (oath, peace terms, limits of liberty, etiquette, etc.), 2 Maccabees enhances through the Greek lens of its author the moral and ethical system behind this war, as well as the interaction between characteristics of the Jewish *politeia* (territoriality, imitation, division and unity, etc.), its values (justice, steadfastness, goodwill, compassion, etc.), and emotions (anger, love, jealousy, etc.). The ethical code of 2 Maccabees is at the end of the day a mirror of this very code in the Hellenistic world shown from the side of the

---

[1] Mendels (2019: 100–31).

subject state itself. Let me discuss conduct and values as they appear in the narrative of 2 Maccabees. I start with loyalty and betrayal.

2 Maccabees 3–5 are dominated by the motif of betrayal, various sorts of betrayal. The story is spread over several years, clearly a description of a chain of events, most of them being fragments of true information and memories, yet all of which are used by the narrator to show how betrayal by leading figures and their supporters of a usually orderly and well-governed *politeia* (3:1) can cause its slide into disorder called by the Greeks *stasis*; even worse, it can lead to a disastrous external intervention by the foreign ruler of the region. Against the background of several betrayals, the description of our author of the conditions in Judea leading to the revolt sounds quite familiar. Similar to the Hellenistic environment we find here betrayal in several of its manifestations, such as betrayal of one leader by another, betrayal of the citizens (for instance, by the failure of a leader to protect their savings and other interests), as well as betrayal of citizens by their fellow citizens and their murder in extreme cases, betrayal of family members (brothers), and the betrayal of one's fatherland and temple by calling in the assistance of a foreign dominating power who harshly acts against confrontative groups in the state, betrayal of the existing law, and finally betrayal of God's law and God himself (by introducing Greek customs into a native temple), customs that were allowed by a former king of the ruling empire.[2] As said, all these betrayal patterns are familiar from the Hellenistic world.[3]

Hence quite symbolically, one of the Jewish instigators is punished by non-Jews outside the state and is left unburied. This in itself is significant. Our author emphasizes that even other nations find the behavior of some of the Jewish factions disagreeable, by that referring to some kind of an international ethical code. It should be underlined here that the fact that the narrator of 2 Maccabees has made his choices of presentation, terminology, and comments (like other Hellenistic historians that I quoted in Part I) does not necessarily discredit the historicity of many of the events described. Let me go into some more detail.

The well-known statement in 2 Macc. 3:1-3 that the city [of Jerusalem] was in perfect peace because the laws were obeyed by the city discloses the idea that the reason for this was the piety and hatred of wickedness of its leader, the High Priest (Onias). Moreover, because of this, the relationship with the super power, the Seleucids, was fine and the latter honored the Jewish subject state and its temple along with many other nations who adored the temple as well. Here is the beginning of a long survey that according to our interpretation reveals a relationship between group characteristics that are the recurrent, hidden, and driving forces behind the actions of human groups (territoriality, split, imitation, hierarchy, etc.), their values (justice, equality, freedom, etc.), and emotions (group love, hate, compassion, anger, etc.)—in short, the triangle.[4] We will see in the following, through the lens of this paradigm how certain triggers, from outside and within the group, ignite the relationship within

---

[2] The narrator mentions betrayal a few times during the description. For instance, at the end of ch. 4, Menelaus is referred to as "betrayer of his fellow citizens" (4:50).
[3] Mendels (1998: 101–26).
[4] Mendels (2017).

this triangle, naturally embedded in all states and empires that I discussed in Part I, which consequently affected the course of history of the Jews as told by the narrator of 2 Maccabees. At the beginning of ch. 3, the relationship between values and law is depicted as being harmonious (characteristics being passive and balanced, namely, no division but unity, no quarrels about authority within a hierarchy, no *pleonexia*, greed, but stability). This balance changes very soon because of a personal feud between the High Priest, the ruler of the state, and the overseer of the market (the so-called *agoranomus*), over the management of the savings of widows and orphans which were deposited in the treasury of the temple. I will not delve into this dispute but only say that the narrator claims that touching the savings of orphans and widows would harm the purity, dignity, and inviolability—all Hellenistic universal values—of the sanctuary "honored throughout the entire world," and that such a plot initiated by the *agoranomus* was utterly unthinkable (3:12). This dispute between two leading authorities within the state caused one of them (the magistrate in charge of the economic affairs of the state) to ask for the intervention of the ruling empire, followed by the king's messenger called Heliodorus, who aimed at extracting money from the temple in Jerusalem. Such intervention of a ruling power or of another state in favor of one party against the other haunted the Greek world throughout the fourth, third, and second centuries BCE.[5] Because of foreign intervention, states and cities lost their independence, or the little autonomy they still had, while others were destroyed (e.g., Corinth 146 BCE). Hence, the relationship of states with super powers and other states within the empire or outside it became a central issue in the politics of the Hellenistic world and its political thought. As we shall see in the following, the issue of *stasis* and its implications constituted one of the burning issues of the Greek world that permeate through the lines of 2 Maccabees. In our story the incident of the visit of Heliodorus to the temple to rob its treasury (3:7-40) became a trigger that caused a long and painful series of interventions of the ruling power in the city of Jerusalem. The first of such interventions was that of Heliodorus himself. However, this intervention failed, first and foremost because of an eruption of feelings of the citizens which according to our narrator brought about a divine intervention. In other words, the Seleucids through their messenger Heliodorus trespassed the temple, thereby hurting the perhaps most important territorial and religious symbols of Jewish national identity, while violating the most precious Jewish values (some of which were universal and shared by pagans in other cities, as we have encountered in Part I). This caused their feelings to be aroused, presented by the narrator as a cardinal factor in the events that evolve. Some examples: In 3:14 our narrator speaks of "no small anguish throughout the entire city [of Jerusalem]," "the countenance [of the priest] change color," and his "anguish of the soul" (3:16); "fear and trembling had seized the man making it plainly evident … what pain was in his heart" (3:17), representing the feelings of part of the community;

---

[5] In theory this phenomenon was treated as well. Aristoteles in his *Politica* Book 5 points to the most trivial causes for civil strife, among others, intervention of a foreign power, and even suggests how to avoid it. The Third Macedonian War as we have seen above occurred because of such an intervention of the Macedonian king in Greek cities and states. Cf. Mendels (1998: 158–99), and in general Gruen (1984).

and then follows a detailed description of "supplication" and "prostration" in a pitiful manner that were considered emotional ways to express fear and sorrow combined, in order to get the attention of the deity (3:22). In v. 30 the narrator speaks of "tumultuous fear" that was transformed into "joy and gladness" when the treasury was saved. In such an atmosphere, the pro-Seleucid party was overcome as well with feelings (fear and awe, 3:24) that were caused by the active intervention of God. This episode presents us with a typical example of what I call elsewhere a symbiosis of values and emotions that supports the characteristic of territoriality.[6] A pagan reader could have seen in the affair of Heliodorus a piquant story, common in Greek historiography, about a deity that protects his or her temple (and example of which appears even in our book concerning Antiochus IV and his sacrilegious behavior in a temple in the east). God's intervention throughout ch. 3 was certainly not surprising to Greek pagans, who from times immemorial were used to authoritative gods who constantly intervene in human action through miracles and other means. Even God is mentioned in this group of chapters, as we will see in the following, in a familiar garb in pagan eyes, since like Greek gods, he is mentioned with several titles. God is according to this chapter the "brain" (the governing power of the *politeia*), a circumstantial force that at the end of the episode brought the tumultuous triangle—relationship of characters, emotions, and values (ethical code)—yet again to a temporary harmonious position (3:22-39).

In the continuation of the narrative in ch. 4, the narrator adduces some new aspects to which a pagan reader could have easily related since it refers to a universal Greek value system as distinguished from the barbarian one (see Part I for this distinction in Livy). Its description uses terms from the politico-theological arsenal of the Greek world and explicitly distinguishes it from the world of barbarians. This in itself is important for our case, since the narrator includes the Jewish *politeia* within the Greek world rather than the barbarian one.[7] If we look again at our triangle—values (ethics and law), human characteristics, and emotions—the interaction between them comes to the fore once more in the narrative that follows in ch. 4. This chapter is quite complex, although its narrative is smooth and clear. As already said, its leitmotif is betrayal (and some unjust killings). Yet this is only the more obvious layer of the story, which in fact is a continuation of ch. 3 but adds some new elements. The description abounds with terminology that specifies actions against the law and state (*ta pragmata*), and elaborates on the tyrannical behavior of its leaders, Jason, Menelaus, and Lysimachus, with bold negative comments intertwined in the narrative, competing with similar descriptions on tyranny in ancient literature.[8] In terms of the interaction within the triangle, our narrator moves from the characteristic of territoriality (acquisitiveness) that he emphasized in the former chapter as a motivation for action of both sides to the conflict, to the dominance of the characteristic of imitation, active in but a section

---

[6] Mendels (2017).
[7] Except for one time in 3 Macc. 3:24, 2 Maccabees is the only book within the corpus of the Septuagint that uses this term four times to denote the dichotomy.
[8] Cf. for instance Plato *Politeia* Book 9, Aristoteles *Politica* Book 5, and Polybius Book 6. See cases in Part I.

of the Jewish population, as I already showed elsewhere.[9] In our case, the imitation of Greek customs and ethics by the Jerusalem elite brought about the activation of rift, yet another characteristic, as we have already seen in Part I, imbued in sociopolitical groups, a divide that became henceforward an almost constant factor during the Maccabean upheaval. The rift that started with a divide within the ruling Hellenistic leadership develops, according to our narrator, into a more serious rift of the whole Jewish state. In other words, the value system of the state, embedded in the ancestral law—which was uninterrupted, according to 3:1—was challenged by one powerful group of the city (part of the priestly elite), and this abrupt change in the current value system caused a rift.

But how does the narrator view the sharpening of this rift within the *politeia*? First and foremost, he narrates a chain of events in which treachery and unfaithfulness bring about a change of leadership, from Onias, to Jason, and from him to Menelaus (and Lysimachus). I will not delve into the historical details but mention three important aspects of the relationship of empire with the subject states. First, the leaders of the Jewish state who cheat each other in order to win power within the *politeia* do this with the approval and support of the Seleucid king and his bureaucrats—in one extreme case three Jews were killed unjustifiably by the Seleucid magistrate by instigation of a Jewish leader, Menelaus (ch. 5). Also leaders of the subject state were obliged as a rule to send regular accounts to the king and when returning to Jerusalem from visits in the king's court had to carry along his written orders. Second, the chain of events that resulted from the intervention of the Seleucid king and his representatives brought about unjust massacres of Jews, who were opponents of the treacherous leaders of the emerging Jewish state. And third, since the Jews of Jerusalem were active participants in the stormy events, the group's emotional factor is portrayed as having a crucial effect on their course.

In spite of the fact that my story here is based on very different historians from each other, the account of 2 Maccabees is reminiscent of affairs that I portrayed in Part I, such as in Boeotia, Demetrias, and so on. We are probably not dealing here with topoi of historiography, but patterns of conduct that occurred in the reality of the years 200–160 BCE and beyond. I have already mentioned the fact that if we take out typical "Jewish" aspects of the narrative of 1–2 Maccabees, we will get close to narratives of relationships with a ruling empire elsewhere in the Hellenistic pagan world. For instance, 4:39-42: "many instances of sacrilegious plunder had been committed in the city … the report of this spread abroad … crowds began to riot … they were filled with increasing rage … some picked up stones, others sticks of wood … causing utter confusion. In this way they wounded many of them." Moreover, the inner rift in the city brought about an intensification of the intervention of the ruling power, a well-known phenomenon in the Hellenistic world, that became an almost constant outer trigger for increased negative interactions within the inner triangle. The narrator of ch. 4 emphasizes how an orderly polis (city-state) that was living in peace can be disrupted by a group from within, assisted by the outside ruling power, that makes attempts

---

[9] Mendels (2017).

to establish a competing set of values that are alien and not acceptable to the other faction. In such a situation, rift is unavoidable and *stasis* persists.

The narrative of betrayal continues in ch. 5, where various patterns of betrayal are adduced. Jason, a member of the Jerusalemite Hellenistic elite, attacks the city and slaughters his "own countrymen unmercifully, not realizing that advantage gained over one's own kindred is the worst kind of disadvantage, imagining that he was winning trophies from his enemies rather than from his own countrymen." And the narrator adds, "he did not gain control of the government (*arche*). He finally reaped only disgrace for his conspiracy" (5:6-7). In this passage, our narrator not only uses a universal political and ethical language but also involves the (putative pagan) reader within his world of ideas when he exhibits the punishment of the villain Jason in a pagan environment by saying that "all" (nations) participated in the understanding of the bad and wayward actions of Jason ("all" referring to other *ethne* that Jason was visiting during his flight): "Jason had to flee from city to city pursued by all, an object of hatred as a rebel against the laws, despised as a tormentor of his fatherland and as a public executioner of his fellow citizens ... He who had banished so many people from their own country" (5:7-9). He who left so many unburied was gone without any mourning rites and was not buried in the sepulcher of his fathers. This is a heavy punishment, perhaps reminiscent of the leitmotif in the tragedy Antigone. Be that as it may, this important passage about Jason's death reveals yet again a glimpse of the narrator's thought, namely, that there existed outside the Jewish state some sort of universal ethical system shared by many of its units (states). Jason pays a heavy price for his tyrannical behavior, such as execution of citizens within the state, arousal of hatred, banishment of opponents, and the policy of humiliation, all of which we have already encountered in Part I. The presentation of the disruption of normality in the state is somewhat ironic, since the riot was against Menelaus, who was a leader at that time in the state and is portrayed by the narrator as being "a traitor both to the laws and to his country" (5:15).

History is repeated, since the Seleucid king, as a result of the chain of disruptive events in the city, decided to intervene, causing much damage. Yet the main theme of the second part of this chapter, except for some details about the destructive results of the intervention of the super power, is the temple. As we have seen in Part I, temples were an indispensable religious and political ingredient of the Greek state. The temple of the Jewish state is here described as the most "renowned and glorious temple in the world honored by kings"; the political theology of gods and temples had an active role in an existing ethical world and a place of rivalry and confrontation. The author emphasizes that King Antiochus IV, being responsible for the transgression of the Jerusalem temple, was thinking, certainly as a result of his hubris (v. 21), that he was so powerful that he could bypass and actually ignore the protector of the temple, God. Yet the king was not aware of the fact that this became possible because God himself punished the wayward Jews by letting him in (Greek and Roman gods also "punished" their believers from time to time). When the temporary "anger" of God toward his sinning people was gone and God was reconciled, the temple rose again "in all its glory." Pagans were familiar with gods' role and influence on value systems all along, and gave gods titles that symbolized real ethical values and at times disrupted the balance between value characteristics and emotions, yet at other times fixed confrontative relationships within the triangle. Be that as it may, the end of the chapter is yet again a story about betrayal, but this time performed as a tactic by the intervening Seleucid army. In sum, betrayal and unfaithfulness of leaders, citizens, and foreign rulers alike are seen by our narrator as being a menace to the normality of the current constitution of the state, a subject that was on the agenda quite a bit in the assessment of relationships between ruling empire and its subject states.

Steadfastness and Bravery (*andreia*)

Chapters 6–7 have been discussed ad nauseam from many different angles, inter alia against the backdrop of their reminiscence of Classical Greek motifs (Antigone springs to mind, but also other tragedies were mentioned). The chapter relates the story of the martyrdom of old Eleazar and seven sons and their mother. They refused to adhere to the king's representative and eat pork, prohibited to Jews. Read from a pagan point of view, the story accords with what we have encountered in Part I, namely, that a rejection or opposition to the ruling empire is understood by the latter as a riot. This was the case in Abydus and other places dealt with above. Refusal by a subject state was answered by the ruling power either by persuasion or, if this did not help, by force. This is what happened in our case here. Torture was common in the Hellenistic world and used usually when persuasion failed.[10] Hence the drama of the martyrs appearing in our chapter was a procedure used later by the Romans in their torture of Christians. Yet what is important for my theme is that the author, through the story about the torture of the ones who refused to adhere to an external law system of the ruling power, adduces a strong view of how a value system operates when it is triggered from without, namely, by putting it on trial. Our author criticizes the bold and ruthless intervention of a super power in the affairs (laws) of a subject state on the one hand, yet praises the stubborn and painful adherence to a dominant value system in this same *politeia* on the other. Ironically, the story about the suicidal act, whereas it shows a breach of international ethics, advertises values that were part and parcel of the inter-state value system, such as steadfastness, heroism, honesty (embodied in Elazar), justice, bravery, all of which lead to glory of the state, compassion, and wisdom on behalf of God, the one who protects the laws of the state.

Mercy (*eleos*)

Chapter 8 takes us in a sharp turn from steadfastness and heroism, facets of an ideal value system of a *politeia* and inter-state ethics, to the battlefield, where the Jews are

---

[10] For instance, King Nabis of Sparta's notorious torture machine (Polybius 13.7). Another example is the one adduced by Polybius 38.18: Philinus of Corinth was accused of being a partisan of the Romans and hence flogged and racked along with his sons "before each other's eyes until both the father and the boys gave up the ghost."

successful. Although in the Hellenistic period it was quite natural for a state to be only partially free, since almost everyone was under the yoke of one of the ruling empires, *eleutheria* (*libertas*, liberty) remained an essential ingredient, and high up in the value scale of constitutions and of the international ethical discourse. Hence, as I already mentioned, it was not accidental that the war for liberty of the Jewish state started between the end of the Third Macedonian War (168 BCE) and the Achaean war of liberation against Rome that ended in 146 BCE. Hence a Greek reader of 2 Maccabees, who knew a thing or two about the political whereabouts and politics of resistance against the ruling powers in the second century BCE in the eastern Mediterranean, eventually looked on the riot of Jews as déjà vu, yet with great awe. It will not be too risky to say that liberal pagan readers of ch. 8 read it with much admiration, and understood its message well against the general political backdrop of the second century BCE, of which our author as a learned and alert person was surely aware. That is, like elsewhere in the Hellenistic world (Part I), a transgression of the state's constitution or parts thereof by a foreign ruler (8:17) was actually seen by many pagans as a justified opportunity to fight him (8:20). Others, most of the well-to-do, yearned for compromise and a status quo. Both of these opinions concerning the relationship of a subject state with the empire, as we shall see in the following, appear in 2 Maccabees, whose author preferred the more moderate stance (15:37). A success in battle with the slogan of complete religious and political freedom or socioeconomic relief was in the Greek world associated with the notion that the gods were helping the state or one of its parties, as we learn for instance from *The Persians* of Aeschylus and the Melian dialogue (Thuc. 5). Yet our chapter associates God's help with compassion toward the freedom fighters. This emphasis can be detected in the direct comments about compassion and mercy.[11] At this point, I should emphasize that the actions of the Jewish group under Judah (and his brothers) are seen in this chapter as an interplay between the values of heroism, liberty, and compassion and the war for religious freedom (characteristic of territoriality). Reminiscent of the embodiment of mercy and victory in two gods are Athena as Nike (victory) and Eleos, who was the goddess of mercy, both significant in the scale of values of the *politeia*.[12]

Liberty (*eleutheria*)

Chapter 9 is extremely important for our theme since it adduces the nature of relationships of a Hellenistic empire with a subject state in high resolution. The following picture has its typical Jewish aspects; however, as we shall see it can well instruct us on relationships of that kind in the Hellenistic world at that time.

Interestingly, our author does not exemplify the kind of rulership that the Jewish state should have. In contradistinction to 1 Maccabees, where the succession of the Hasmoneans is an important issue, in our book—perhaps because it was composed

---

[11] Coetzer (2017: 419–33) argues that the fate of the Jews is intimately connected to the scale of God's wrath and mercy.
[12] Mendels (2017).

before the succession of the Hasmoneans was on the agenda—the leadership of the High Priesthood is a given, even if it is not always presented as a positive rulership. However, a typical Hellenistic concept comes to the fore in this chapter (and will appear later). I have already mentioned that our author emphasizes the fact that liberty (*eleutheria*) was an aim of the war of Judah Maccabee and his supporters, only one sector of the citizen-body of the state. Since our author knew quite well what this kind of liberty meant, he ends the book when autonomy was achieved (15:37). It seems that complete independence of the Jewish state was not on his agenda. This latter pattern required, as expressed by the political theory of the times, a good relationship between king and his subject states (Part I). The ruler of the empire should first and foremost be a good king in line with Greek standards expressed in political thought about kingship.[13] Thus, in ch. 9, it becomes clear that a king who disrupts even the limited liberty of the state is considered a bad king. A king who behaves with hubris is considered a bad king as well. When ch. 9 is interpreted as a gentile Greek would have done, it becomes quite understandable. The author does not put forward a rejection of the given situation, namely, of a legitimate rule of an empire over the Jewish subject state. Yet, mostly implicitly, he promotes the idea of the necessity to reach the right equilibrium between limited *eleutheria* and the degree of intervention of the ruling king and his generals. The king should guard the autonomy of a subject state rather than attempt to transgress or even abolish it. Thus, when the king in our story is punished (by God), suffers a great deal, comes to his senses, and repents, only then does he promise to guard the *eleutheria* of the Jewish state and even extend it. Let us go into some detail.

For a pagan Greek reader, this chapter is a good read since it tallies with the familiar nuanced literature of Greek political thought. The story itself of Antiochus IV who is punished because of his hubris is in some ways reminiscent of the confession of Xerxes in *The Persians*. The Seleucid king even expresses his wish to become a Jew. A pagan, one might speculate, did not understand this thought of the king as a wish to convert to monotheism but as the willingness on behalf of a Hellenistic king to accept yet another religious identity, in the wake of, for instance, Alexander the Great in the temple of Siwah, who became the son of Ammon. Seen from the Seleucid side this behavior was but natural in the case of Antiochus IV. The story here concerns a wayward arrogant king who is punished, similar to the one in the tragedy *The Persians* where the king's punishment is the defeat and loss of his army. Here, as in *The Persians*, the king repents, and moreover recites himself what he should have been, namely, a good king. Darius on the other hand regrets the succession of his son to the throne (this is comparable to the letter of Antiochus adduced here, who warns of a bad succession). In *The Persians*, it is Xerxes who confesses and mentions his father as the good king. Here it is Antiochus IV who confesses and writes a letter about himself as being a good king. It is not accidental, I believe, that the author did not cause his hero to convert subsequent to expressing his wish to do so. Yet "he spread God's fame and authority all over the world," a comment addressed to

---

[13] For Polybius's standard views on kings and benevolence, see Book 6, and Eckstein (1995: 274–84).

a pagan publicum. Conversion to Judaism is different than just acknowledging it. At the same time, it is Antiochus IV who wants to announce the power of God, namely, acknowledging God's superiority (which is already announced in v. 8). This itself is interesting from our point of view, since the book repeats this dictum and exemplifies it by historical examples.[14] Such idea is self-evident for Jews who know their Bible, but for a pagan, it constitutes a support for many sceptic views about pagan gods that are in fact breathless.[15] The nature of the bad king in reference to his international relations becomes quite clear from the story about King Antiochus IV, who, because of his arrogance, harassed not only believing Jews in Jerusalem but also pagan gods and their believers. He profaned a temple in Persia, an episode not accidentally adduced as the first anecdote in our chapter. Yet the features of the good king that were common in Greek thought come to the fore in the letter sent to the Jews by the very same (wicked) Antiochus IV (comparable to Xerxes's confession).[16] Whether this letter is a fabrication or not does not matter for our case here. What interests us in this letter is the nature of a good king, his traits, and conduct toward his subject states. As already mentioned, this is a revealing passage about the views of the Seleucid side (even if presented by the Jewish author, the views accord with Seleucid policies elsewhere). Whether this is a wishful list of a Jewish writer, namely, how a relationship between empire and subject state should be, or reflects authentic thoughts of the Seleucid king, it shows that there was an awareness on both sides that such a master–subject relationship was on the inter-state political agenda all the time. That the king himself recites this wisdom grants it special authority in the eye of the reader, Jewish and pagan.

According to the king's letter, it is expected of the citizens and their children to be in good health and well-being (under the rule of the good king). The affairs of state should be performed by the citizens. They should show goodwill and esteem toward the king. A good king should think about the common welfare of the public. A good king will not be punished by god but will recover from an occasional illness. The affairs of state (*ta pragmata*) could only be in good order if a successor to the king is appointed while the king is still alive so that a smooth transition of rulership will occur. Whereas in 1 Maccabees the succession of the Hasmonean rulership was crucial, here the succession of the king of the ruling power becomes the cardinal issue (succession in dynasties is a central motif in "On Kingship" compositions, see obituary of King Attalus in Part I). Hence according to the letter of Antiochus, it is indispensable for a king to appoint his successor while he is still alive, since neighbors of the state always look for opportunities to invade and conquer it (characteristic of territoriality). Yet, the citizens should always remember the public and private instances of kindness they have received and be persistent in their goodwill toward the king and his successor. The latter, the king's son in this case, is expected to follow

---

[14] One famous example is the story of Heliodorus, where he tells the king how powerful the god of Jerusalem is: "the sacred Place is haunted by some divine power" (3.38); he implicitly doubts the power of other pagan gods; also later in ch. 10.

[15] See the Athenian hymn in honor of Demetrius Poliorcetes from 291/290 BCE (Athenaeus 6.253 b-f).

[16] 9: 19-27 Mendels (1992: 55–79).

the kind and moderate policy of his father and accommodate himself to the interests of the citizens. In short, the letter can be read as a kind of "On Kingship" document that is in complete discrepancy with the narrative telling us about the sender himself, who was punished for his arrogant behavior. The letter is a result of the king's repentance and adduces in familiar Hellenistic political jargon the positive universal principles of good kingship with a clear reference to the king's inter-state relations. Moreover, in between the letter of Antiochus IV and the narrative of the bad king, there is a passage written by the author (9:13-18) who recites the good deeds of the king toward the Jewish state in particular, such as granting Jerusalem liberty (namely, autonomy under a foreign king), equality of status with the Athenians, and financial support of the temple. In 9:13-27, good deeds of a king, real and theoretical, get a place of honor, a passage that would have been intelligible to every learned pagan reader who was acquainted, as it were, with the ruling power–subject state relations in the surrounding Hellenistic world. The arrogant king, as opposed to the good king who brings order and welfare to his citizens, is a familiar theme in Classical and Hellenistic political science. Yet our author gives it a certain twist, and instead of referring to the ruler of the state itself, it is applied to the ruler of the empire to whom the state is subjected. There is nothing particularly Jewish in this presentation—even the promise to support the Jerusalem temple could be applicable to any Hellenistic temple, as we know also from inscriptions concerning other Hellenistic temples (and see Part I). This leads us to ch. 10.

Moderation (*epieikeia*)

Following the passage about the inauguration of the temple of Jerusalem, the author writes a summary of the subsequent battles of Judah Maccabee (v. 10), but never within the narrative does he forget the vocation of a historian who writes a moral and ethical narrative. Whether the battles of Judah are described accurately or not, one thing is clear: the battles are portrayed in a quasi-Hellenistic mode of accounts of battles, but lacking its precision and detail, and present two armies equal in status (not in numbers); their didactic purpose is quite obvious. As our author frequently does when he wants to teach a lesson, he tells a story of treason—so common in Hellenistic historiography—in two parallel modes, one of a pagan case and the other of a Jewish one (as he does, for instance, in his description of the eastern temple and Antiochus as against the incident of Heliodorus in the temple). Thus, a governor who is in favor of the Jews (Ptolemy) is accused by the Seleucid king of being a traitor, since he "was not successful in maintaining the honor of his position." He killed himself. Yet his deed is enhanced by the author as a positive action on behalf of the Jews in line with his concept of how the right political relationship between the ruling empire and a subject state should be. The governor was taking the lead in "preserving justice for the Jews," and hence "dealt peacefully with them," namely, acted according to an ethical inter-state system (v. 12). This in itself was seen by the Seleucid king as an act of treason, hence it is in line with the notion of the negative role of the king in his treatment of subject states in his realm.

A meticulous ethical stance can also be found in the parallel story of betrayal that concerns with the Jewish side. It is an anecdote about informing the enemy in exchange for money; this happened in the Jewish army (intentional breach of secrecy). The punishment that Judah inflicts on the unfaithful traitors is public, in front of the leaders of the people (publicity and testimony). He accuses them of "having sold their brothers for money by releasing their enemies to fight against them." The latter story is not necessarily Jewish and could be well-understood by pagans who were among its readers, since stories of betrayal appear frequently in descriptions of war in classical and Hellenistic literature (Part I).

In ch. 10, the role of God is yet again emphasized. God is portrayed, like in many cases that we encountered in pagan societies, as the "brain" who manages his people (the triangle) from above. His mercy is yet again enhanced (10:26), and some values of the ethical system are mentioned concerning the driving force behind the Jews in the battlefield. Whereas their enemy was animated by "unrestrained passion" (*thumon*), the Jews with God as their ally (*summachos*), "being an enemy to their enemies and adversary to their adversaries" (a formula taken from formal pacts; see 1 Maccabees 8), relied on the Lord as their refuge for good fortune (*euemeria*) and victory (*nike*) along with excellence (*arete*) (10:26, 28). In an intriguing manner, a value system that is dominant in the state (*politeia*) is juxtaposed with a case where the emotions are overshadowing the good judgment of the leader. *Arete* (virtue, excellence) is victorious, since the activity of *thumos* on its own is negative, while *thumos* in conjunction with *arete* (10:35), namely, a balance between value and emotion, can be positive. Judah has of course the upper hand against the Asiatic "blasphemous barbarians." Yet both warring parties are clearly motivated by the characteristic of territoriality. The effective harmonious interplay within the Jewish "triangle" is what brought about Jewish victory. We have seen in Part I that this kind of harmony within the state was an ideal prerequisite for a good relationship with the ruling empire. The chapter ends with confessions of gratitude. The Jews praise their God and His benefits, which is reminiscent of Hellenistic kings some of whom were titled *euergetes*.

Good (*agathos*)

Making peace with the enemy at the opportune time is a dominant theme in ch. 11 (and in Part I above). In order to convince his audience, the author adduces a correspondence that exemplifies this point. It goes without saying that peace-making and its additional values were one of the main themes during war at that time. I will not go into detailed analysis but just emphasize how a Greek pagan with some knowledge on his recent history of war and peace could have interpreted this chapter. That our author had this particular audience in mind is made clear by the statement in v. 3 that Lysias, the Seleucid general, "also intended to levy a tribute on the Temple, as he had done with the rest of the sacred precincts of the nations." For a Jew, 11:1-4 indicates a trespass of Jewish religion concerning his temple, whereas for a pagan the *dicta* are familiar, in particular when they are read against the background of a Hellenistic king's relationship with his subject states. Moreover, as has already been observed in our discussion of ch. 9, that a Hellenistic king sends an army to fight his riotous subjects was no surprise for a pagan reader. The victory of the Jews in this battle, the battle of Beith Zur, is assigned to the mercy of God (twice mentioned in 11:9-10). We have already observed this motif elsewhere in the book. Mercy and compassion as significant values of the state are here activated, transformed into emotions, by the real manager of the *politeia*, God. Since the Greeks even had a goddess who was mercy personified, Eleos, and the gods were sometimes perceived as allies of human beings in battle, every pagan who might have read this chapter could well understand the mention of God in v. 13 as yet another god who helps his people that are in trouble; here these people are called "Hebrews" (a term to be repeated in 15:37). Our book presents God as the symbol of an ultimate ethical system, since he is justice incarnate, compassionate, steadfast, heroic, loving, keeper of law and good behavior, and so on. These values are familiar to pagans from the Hellenistic universe, in particular when expressed by our author in a universal political and ethical terminology.

The overtures for peace are initiated by the Seleucid general (since he realized how strong the Jews were). Here comes the crux of the chapter: The comprehensive settlement that is proposed by Lysias is presented as "just" and as an initiative of a local governor (general) who was apparently clever (v. 13). From here onward much of the "pagan" stance of the author comes to the fore. He argues that "the time was opportune" (11:15). It was a wise consideration of Judah to accept the proposal of the Seleucid general, Nicanor. Four letters follow, Lysias to the Jews, the king to Lysias, the king to the Jews, and the Romans to the Jews. The letter of Judah to Lysias, mentioned by the author in v. 15, does not appear. I cannot enter here the complicated issue of the credibility of this correspondence but will just emphasize what a pagan reader could have learned from the letters, or how do these letters accommodate with his own political and ethical knowledge of his world. He or she could have deduced that they are quite general in tone and meagre in the information they provide (if, for instance, compared to Demetrius's letter in 1 Maccabees 10), and that they provide a clear message in Greek political and theological political thought when read together: a peaceful channel of deliberation during a war is an option, as we have encountered as a cardinal theme in Part I. A correspondence between enemies should be seen as an effective means of achieving peace. This peace strategy of talk rather than fight is seen as orderly and hierarchical (see, for instance 11:18, 20). Second, there is an interrelation between the goodwill (*eunoia*) toward the state affairs (*ta pragmata*) and the good of the *politeia* (*agathos*). Third, it emphasizes yet again what an autonomy meant for a state subject to another power: no independence but limited freedom to act in certain domains of its inner political life. Here, in the letter of the king to Lysias, a typical political language from the period is used and delivers the message that the Jews will be permitted to follow their own religious customs and will be exempt from following Hellenic rules. The letter also emphasizes that the wish of the king is that the nation of the Jews will be undisturbed (corresponding with the disturbance of the city in ch. 3). Needless to say, when seen from the side of the dominating power these grants were just partial and certainly not seen as complete independence to a subject state.

A pagan no doubt understood that the Jewish state as defined by the letter was allowed from now on to abide by the customs of their fathers and laws (*ta nomima*). Nothing in particular alludes to the Jewish nature of these customs and laws, and the language of the message remaining quite universal. Verse 26 mentions the autonomy of the *politeia*, and pledges are given by the king so that their good cheer and free mind will occur.

The letter of the king to the Jews presents us with an additional ingredient to the issue of opportune peace-making: an amnesty, that is, letting the Jews go back to their fatherland. Amnesties of this kind were popular in the Greek world, known, for instance from the revolution of 404/3 BCE in Athens.[17] Yet again, the autonomy that the king grants to the Jews, namely, that they can abide by their own laws, is enhanced. In order to make the story even more convincing, the author adds a letter from the Roman senate that assures the agreement of the Seleucids with the Jews, which was either fabricated by the author, partly or wholly, or is authentic. Many expressions used here were taken from the standard political arsenal of the Greek language. Judah is, unlike in the former chapter, operating without the explicit help of God and is praised all along for his wise decision, whereas King Antiochus is indirectly praised for his restoration of exiles, a policy which was seen as noble and positive in Greek historiography.[18]

These two last chapters, as my reader already observed, are a substantial contribution to our survey regarding (Hellenistic) patterns of behavior and thought that are revealed by 2 Maccabees. They design a state which, according to standard Hellenistic descriptions on subject states, is free (*eleutheros*)—freedom not in its meaning in classical Athens (Perikles' funeral speech, for instance)—but with the familiar limitations imposed by the ruling empire in charge. When even this limited freedom of the state is transgressed by the latter, it is almost natural and/or legitimate for the state to use force in order to restore its autonomy—this is done not only in our case but all over the Hellenistic sphere quite frequently as we have seen in Part I. Yet the war for independence brings to the fore several political and ethical rules that are defined as an ethical code of the state during its search for a value system, if the latter is not already embedded in their law code and/or group awareness. The author cares to emphasize that some of these ethical values are created by humans, and others are broadcast by God. The awareness of a value system that guards the state from wild and unjustified outbursts of characteristics that are imbued in the group of citizens (such as territoriality, imitation, split) is promoted implicitly and explicitly by the author, who is also quite attentive to the role of emotions within the state. Using the example of passion, he makes an attempt to demonstrate that good leadership can manage, restrain, and channel its group's emotions. In the relationship between characteristics, values, and emotions, the balance was temporarily restored at the end of ch. 11, we will return to this issue in the following.

---

[17] Other cases of amnesties include Plutarch *Solon* 19; Aristoteles *Athenaion Politeia* 39.6; and *SIG* 633.1.36 (second century BCE, Milesian inscription).

[18] Eckstein (1995: 84).

Goodwill (*eunoia*)

I have already dealt in Part I with ethics in inter-state wars, not necessarily linked to the relationship with the ruling empire/s. Yet the ethical inter-state system comes to the fore in the internal war, namely, between states that are ruled by one and the same empire. An example of this is in 2 Maccabees 12, which is a collection of *exempla* that are adduced by our author as a code of the right conduct of a state during times of war. They have no doubt a historical kernel, like much of the book, but they are presented in such a way as to convey a clear message that every pagan who knows the Hellenistic background could easily grasp. Judah is called at the end of the chapter "the noble Judah," since he operated in accordance with the ethical code suggested by the author. Yet it is not a typical Jewish code, even if some of its ingredients can be found in the Bible, but presented as a universal one (see, e.g., 12:42 in connection with the bringing of his people to burial). What, then, could the pagan reader learn about the Jewish state from the catalogue of modes of decision-making and behavior during war?

First, revenge is indispensable and natural (the case of Joppa), yet even revenge should remain proportional and logical, not exaggerated. It should have its limits, exemplified by v. 7, where it seems that the author was quite content with the fact that Judah's intention of pursuing the destruction of the city further did not materialize, namely, to annihilate the "barbarous" people of Joppa completely. The case of Jamnia serves as an instruction for future leaders. A city that shows just bad intentions should immediately be treated harshly.

Second, if your army is being attacked (by Arabs, nomads) and you defeat the other side, then you should conclude a peace, if you think that this enemy can be useful in the future (12:10-12). By no means continue an unnecessary war.

Third, rely on your god whoever he or she is, since when the enemy is much stronger than your army (because of the numbers of your army, or well-built strongholds of the enemy positioned in a strategic spot), your god, who is a constant reminder of the good value system of the state, can, when he wants, win a war, in particular when the enemy fights for bad values, such as blasphemy and scoff (12:13-16, 26-28).[19] Pagans knew very well what the intervention of gods could cause during war.

Fourth, in 12:24-25 the author gives an example of a pact under oath during the war to free a general of the enemy, who was taken captive in order to save the Jewish families from harm while still in the enemy's hands. He let him go free in order to save their brothers (12:25). This is a typical example of ethical behavior during times of war, which even in modern wars is not always adhered to.

Fifth, goodwill (*eunoia*), as I have already mentioned, was a central value in the state in its different manifestations. Here, our author returns to this important term and demonstrates how *eunoia* can provide unity and good citizenship when two different nations share one and the same city (mixed cities were quite common in the land of

---

[19] As we have already noted in Part I, Greek and other Near Eastern gods represented values taken from the scale of values of the society that worshiped them. The gods are there to remind human beings of what these values really mean they also constituted a warning addressed at humans that should adhere to a value system. Athena, for instance, represents both valor and wisdom

Israel at that time and probably elsewhere in the ancient Near East, see also 12:27). The city mentioned is Scythopolis: "The Jews who were located there testified that the Scythopolitans held them in good will and maintained a civilized approach in times of misfortune, with the result that they thanked them and urged them to preserve their good will to their race (*to genos*) for the future also" (12: 30-31).

Sixth, as we have already seen in the above, war is always associated with ethical issues, such as killing the innocent and burying the fallen. At the end of our chapter, the author refers to these issues. The attentive pagan reader (or, for that matter, the Jewish one as well), is handed the solution to such issues on a silver platter. However, even sinners who die in battle should be buried and not left on the battlefield. In the ancient world the business of burial in general was a crucial principle of communal life in the state and is frequently a leitmotif in ancient literature (Sophocles, *Antigone*). It should be noted that the explanation of the author in v. 40 shows yet again that this is a comment adduced for pagan readers. Jews did not need comments, such as that the Jews "singing hymns in their traditional tongue" (12:37), and "Then it was that they discovered under the shirt of each of the slain, consecrated objects of the idols of Jamnia, which the Law forbade to the Jews" (12:40).

Seventh, here as elsewhere in the book, God, like the multifunctional gods of the Greek pantheon, is again presented in a manner that pagans could have understood easily. Our author implicitly claims that believers should approach him, since he is an active righteous judge (12:6), a helper (12:11), the ruler who has power (12:28), and an ally (12:36). As we have already observed, these latter functions are just a few out of many others that are mentioned in 2 Maccabees.

In sum, serious ethical issues were included in the catalogue of the right behavior of the state and its army during war—there were perhaps many other issues of that sort mentioned by Jason of Cyrene but left out and abridged by the *epitomator*.

Daring Valor (*eutolmia*)

In ch. 13, we read of yet another invasion at the time of a Seleucid king, Antiochus Eupator. This in itself could arouse the sympathies of some pagan readers who saw in the Hellenistic ruling dynasty a legitimate power that creates and keeps order in the realm (see the support the Macedonian invading kings, Philip V and Perseus, received in Greek cities). Others, like the liberty fighters in Greece in the third and second centuries BCE, might have resented it. As already emphasized, liberty was limited to what we would call autonomy. At any rate, without getting into a discussion of the battles described in this cluster of chapters, I wish to emphasize that several precedents of ethical behavior and law are adduced in ch. 13 that underline secular universal lessons in ethics, not necessarily linked to Jewish religious law. Hence, like elsewhere in the book, we find first and foremost ethical terms familiar from the Greek world that are expressed either through the author in his own comments or adduced by other actors. They appear in pairs, good and bad ones, such as hypocrisy and treason as against faithfulness and honesty, steadfastness as against feebleness, sacrilege as against purity, abiding by the law versus breaking of the law. The first of such moral lessons that relates to the leadership of a state is told in 13:1-8, the events leading to Menelaus's death. The latter was one of the wayward leaders of the city, taking the leadership (High Priesthood) by mischief, as related in earlier chapters of the book. The narrative lingers on the fact that he was sentenced to capital punishment by the king because of his selfishness (having "not any idea of saving his fatherland," using *soteria*, a famous politically and theologically charged term; 13:3). Similar to another bad leader of the state, Jason, he was killed by foreigners and left unburied, a shameful death in paganism and Judaism alike. Yet Menelaus, the villain and "hypocrite" (13:3), was tried by foreigners "in accordance with local custom" (13:4). The procedure of his death is interesting, when read against the background of the virtual ethical universal code. Menelaus is accused of "the trouble" (13:3-4), that is, the current massive intervention of the Seleucids and the disruption of the normal relationship between empire and subject state. Then he is put to death in Beroea in a cruel manner, quite common in the Hellenistic world.[20] Since Menelaus was sentenced and punished according to "local custom," he received the same punishment as pagans did in Beroea because of their "sacrilege" (13:6, 8), and because he was a "lawbreaker." The local custom is presented here as being universal and was meant to moralize pagans alongside Hellenistic Jews. In the following, we read again about God the helper in battle (*boetheia*) and *theou niken* (the slogan of the Jews in this war) certainly evokes the familiar title of Athena who was *Athena Nike*. Then a short passage about a betrayal in the Jewish army follows that probably corresponds to the betrayal of Menelaus and others mentioned in the book, yet the guilty person is treated humanely by Judah (the traitor in the battle of Beith Zur was "only" imprisoned). It is a perfect lesson for the necessity to be endowed with faithfulness in a state and its army.

Another story is about the Seleucid general who decides to stop the battle in Judea because of an alert of a revolution in the Seleucid court. Judah accepts the cease-fire, since he was pragmatic and could only win by the cessation of hostilities at that particular juncture of the war. The narrative in ch. 13 reveals processes of deliberation and consent, reminiscent of such procedures in the Hellenistic world during war discussed in Part I above. Judah deliberates "privately" with the elders whether to accept the cease-fire (13:13, 22), and in 13:18-26 a peace initiated by the Seleucid general is concluded. Ratifying it himself, it was brought to an assembly in another Hellenistic city (a provincial capital, Acco-Ptolemais), where it is rejected, but then ratified as a result of a persuasive speech of the Seleucid general. The quasi-democratic procedure is presented by our author as a common feature within a normal relationship of a subject state with the empire. This could have been any description in pagan Hellenistic historiography, leaving out some Jewish details. The "daring valour" of the Jews described throughout the chapter is universal in nature and narrated quite clearly for Hellenistic Jews as well as for the pagan reader (13:18).

It was Alcimus who, in contradistinction to Menelaus, representing "the best of interest for the state" (ch. 14), expressed the views of a politician about the right relationship of the ruling empire and a subject state (14:6-10). This latter relationship

---

[20] Menelaus was put to death in the style of Nabis; cf. Mendels (1998: 223-48); this exemplifies an eye for an eye punishment (13.8).

was already elaborated upon in the text before by the letters of the king in ch. 11, yet this time it is presented by a former Jewish leader, a member of the subject state, and opponent of Judah and his freedom fighters. Thus, according to him, a state can be balanced under foreign rule without causing conflict only when the sense of responsibility is activated, in order for the state to be fortunate without revolution (*stasis*). Moreover, the state should on the one hand regard the interests of the king of the ruling power, and on the other be mindful of the welfare of its citizens. The revolutionaries within a subject state are those who damage the stability of the whole empire and its peace (14:10). The king of the ruling empire for his part should be benevolent and think about the interests of the nations in his realm. This is an interesting presentation by our author. On the one hand, he supports the Maccabean revolt of Judah and his brothers, yet on the other, he promotes the idea throughout the book that a correct, peaceful, and balanced relationship between Judea and the Seleucid empire should be restored. In these chapters, therefore, we hear yet again a story about the wisdom of the human being (without the help, or rather explicit help, of God), who apparently knows the right time to cease fighting and conclude a peace, even if this involves deliberating with one's fierce enemy (nevertheless, one has to be cautious). In addition, we get in these chapters a recitation of two opposite values exemplified by two different stories. The one exemplifies yet again a treacherous behavior of a leader, Menelaus. The other depicts a brave suicidal act by Razis, called "the father of the Jews" (14:37-46). It is no accident that the latter hero does not die as a result of some kind of religious persecution, as the seven brothers underwent, nor does he die an intellectual death such as that of Socrates. Instead, he dies as a hero by committing suicide in a horrible manner, since he refuses to fall into the hands of the enemy.[21] Whereas Fukuyama speaks of the "politics of identity," I would speak of 2 Maccabees as a book that broadcasts the idea of "the politics of the right balance" (between characteristics, values, and emotions managed by rulers and super rulers such as gods). Since the stories are first and foremost ornaments for conveying a message (ch. 2), or rather messages meant for a double audience, they are narrated with a view to enable pagans to read much of them like events narrated by Hellenistic historians. This is also the reason, as mentioned earlier, why the book makes the typical Greek distinction between barbarians (the Seleucids and their friends) and the Greeks, to whose cultural world the Jews belong. For a pagan reader, unlike for a Jewish one, the heathen that join the forces of Nicanor's army during this invasion into the land of Israel are called *ethne*, (foreign) nations. The phenomenon of nations within an empire supporting the ruling power's military intervention against other nations who fight for their liberty or are causing socioeconomic unrest was still common in the Greek world a couple of years before our events took place as I have related in Part I. To get back to the division between barbarians and Greeks (the civilized world), the incorporation of the Jewish state within the civilized world of Greek culture may have been intentional on the part of the author who wanted to

---

[21] Stern (1991: 313-43).

fend off the anti-Semitic rhetoric that positioned the Jews as the ultimate "other" and to demonstrate their being part of the Hellenistic ethical system.[22]

Virtue (*arete*)

Chapters 14–15 are a turn from the events described in ch. 13. Here, we find the story of the Seleucid general Nicanor's appearance in Judea and his shameful death there, which marks the end of the narrative. As already said, I am not going to deal with the reasons why the author ended his story here, although it seems quite obvious that the book reached a climax, showing the victory of a state within an empire over the empire itself, or rather its turn to a normal relationship of empire and subject-state: "From that time the city [Jerusalem] has been in the possession of the Hebrews" (15:37).[23] The scene is presented as a match between equals and ends in peace for the state. The account of the intervention of Nicanor in Palestine presents us once again with an opportunity to learn about the relationship between empire and subject state; the story presents us with ethical issues that are linked to political actions. First, it conveys a clear message that when a battle can be avoided, one should opt for peace. This is not the first time that this motif appears in the book. It shows yet again that the empire in this particular case was not necessarily bloodthirsty (and was ethical when it served its interests). Second, it presents us with a universal ethical problem that has political repercussions: a promise has been made (in this case by Nicanor to Judah), yet the king is persuaded by Alcimus, Judah's adversary—a former High Priest who "through his own fault had disgraced himself" (14:3)—that he should renege on this promise. The king, the highest authority in the scene, overturns this promise and Nicanor has to act in accordance with his king's ordinance, but he does so reluctantly because of his former obligation. 2 Maccabees presents this as a blunt breach of oath. Politics is portrayed here as the opposite of ethics, a familiar phenomenon in the Hellenistic reality. Third, the power of gods, as any Jew and pagan would have known already, overrules the power of any human being, including a king. The whole episode where the authority (*exusia*) of God is pitted against that of the king, which is exemplified as well in the supercilious appearance of the Seleucid general in the temple, shows clearly who the real boss on earth is. It argues against the dictum of Nicanor, who says, "It is I, a sovereign on earth," reacting against Jews who say that "God is the Sovereign in heaven" (15:3-5). But what is the identity of this god? Having pagan readers in mind (alluded again in 15:36), his several references to God, as elsewhere in the book, are crucial. As I already mentioned, Jews read these chapters with the full understanding that in line with their Bible their one and only God has various titles. Yet a pagan Greek could interpret this same god somewhat differently, namely, in line with his perception of a world full of gods and/or one god with several titles. Since I have mentioned this

---

[22] For the Jew as the "other," see Bar-Kochva (2010).
[23] To remind my reader, the narrative about the events leading to the Maccabean revolt starts with: "Time was when the holy city was governed in a perfectly peaceable manner and the laws were preserved as well as could be."

already, I will only refer here to God's title in these chapters. He is named here *Ourano dunastes*, "Sovereign of the heavens." For a pagan, this sounded familiar, since Zeus was the head of the hierarchy of the Greek pantheon. Moreover, these last chapters abound with nomenclature that was drawn from the Greek political and ethical arsenal of terms. This aspect requires another article, if not a book.[24]

The central scene of the last chapters of 2 Maccabees takes us to a conference where deliberations between two belligerent sides took place. In contradistinction to the strategy of humiliation so common in the Hellenistic world (14:40), there was a strategy of civil talk as we have encountered frequently in Part I. The conference between Nicanor and Judah introduces a well-known tool of Hellenistic diplomacy in which enemies talk. The conference of two famous enemies, Titus Flamininus and Nabis, one of many such conferences, springs to mind.[25] The author remarks that the conference between Nicanor and Judah was a "harmonious conference." Yet later we read that Nicanor went back to the path of war and was then defeated by the Jewish army. This description has not much that is Jewish; every pagan could easily connect to it.

The book ends with the crucial sentence: "at that time the city has been in the hands of the Hebrews" (15:37). Scholars disagree on why the book ends here. I will not make an attempt to adduce my own speculations but suggest a solution that is in line with what I have argued so far. The author presented his vision of a state and its relationship with the ruling empire in such a way as to demonstrate to Hellenistic Jews, as well as to Greek-reading pagans, what a Jewish *politeia* in a Greek garb was like. Its characteristics, values, and the role of group emotions are enhanced. On a theoretical level, the interaction between these three angles of the triangle and their rulers, earthly and/or heavenly, is what interested the author of 2 Maccabees. Thus, when autonomy was achieved at last, no further intervention of the foreign power was secured, and a harmony within the subject state was reached after the battle of Nicanor, this was for the author (by now we can call him a political thinker) the ideal political *arete*—a central term in the political philosophy of Aristoteles (2 Macc. 15:12, 17). The harmony within the cities and states was a key concept when relations of empire and its subjects were on the agenda, as we have seen in Part I. 2 Maccabees is an important cornerstone in the history of political science of the Hellenistic era. Scholars should give much more attention to the composition as a set of universal ideas meant inter alia to fend off animosity against the Jews based on the notorious claim that they were an awkward nation (14:39).

---

[24] See Mendels (2019: 129) for a list of terms and expressions, some of which are: "warmongers and revolutionaries," "enjoy stability," "interests of the king," "welfare of my countrymen," "complete irresponsibility," "the nation is unfortunate," "interest of our country," "beleaguered nation," "spirit of courteous benevolence," "to inflame the king," "misfortunes and calamities," "manifestation of divine power," "shrank from taking the decision on the bloody contest," "authority to propose and accept a truce," "unanimous consent," "harmonious conference," "under surveillance," "subversive to the government," "traitor to the kingdom," "dissatisfied with the treaty," "break his promises although the man had done no wrong," "not possible to oppose the kings' command," "treating with more formality," "disclaimed under oath," "swore this oath," "the one who had ever been Ally of their nation," "devoted patriot," "fine reputation," "public decree."

[25] Mendels (1998: 261–8).

In conclusion, whereas Part I is a survey of the inter-state ethical system that emerged in the Hellenistic world during the three decades that preceded the Hasmonean conflict with the Seleucid empire, Part II showed its correspondence with the remnants of this system. It also enhanced the patterns of relationship between empire and subject state current in the Hellenistic world and their similarity to the interactions between Judea and the empires that were active in the region.

Bibliography

Almagor, E., and J. Skinner, eds. 2013. *Ancient Ethnography: New Approaches*. London: Bloomsbury.
Badian, E. 1958. *Foreign Clientelae (264-70 B.C.)*. Oxford: Clarendon Press.
Bar-Kochva, B. 1989. *Judas Maccabaeus: The Jewish Struggle against the Seleucids*. Cambridge: Cambridge University Press.
Bar-Kochva, B. 2010. *The Image of the Jews in Greek Literature: The Hellenistic Period*. Berkeley: University of California Press.
Bell, D. 2010. *Ethics and World Politics* Oxford: Oxford University Press.
Blondheim, M., and H. Rosenberg, eds. 2020. *Communication in the Jewish Diaspora: Two Thousand Years of Saying Goodbye without Leaving*. New York: Israel Academic Press.
Briscoe, J. 1981. *A Commentary on Livy Books XXXIV-XXXVII*. Oxford: Clarendon Press.
Briscoe, J. 1989. *A Commentary on Livy Books XXXI-XXXIII*. Oxford: Clarendon Press.
Briscoe, J. 2008. *A Commentary on Livy Books 38-40*. Oxford: Oxford University Press.
Briscoe, J. 2012. *A Commentary on Livy Books 41-45*. Oxford: Oxford University Press.
Brown, A. 2009. *The Rise and Fall of Communism*. London: Bodley Head.
Burset, Ch. R. 2019. "Why didn't the common law follow the flag?" *Virginia Law Review* 105 (3): 483-542.
Buzan, B., and R. Little. 2000. *International Systems in World History: Remaking the Study of International Relations*. Oxford: Oxford University Press.
Coetzer, E. 2017. "Heroes and villains in 2 Maccabees 8:1-36: A rhetorical analysis." *OTE* 29 (3): 419-33.
Dahlheim, W. 1968. *Struktur und Entwicklung des römischen Völkerrechts im dritten und zweiten Jahrhundert v. Chr.* Munich: C. H. Beck.
De Ste. Croix, G. E. M. 1981. *The Class Struggle in the Ancient Greek World: From the Archaic Age to the Arab Conquests (1981)*. London: Duckworth.
Doran, R. 2012. *2 Maccabees: A Critical Commentary* (Hermeneia). Minneapolis, MN: Fortress Press.
Eckstein, A. M. 1995. *Moral Vision in the Histories of Polybius*. Berkeley: University of California Press.
Eckstein, A. M. 2006. *Mediterranean Anarchy, Interstate War, and the Rise of Rome*. Berkeley: University of California Press.
Frank, T. 1921. *Roman Imperialism*. New York: Macmillan.
Fukuyama, F. 2018. *Identity: The Demand for Dignity and the Politics of Resentment*. New York: Farrar, Straus & Giroux.
Gamble, A. 2010. "Ethics and politics." Pages 73-92 in *Ethics and World Politics*. Edited by D. Bell. Oxford: Oxford University Press.
Geuss, R. 2008. *Philosophy and Real Politics*. Princeton, NJ: Princeton University Press.
Grainger, J. D. 2019. *Great Power Diplomacy in the Hellenistic World*. Abingdon: Routledge.
Green, P. 1990. *Alexander to Actium: The Historical Revolution of the Hellenistic Age*. Berkeley: University of Californian Press.

Gruen, E. S. 1984. *The Hellenistic World and the Coming of Rome*. Berkeley: University of California Press.

Harris, W. V. 1979. *War and Imperialism in Republican Rome, 327–70 B.C.* Oxford: Clarendon Press.

Herman, G. 1987. *Ritualised Friendship and the Greek City*. Cambridge: Cambridge University Press.

Herman, G. 2006. *Morality and Behaviour in Democratic Athens: A Social History*. Cambridge: Cambridge University Press.

Isaac, B. 2004. *The Invention of Racism in Classical Antiquity*. Princeton, NJ: Princeton University Press.

Kissinger, H. 2014. *World Order: Reflections on the Character of Nations and the Course of History*. London: Allen Lane.

Klawans, J., and L. M. Wills, eds. 2020. *The Jewish Annotated Apocrypha*. Oxford: Oxford University Press.

Kohn, M. 2010. "Post-colonial theory." Pages 200–18 in *Ethics and World Politics*. Edited by D. Bell. Oxford: Oxford University Press.

Koselleck, R. 2004. *Futures Past: On the Semantics of Historical Time*. New York: Columbia University Press.

Larsen, J. A. O. 1968. *Greek Federal States: Their Institutions and History*. Oxford: Clarendon Press.

Livy Books 31–45 (Loeb edition). The Loeb Classical Library. London: Heinemann.

Livy Books 31–45 (Loeb edition). *Volume IX*: E. T. Sage (1935).

Livy Books 31–45 (Loeb edition). *Volume X*: E. T. Sage (1935).

Livy Books 31–45 (Loeb edition). *Volume XI*: E. T. Sage (1936).

Livy Books 31–45 (Loeb edition). *Volume XII*: E. T. Sage and A. C. Schlesinger (1938).

Livy Books 31–45 (Loeb edition). *Volume XIII*: A. C. Schlesinger (1951).

Ma, J. 1999. *Antiochus III and the Cities of Western Asia Minor*. Oxford: Oxford University Press.

Mendels, D. 1992. *The Rise and Fall of Jewish Nationalism: Jewish and Christian Ethnicity in Ancient Palestine*. New York: Doubleday.

Mendels, D. 1998. *Identity, Religion and Historiography. Studies in Hellenistic History*. Sheffield: Sheffield Academic Press.

Mendels, D. 2004. *Memory in Jewish, Pagan and Christian Societies of the Graeco-Roman World*. London: T&T Clark.

Mendels, D. 2013. *Why Did Paul Go West? Jewish Historical Narrative and Thought*. London: T&T Clark.

Mendels, D. 2017. *History as Repetition: Can We Affect Its Course?* Amazon, Kindle edition.

Mendels, D. 2019. "An overlooked treatise in Greek political thought: An essay on 2 Maccabees as a Hellenistic politico-theological manifest." *Journal for the Study of the Pseudepigrapha* 29 (2): 100–31.

Mendels, D. 2020. "The Hasmonean State and Ancient Jewish Nationalism." Pages 564–70 in *The Jewish Annotated Apocrypha*. Edited by J. Klawans and L. M. Wills. Oxford: Oxford University Press.

Mendels, D. 2021. "1 Maccabees." Pages 150–68 in *The Oxford Handbook of the Apocrypha*. Edited by G. Oegema. Oxford: Oxford University Press.

Moore, J. M. 1975. *Aristotle and Xenophon on Democracy and Oligarchy*. London: Chatto and Windus.

Pensky, M. 2010. "Ethics and Critical Theory." Pages 35–53 in *Ethics and World Politics*. Edited by D. Bell. Oxford: Oxford University Press.
Polybius (Loeb Edition). The Loeb Classical Library. London: Heinemann.
Polybius (Loeb Edition). *Volume V*. W. R. Paton (1926).
Polybius (Loeb Edition). *Volume VI*. W. R. Paton (1927).
Price, J. J. 2001. *Thucydides and Internal War*. Cambridge: Cambridge University Press.
Schama, S. 1989. *Citizens: A Chronicle of the French Revolution*. London: Penguin Books.
Schmitt, H. H., ed. 1969. *Die Staatsverträge des Altertums* vol. 3. *Die Verträge der griechisch-römischen Welt von 338 bis 200 v. Chr.* Munich: C. H. Beck.
Scholten, J. B. 2000. *The Politics of Plunder: Aitolians and Their Koinon in the Early Hellenistic Era, 279–217 B.C.* Berkeley: University of California Press.
Schwartz, D. R. 2008. *2 Maccabees* (Commentaries on Early Jewish Literature [CEJL]). Berlin: Walter de Gruyter.
Scullard, H. H. 1951. *Roman Politics 220–150 B.C.* Oxford: Clarendon Press.
Sherk, R. K. 1984. *Rome and the Greek East to the Death of Augustus*. Cambridge: Cambridge University Press.
Stern, M. 1983. *The Documents on the History of the Hasmonean Revolt with a Commentary and Introductions* [in Hebrew]. Tel Aviv: Ha'kibutz Ha'meuchad.
Stern, M. 1991. *Studies in Jewish History* [in Hebrew]. Jerusalem: Magnes Press.
Sulimani, I. 2011. *Diodorus' Mythistory and the Pagan Mission: Historiography and Culture-Heroes in the First Pentad of the Bibliotheke*. Leiden: Brill.
Sussman, Y. 2020. "The Simple Meaning of 'Oral Law', or the Power of the Tip of a 'Yod.'" Pages 29–53 in *Communication in the Jewish Diaspora*. Edited by M. Blondheim and H. Rosenberg. New York: Israel Academic Press.
Vasaly, A. 2015. *Livy's Political Philosophy: Power and Personality in Early Rome*. Cambridge: Cambridge University Press.
Walbank, F. W. 1957. *A Historical Commentary on Polybius*. Oxford: Clarendon Press.
Walbank, F. W. 1967. *A Historical Commentary on Polybius*. Oxford: Clarendon Press.
Walbank, F. W. 1979. *A Historical Commentary on Polybius*. Oxford: Clarendon Press.
Weber, M. 2015. *Wirtschaft und Gesellschaft*. Tübingen: J.C.B. Mohr (Paul Siebeck).
Wirszubski, Ch. 1950. *Libertas as a Political Idea at Rome during the Late Republic and Early Principate*. Cambridge: Cambridge University Press.

Index of Ancient Sources

Apocrypha

1 Maccabees
1:41-64	129
1:52-53	129
2:19-22	130
2:29	131
2:31-41	131
2:44	131
3:1-9	105, 140
3:8-9	18
3:17	131
3:18-20	131
3:46	27
3:50-52	132
4:1-35	132
4:9	132
4:17-18	132
5	112, 133
5:58-68	133
5:63-64	133
6:5-8	133
6:18-27	134
6:57-59	134
6:60-63	135
7:3-4	135
7	76
7:5-7	135
7:9	136
7:15-18	136
7:19	136
7:25	136
7:29	137
7:33-35	137
7:38	137
7:47	137
8	74, 80, 138, 154
8:12-13	138
9	113–15, 138
10	138
10:46	45
10:59-60	25
11	139
14	27, 105, 139–40
14:4-15	140
15	49, 73, 135, 139
15:33-35	43
16:11-22	22

2 Maccabees
2	160
3-5	144
3	12, 27, 145, 155
3:1	144, 147
3:1-3	144
3:7-40	145
3:12	145
3:14	145
3:16-17	145
3:22	146
3:22-39	146
3:24	146
3:30	146
3:38	152
4	146
4:39-42	147
5:6-7	148
5:7-9	148
5:15	148
5:21	148
6-7	149
8	149
8:17	150
8:20	150
9	150–1
9:13-18	153
9:13-27	153
10	155
10:10	153
10:12	153
10:26	154
10:28	154

10:35	154	*Plato*	
11:1-4	154	*Politeia*	
11:3	154	9	146
11:9-10	155		
11:13	155	*Aristotle*	
11:15	155	*Politica*	
11:18	155	5	145–6
11:20	155		
11:26	156	*Polybius*	
12:6	158	*The Histories*	
12:7	157	2.37.10-11	15
12:10-12	157	2.58.10	17
12:11	158	6	146
12:13-16	157	7.14.3	17
12:24-25	157	13.7	149
12:26-28	157	16.25.5-6	13
12:27	158	16.26.7-8	13
12:30-31	158	16.29-35	14
12:36	158	16.32.1	14
12:37	158	18..13-15	27
12:40	158	21.11	82
13	158	27.1-2	101
13-15	161	27.4-5	103
13: 1-8	159	27.9	107
13:3	159	29.1 (11)	113
13:4	159	30.6	122
13:6	159	30.13 (10)	122
13:8	159		
13:13	159	*Livy*	
13:18-26	159	*Ab Urbe Condita*	
13:22	159	31.2.3-4	10
14:3	161	31.5-6.6	11
14:6-10	159	31.7	11
14:10	160	31.8	11
14:37-46	160	31.9.1-5	10
14:39-40	162	31.9.5	12
15:3-5	161	31.9.8	11
15:12	162	31.10-20	17
15:17	162	31.11	11
15:36	161	31.11.10-12	12
15:37	150–1, 155, 161–2	31.14-15	12
		31.14.7-9	12
Greek and Latin Authors		31.14.10	12
		31.14.12	13
Thucydides		31.15.6-7	12
The History of the Peloponnesian War		31.16.4-5	13
1.70-71	118	31.18.3-4	14
5	150	31.18.7-8	15
		31.25	15

Index of Ancient Sources 171

31.25.9-10	15	33.32	37
31.28.6	16	33.33	38
31.29.6-16	16	33.34	38
31.30	17	33.35	38
31.30.2-4	17	33.38.1	41
31.31	17	33.38.2-3	42
31.32.2	18	33.38.3	42
31.34.2-3	18	33.38.5-6	42
31.43.5-7	18	33.38.7	42
31.44	18	33.38.14	42
31.44.2-3	18	33.40	43
31.45.1-2	19	33.40.3-4	43
32.10.3-6	19	33.40.6	43
32.19-23.3	20	33.41.5	44
32.20.3	113	33.45.3-4	44
32.20.3-4	20	34.32.4	44
32.22.8-12	21	34.48.2	45
32.29	12	34.49.5	46
32.32-36	22	34.49.6	46
32.33.10-14	25	34.49.7-10	45
32.34.4-7	23	34.49.11	46
32.34.8-10	24	34.50.3	46
32.34.11-13	24	34.51.4-5	47
32.38	25	34.51.6	47
32.40.5-7	26	34.57.5	47
33.2	27	34.57.7-9	47
33.3	27	34.57.10-11	48
33.3.11-12	27	34.58.2-3	48
33.5	27	34.58.4-5	48
33.11.7-9	28	34.58.4-7	48
33.12	28	34.58.8-12	49
33.12.6-9	28	34.59.1	49
33.13	29	34.59.4-5	49
33.13.6-14	30	35.16.2-6	51
33.14-15	30	35.16.7-13	52
33.13.15	30	35.17.1-2	52
33.16.2	31	35.17.3-4	52
33.16.4-9	31	35.17.9	52
33.16.10-11	31	35.18.1-5	53
33.20.7-13	32	35.31.1-2	53
33.21.1-5	33	35.31.3-4	53
33.27.5-9	34	35.31.8-10	53
33.27.10-11	34	35.31.12	53
33.28.1	34	35.31.13-16	54
33.29.8	35	35.32	54
33.30	36	35.32.8-11	55
33.31.2-5	36	35.32.9	55
33.31.7-9	36	35.33. 1-3	55
33.31.11	37	35.33.4-6	55

35.33.7-8	56	36.28.2-6	71
35.33.9-11	56	36.28.9	71
35.34	56	36.29.1-3	71
35.34.3-4	56	36.30	71
35.35.2	58	36.31	72
35.36-38	64	36.31.3-5	72
35.37-40	57	36.31.8	72
35.38.4-6	57	36.31.9	73
35.38.7-10	66	36.31.9-10	73
35.38.8-10	57	36.32	73
35.39.4	58	36.32.5-8	73
35.39.7-8	58	36.32.9	73
35.42.4-5	58	36.33.1-3	75
35.43-44	59	36.33.4-7	76
35.43.2-3	58	36.34.1-4	76
35.45	59	36.34.5	77
35.46.5-6	59	36.34.8-10	77
35.46.7	59	36.35.1	77
35.46.9-11	59	36.35.2-4	78
35.46.13	59	36.35.7	78
35.48-49	60	36.35.8	78
35.48.2-3	60	36.35.8-11	79
35.48.7-11	61	36.35.12-13	79
35.49.1-13	61	36.41	79
35.50.1-2	61	37	80
35.50. 4	61	37.1.2-6	79
36.3.10-12	63	37.7	81
36.5.3	64	37.8	81
36.5.5-7	64	37.17.7	81
36.5.8	64	37.19	81
36.5.3-8	78	37.20-21	81
36.6.1-3	64	37.25.4-7	81
36.6.1-4	65	37.25.8-12	82
36.6.6-10	65	37.35.5-10	82
36.7	65	37.36.3	82
36.7.11	66	37.45.1-3	83
36.7.3-13	65	37.45.6-9	83
36.8.1	66	37.45.10-18	84
36.8.2	66	42.2.1-2	85
36.9.1-2	66	42.5.1-2	86
36.9.4-7	67	42.5.3	87
36.9.9-15	67	42.5.4-6	87
36.15.1	67	42.6.2-3	87
36.20.1-4	68	42.11.2-3	87
36.22.1	68	42.11.4-9	88
36.22.2-4	69	42.12.1-7	89
36.27.2-3	69	42.13.1-3	89
36.27.5-8	70	42.13. 4-11	90
36.27.6	70	42.25.2-3	92
36.28.1	70	42.25.4-13	92

42.26.7-9	94	43.8.8-10	109
42.29.1-4	94	44.22	112
42.29.5-7	94	44.22.6-15	113
42.29.11	94	44.23.1-2	109
42.30	90	44.23.3-6	110
42.30.1-6	90	44.23.7-9	110
42.36	93	44.24.1-6	110
42.36.1	93	44.24.9-11	111
42.36.2-3	93	44.24.7-8	111
42.37.5	94	44.34.1-5	113
42.37.6-9	95	44.34.6	114
42.38.1	95	44.34.8-9	114
42.38.3-4	95	44.36.13	114
42.38.5	95	44.37	114
42.38.6-7	96	44.38.1-4	114
42.38.8	96	44.39.3-4	115
42.39	96	45.8.3-5	116
42.39.2-8	96	45.8.6-7	116
42.40.1-11	97	45.13	116
42.41.1-3	98	45.17.7-18.2	116
42.41.5-7	98	45.18.6-7	116
42.41.7-14	99	45.23-24	118
42.42.1-5	100	45.23.1-6	117
42.42.6	100	45.23.7	118
42.42.7-9	100	45.23.8-9	118
42.43.1-2	101	45.23.10-15	118
42.43.4	101	45.23.16-19	118
42.45	102	45.24.2-4	119
42.45.1-2	102	45.24.4-7	119
42.45.3-5	102	45.24.8-14	119
42.46.2	103	45.25	120
42.46.3-5	103	45.25.11-13	120
42.46.6	103	45.29.4	121
42.46.7-9	104	45.29.4-12	121
42.47.9	104	45.29.13-14	121
42.49.1-7	105	45.30.1	118
42.50	105	45.30.1-2	121
42.50.1-3	105	45.31	121–2
42.50.4-5	106	45.31.1	121
42.50.11-51.2	106	45.31.3	121
42.52.8	106	45.31.4-8	122
42.52.13-16	106		
42.53	106	*Plutarch*	
42.53.1	106	*Titus Flamininus*	
42.53.1-4	107	10-11	37
42.63.1-2	107		
43.7.10-11	108	*Aemilius Paulus*	
43.8.1-2	108	17	114
43.8.3-4	108	28	121
43.8.6-7	109		

Index of Authors

Almagor, E. 80

Badian, E. vii, 6, 48, 102, 128
Bar Kochva, B. 18, 161
Bell, D. 21, 24, 28, 44
Briscoe, J. vii, 9–10, 12, 17, 19, 21, 27, 45, 52, 63, 80, 87, 108–9, 115
Brown, A. 1
Burset, Ch. R. 6
Buzan, B. 1–3, 99, 101–2

Coetzer, E. 150

Dahlheim, W. 6
De Ste. Croix, G.E.M. 85
Doran, R. VI

Eckstein, A. M. 3–4, 53, 62, 76, 93, 112, 140, 151, 156

Frank, T. vii
Fukuyama, F. 54

Gamble, A. 24, 33, 74
Geuss, R. 24
Grainger, J. D. 9
Green, P. 51
Gruen, E. S. vii, 6, 10, 16, 37, 85, 102, 128, 145

Harris, W. V. vii, 74
Herman, G. vii, 21

Isaac, B. 135

Kissinger, H. 81

Kohn, M. 44
Koselleck, R. 109

Larsen, J. A. O. 15–16, 53
Little, R. 1–3, 99, 101–2

Ma, J. 32
Mendels, D. vi, 12, 15, 26, 33, 35, 63, 76–7, 80, 85, 89, 100, 102, 127–8, 130–1, 133, 137–9, 143–7, 150, 152, 159, 162
Moore, J. M. 44

Pensky, M. 3
Price, J. J. 7, 24, 35, 37

Schama, S. 1
Schmitt, H. H. 6, 117
Scholten, J. B. 16, 80
Schwartz, D. R. vi
Scullard, H. H. vii
Sherk, R. K. 1, 6, 20, 38, 48, 72, 138
Skinner, J. 80
Stern, M. 4, 160
Sulimani, I. 131
Sussman, Y. 4

Tolstoy, L. 1

Vasaly, A. 9

Walbank, F. W. vi, 10, 13–15, 17, 19, 101, 103, 111, 113, 122
Weber, M. 41
Wirszubski, Ch. 50, 55

www.ingramcontent.com/pod-product-compliance
Lightning Source LLC
Chambersburg PA
CBHW061835300426
44115CB00013B/2389